Street by Street

EDINBURGH

DALKEITH, LEITH, MUSSELBURGH, PENICUIK

Balerno, Bonnyrigg, Cockenzie & Port Seton, Gorebridge, Loanhead, Prestonpans, South Queensferry, Tranent

3rd edition October 2007
© Automobile Association Developments Limited 2007

Original edition printed May 2001

This product includes map data licensed from Ordnance Survey® with the permission of the Controller of Her Majesty's Stationery Office. © Crown copyright 2007. All rights reserved. Licence number 100021153.

The copyright in all PAF is owned by Royal Mail Group plc.

Published by AA Publishing (a trading name of Automobile Association Developments Limited, whose registered office is Fanum House, Basing View, Basingstoke, Hampshire RG21 4EA. Registered number 1878835).

Produced by the Mapping Services Department of The Automobile Association. (A03384)

A CIP Catalogue record for this book is available from the British Library.

Printed by Oriental Press in Dubai

Ref: ML67y

Key to map pages	ii-iii
Key to map symbols	iv-1
Enlarged map pages	2-3
Main map pages	4-79
Index – towns & villages	80
Index – streets	81-91
Index – featured places	91-93
Acknowledgements	93

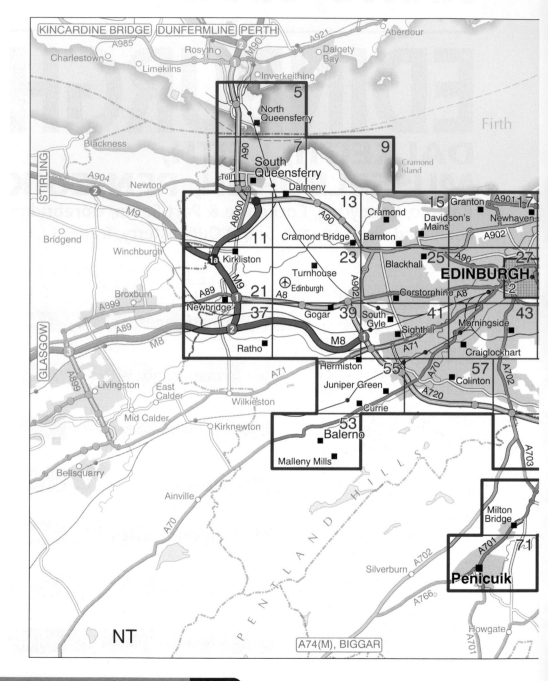

Scale of enlarged map pages 1:10,000 6.3 inches to 1 mile

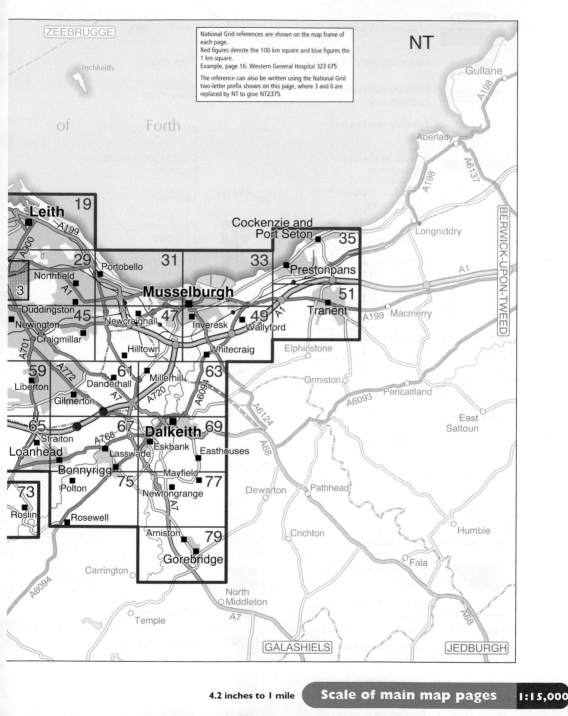

NT

National Grid references are shown on the map frame of each page.
Red figures denote the 100 km square and blue figures the 1 km square.
Example, page 16: Western General Hospital 323 675

The reference can also be written using the National Grid two-letter prefix shown on this page, where 3 and 6 are replaced by NT to give NT2375.

ZEEBRUGGE

Inchkeith

of Forth

Gullane

Aberlady

A198

A6137

A198

BERWICK-UPON-TWEED

Leith — 19

A199

Longniddry

A900

Cockenzie and Port Seton — 35

29 — Portobello — 31 — 33

Northfield

A1

3

Musselburgh

Prestonpans

A1

Macmerry

Duddingston — 45 — 47 — 49 — 51 — Tranent

Newington — Newcraighall — Inveresk — Wallyford

A199

Craigmillar — Hilltown — Whitecraig

Elphinstone

A701

A772

59 — 61 — 63

Millerhill

Ormiston

Pencaitland

A6093

Liberton — Danderhall

A720

A6094

A6124

East Saltoun

Gilmerton — A7

A68

65 — 67 — 69

Dalkeith

Straiton — A768 — Eskbank — Easthouses

Loanhead — Lasswade

Bonnyrigg — Mayfield

Dewarton — Pathhead

Polton — 75 — 77

Newtongrange — A7

Humbie

73 — Roslin

Rosewell

Crichton

Fala

79

Arniston

Gorebridge

A6094

Carrington

North Middleton

A7

Temple

A68

GALASHIELS

JEDBURGH

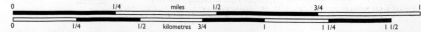

4.2 inches to 1 mile | **Scale of main map pages** | 1:15,000

0 — 1/4 — miles — 1/2 — 3/4 — 1

0 — 1/4 — 1/2 — kilometres 3/4 — 1 — 1 1/2

Symbol	Description
Junction 9	Motorway & junction
Services	Motorway service area
	Primary road single/dual carriageway
Services	Primary road service area
	A road single/dual carriageway
	B road single/dual carriageway
	Other road single/dual carriageway
	Minor/private road, access may be restricted
← ←	One-way street
	Pedestrian area
	Track or footpath
	Road under construction
	Road tunnel
P	Parking
P+🚌	Park & Ride
🚌	Bus/coach station
	Railway & main railway station
	Railway & minor railway station
⊖	Underground station
⊖	Light railway & station
++++++++	Preserved private railway

Symbol	Description
LC	Level crossing
•—•—•—•	Tramway
- - - - - -	Ferry route
....	Airport runway
— · — · — ·	County, administrative boundary
ⱱⱱⱱⱱⱱⱱⱱ	Mounds
17	Page continuation 1:15,000
3	Page continuation to enlarged scale 1:10,000
	River/canal, lake, pier
	Aqueduct, lock, weir
465 ▲ Winter Hill	Peak (with height in metres)
	Beach
	Woodland
	Park
	Cemetery
	Built-up area
	Industrial/business building
	Leisure building
	Retail building
	Other building
IKEA	IKEA store

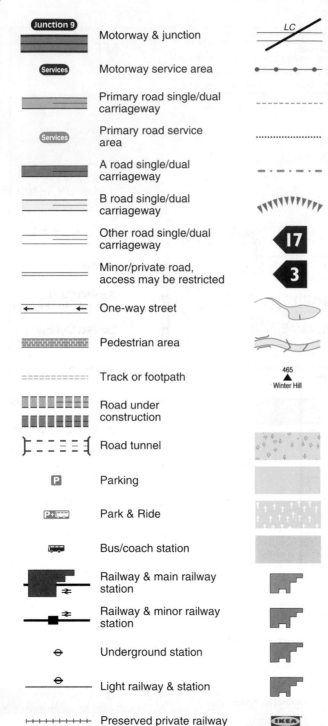

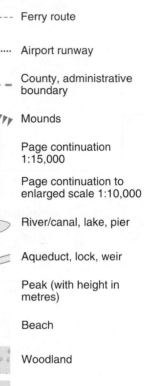

⊓⊓⊓⊓⊓	City wall	Castle	Castle
A&E	Hospital with 24-hour A&E department	Historic house or building	Historic house or building
PO	Post Office	Wakehurst Place (NTS)	National Trust property
	Public library	M	Museum or art gallery
i	Tourist Information Centre		Roman antiquity
i	Seasonal Tourist Information Centre		Ancient site, battlefield or monument
	Petrol station, 24 hour Major suppliers only		Industrial interest
†	Church/chapel	✳	Garden
	Public toilets		Garden Centre Garden Centre Association Member
	Toilet with disabled facilities		Garden Centre Wyevale Garden Centre
PH	Public house AA recommended		Arboretum
	Restaurant AA inspected		Farm or animal centre
Madeira Hotel	Hotel AA inspected		Zoological or wildlife collection
	Theatre or performing arts centre		Bird collection
	Cinema		Nature reserve
⚑	Golf course		Aquarium
▲	Camping AA inspected		Visitor or heritage centre
	Caravan site AA inspected		Country park
	Camping & caravan site AA inspected		Cave
	Theme park		Windmill
	Abbey, cathedral or priory		Distillery, brewery or vineyard

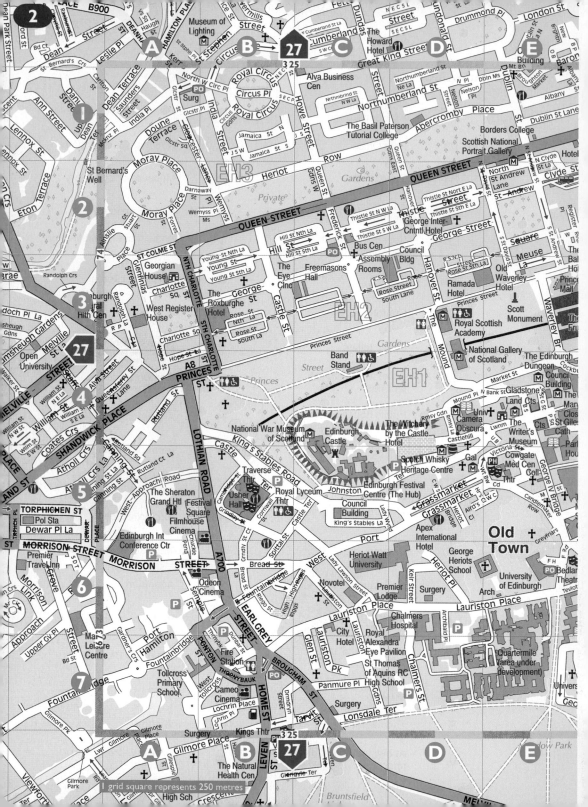

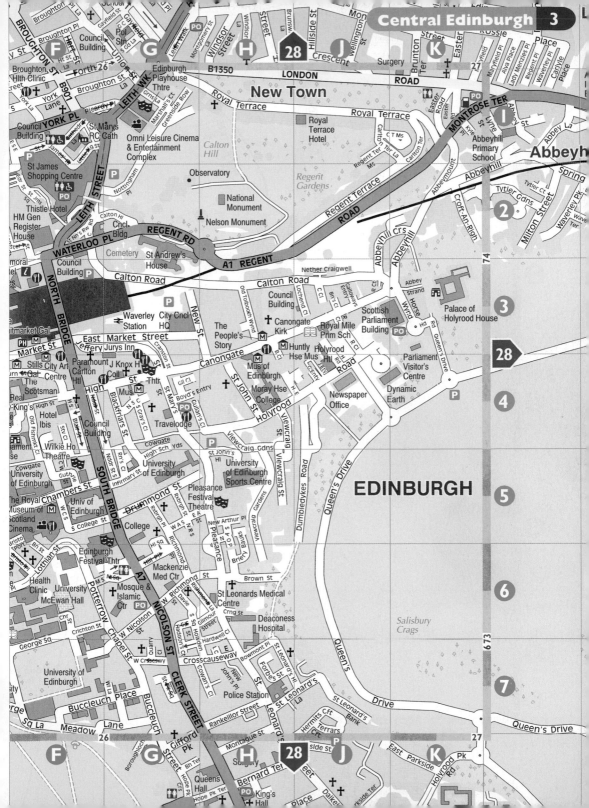

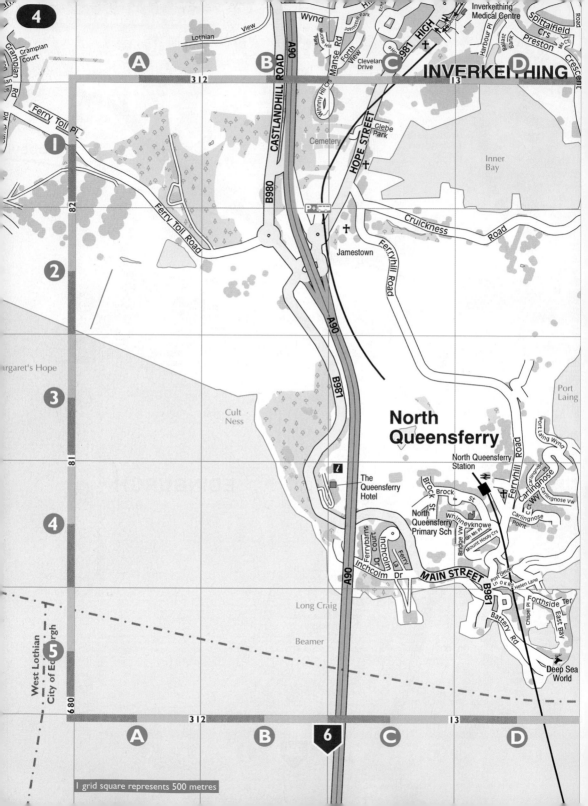

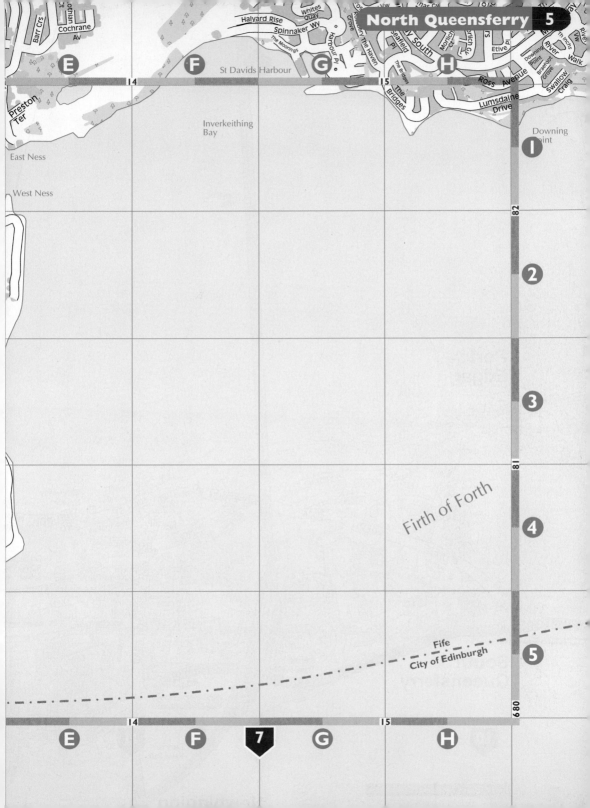

Barr Crs

othian
Cochrane
Av

Halyard Rise
Whites
Quay
Spinnaker Wy
The Moorings

Grove
The Haven
Harbour Pl

y South
Seafield
Pl
The Bridges
Morich
Etive
Pl
Downing
Point
Braefoot
Grove
River
Walk
Swallow
Craig

E

F

St Davids Harbour

G

The
Bridges

Ross Avenue

Lumsdaine
Drive

H

14

15

Preston
Ter

Inverkeithing
Bay

Downing
Point

I

East Ness

82

West Ness

2

3

81

Firth of Forth

4

Fife
City of Edinburgh

5

80

E

14

F

7

G

15

H

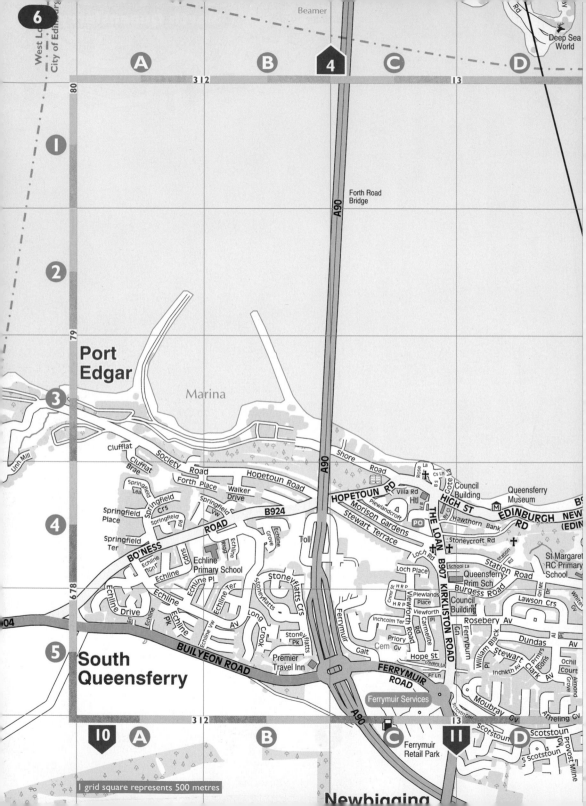

E **F** 5 **G** **H**

14 15

80

I

Hou
Poir

Peatdraught
Bay

Forth
Bridge

Inch
Garvie

2

Whitehouse
Point

79

Long Craig
Pier

Long Craig
Gate

Leuchold

3

8

Innkeeper's
Lodge

Dalmeny

HALLS RD
BURGH RD

HAWES BRAE

924

4

Ashburnham

Ashburnham
Gdns

Ab Gdns

Ashburnham
Gardens

Loan

Bankhead
Grove

Station Rd

B924

678

Asburnham
Road

Queensferry
High School

Dalmeny
Station

Bankhead

Road

5

EH30

Forth Park

Queensferry
Recreation
Centre

B924

Wellhead Cl

Avenue

Easter
Dalmeny

14 15

E **F** **G** 12 **H**

Main Street

PO

Dalmeny

Carlowrie Av

Somerville

Carlowrie
Crs

Dalmeny
Primary School

A   B   C   D

316   17

80

I

Hound
Point

Peatdraught
Bay

Fishery
Cottage

2

79

3

7

Barnbougle
Castle

Dalmeny Park

4

Dalmeny
House

5

B924

678

12   A   316   B   C   17   13   D

Home
Farm

1 grid square represents 500 metres

Barnb...

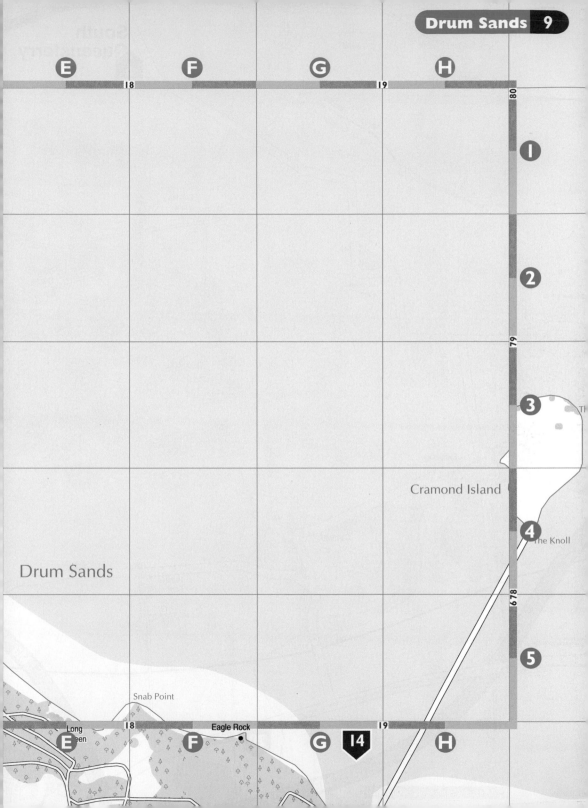

E   F   G   H

18   19

South
Queensferry

Drum Sands

Cramond Island

The Knoll

Snab Point

Long
Green

E   18   Eagle Rock   G   14   H

I

2

3

4

5

10

South
Queensferry

Lawflat

Duddingston

West Lothian
City of Edinburgh

Dundas
Mains

Dundas
Castle

Westfield
Farm

tleywells

Dundas
Loch

Swineburn

Carmelhill

Humbie
Farm

M9

Kirkliston
Sports
Centre

Course

1 grid square represents 500 metres

Snab Point

E   F   G   H   **9**

16   17   18

Long
Green

Barnbougle Ride

Home
Farm

I

77

*Búrnshot
Wood*

*Glenpunty
Wood*

2

A90

East
Craigie

New
Burnshot

3

14

Lowood

Peggy

Avon Rd

Avon P

Hillside   Road
H.R.

Edinburgh
Gate

Avon

76

River
Almond
Walk

Essex
Park

Essex
Brae

4

Craigiehall

Ewerland

Brae Pa

Dowie's Ml
Lane

Braepark

Braehead
Crs

Riverside
Road

Cramond By-Toll

Braehead
Pk

Braehead

**Cramond
Bridge**

Braehead Av

Braehead
Loan

5

Primrose Dr

Strathalmond Rd

strthlmnd
Ln

Nether
Lennie

Strathalmond PK

Cammo Road

strthlmnd
Ct

16   17

E   F   **23**   G   H

Cra
Ter

Cammo R

Strathalmond R

Cammo

Cammo
Brae

Cammo
Pkwy

Cammo
Pl

Cammo
Gr

Cammo H.

Cammo   Grove

Cammo

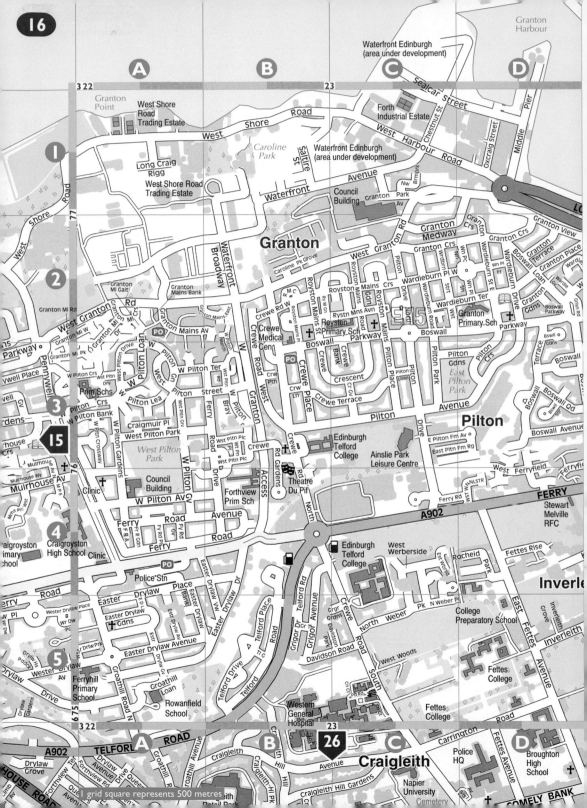

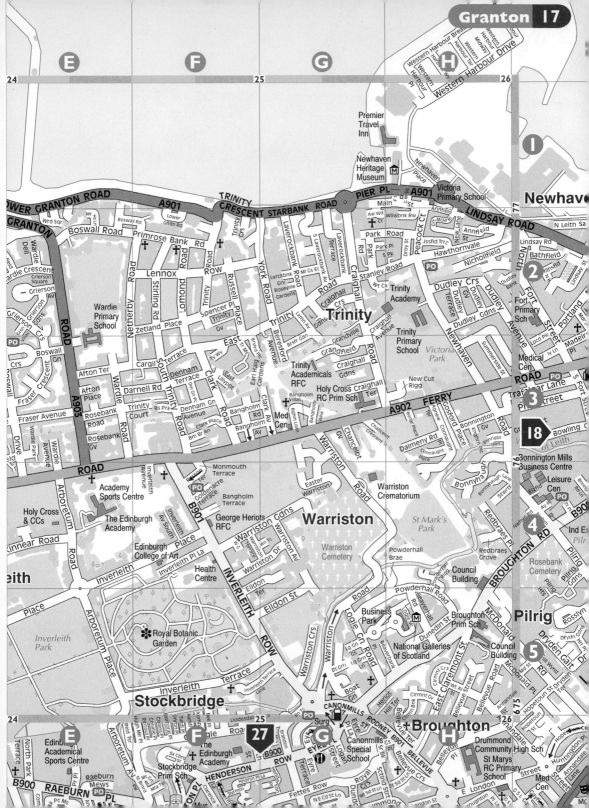

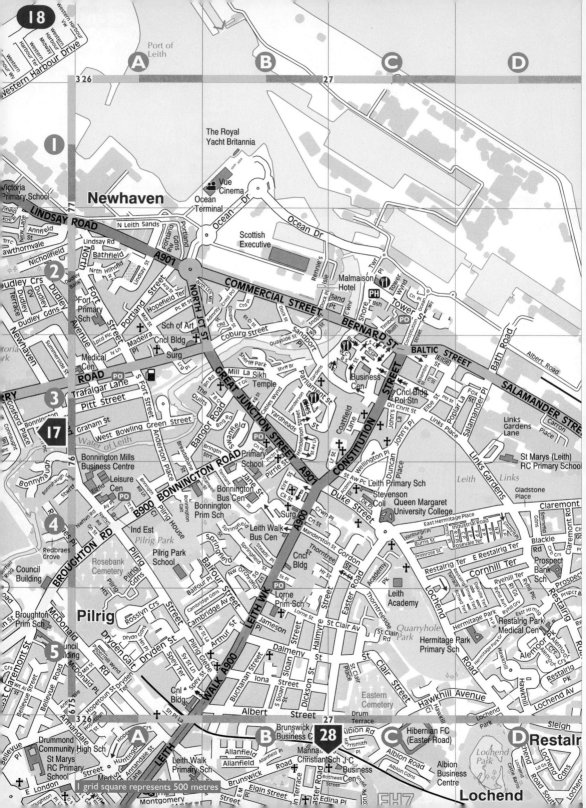

A B C D

3 26 27

I

Port of Leith

The Royal
Yacht Britannia

Vue
Cinema
Ocean
Terminal

Ocean Dr

Scottish
Executive

Newhaven

LINDSAY ROAD

N Leith Sands

2

Lindsay Rd
Bathfield
Nrth Hillsfd

A901

Portland
Street

Fort
Primary
Sch

Victoria
Primary School

Annfield

Nicholifield

awthornvale

Dudley Crs

Dudley

Dudley
Terrace

Dudley
Gdns

Medical
Cen

Newhaven
Road

Trafalgar Lane

Pitt Street

Summerside St

Hopefield Ter

Sch of Art

Madeira
Pl

Cncl Bldg
Surg

Commercial Street

Coburg street

Quayside St

Bernard St

Malmaison
Hotel

PH

Tower St

PO

Baltic Street

Albert Road

Salamander Street

Bath Road

Cncl Bldg
Pol-Stn

Links
Gardens
Lane

Links
Place

Carron
Place

St Marys (Leith)
RC Primary School

3

17

PO

Cosford Place

Bonnington

Graham St

West Bowling Green Street

Water of Leith

Anderson Place

Bonnington Mills
Business Centre

Leisure
Cen

PO

Bonnington
Bus Cen

Bonnington
Prim Sch

Bangor Road

Great Junction Street

Mill La

Sikh
Temple

Parliament St

Sheriff Park

Primary
School

Jane St

Sandport

Shore

Coatfield
Lane

Constitution Street

John's Pl

Wellington Pl

Leith Primary Sch

Duncan
Place

Queen Margaret
University College

Leith
Links

Gladstone
Place

Claremont

4

Broughton Rd

Redbraes
Grove

Council
Building

B900

Bonnington Road

Pilrig House

Ind Est

Pilrig Park

Rosebank
Cemetery

Pilrig Park
School

Springfield

Leith Walk
Bus Cen

Surg

A900

Manderston St

Thorntree

St Gordon
Street

Crwn Pl

Cncl
Bldg

East Hermitage Place

Industrial Road

Vanburg Pl

Burns St

Rosevale Ter

Primrose St

Restalrig Ter

E Restalrig Ter

Cornhill Ter

Blackie
Rd

Prospect
Bank
Sch

Claremont Rd

5

Pilrig

McDonald Road

Broughton
Prim Sch

Council
Building

Dryden Galt

Dryden St

Spey St

Rosslyn Crs

Cambridge Gdns

Balfour Street

Pilrig Gdns

Pilrig Glebe

Arthur St

Leith Walk

Springfield Street

Lorne
Prim Sch

Lorne St

Jameson

Dalmeny
Street

Sloan
Street

Dickson
Street

St Clair Av

St Clair
Place

Easter Road

Thorntreeside

Academy
Pk

Leith
Academy

St Clair Street

Quarryhole
Park

Hermitage Park
Primary Sch

Restalrig Park)
Medical Cen

Alemoor

Restalrig
Pk

Hawkhill Avenue

Lochend
Park

Lochend AV

Hawkhill

Lochend
Road

Restalrig Road South

A B 28 C D Restalr

3 26 27

Drummond
Community High Sch

St Marys
RC Primary
School

Annandale
Street

Bellevue
Pl

L London
St

Leith Walk

Leith Walk
Primary Sch

Allanfield

Brunswick
Street

Albert
Street

Buchanan
Street

Iona
Street

Brunswick
Business
Centre

Mannan
Christian Sch

Allanfield Pl

Annfield Pl

Brunswick
Road

Elgin Street

Montgomery

Hibernian FC
(Easter Road)

Albion Road

Albion
Gdns

Albion Business
Centre

Lochend

Restalrig Road

EH7

I grid square represents 500 metres

E F G H

28 29 30

I

77

2

3

76

4

5

675

Leith

Marine Esplanade

A199

Salamander Yards

Seafield Place

Park

Boothacre Lane

Pirniefield Place

Pirniefield Gdns

Pirniefield Bank

SEAFIELD ROAD

LC

Council Building

Seafield Cemetery

Seafield Crematorium

Prnfld Trrce

Prnfld Gdns

Prospect Bank Rd

Bank

Prospect Bank Place

Prospect Bank Grove

Sq St

Craigentinny Avenue North

A199

Restalrig Circus

PO

Restalrig Crescent

Findlay Cots

Findlay Gardens

Findlay Gv

Findlay Medway

Findlay Avenue

Restalrig Square

Restalrig Road South

Eastern General Hospital

Craigentinny Golf Course

Golf Course

SEAFIELD ROAD

Fillyside Road

Nantwich Drive

Craigentinny Av

Fillyside Terrace

SEAFIELD ROAD EAST

Seafield Rd

Seafield Way

Promenade

Seafield St

E F G H

28 29 30

Craigentinny 29

Drive

Restalrig Gdns

Restalrig Dr

Lochend Quadrant

St Triduana's Rest

St Ninians RC Prim Sch

Loaning Crescent

Loaning Drive

Cyr Rd

Craigentinny Road

Stapeley Avenue

Nantwich Dr

Wakerield

Vane

Kekew

A199

Seafield Industrial Estate

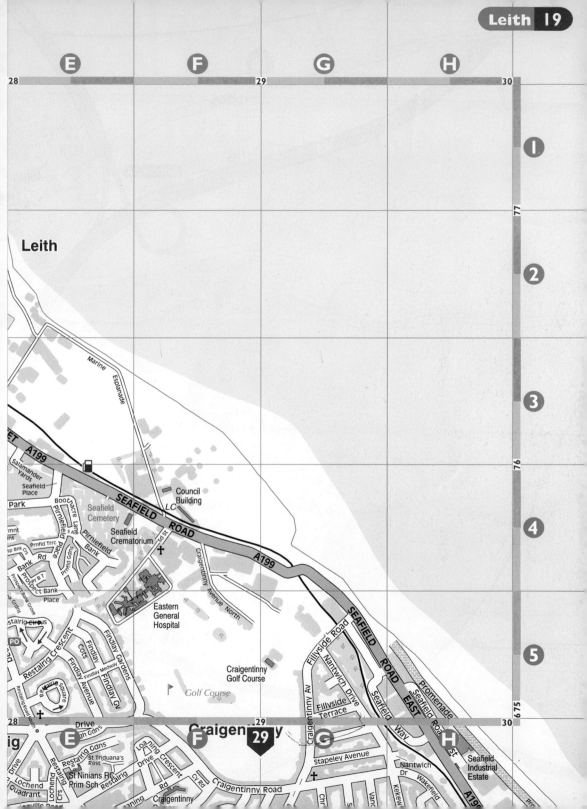

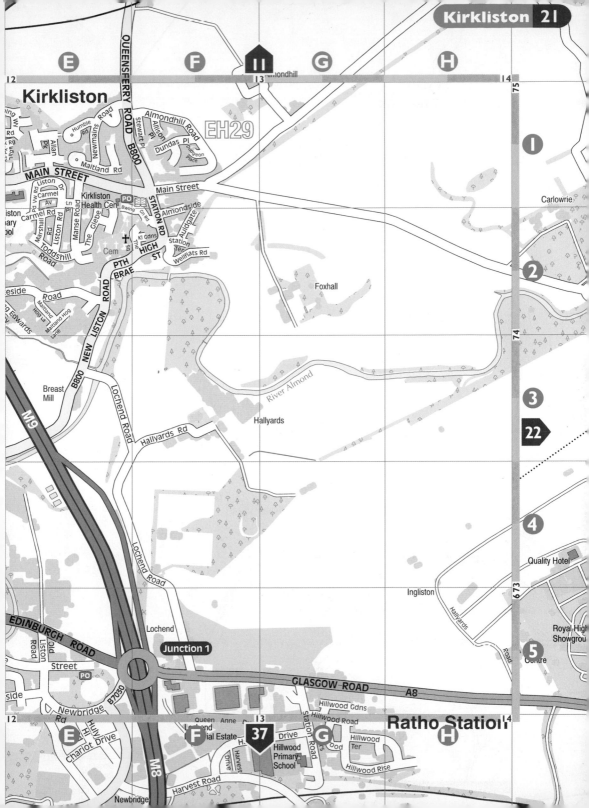

22

314
75

A   B   **12**   C   D
15

Wheatlands

I

Carlowrie

2

74

Boathouse
Bridge

Lenniemuir

Masefield Wy

Turnhouse Road

Edinburgh
Airport

Edinburgh Airport
Terminal Building

P

Gogar Bridge Road

3

21

Jubilee

Burnside Rd

P

P

P

Almond
Road

P

Almond
Av

P

Eastfield Avenue

Gogar Burn

4

673

Quality Hotel

Exhibition
Hall

Fairview   Road

Ingliston   Road

Eastfield   Road

Royal Highland
Showground

Hallyards Road

5

Rural
Centre

P+

East Mains
of Ingliston

314

A   Middle Norton   **B**   **38**   C   D
15

A8

Gogar
Stone

Gogarsto

Gogar
Mount

River A

1 grid square represents 500 metres

Primros

Nether
Lennie

E

F

13
17

G

Cammo Road

H

Almond Rd
Strthlmnd
Strthlmnd
Strthalmond Pk

16
17

Cammo Road

Craigiehall
Temple

Cammo

Cammo
Brae
Cammo Pl
Cammo
Grove

Cammo Hi

Cammo Pkwy

Lennie
Mains

Cammo Road

Cammo

I

Cammo Walk

Turnhouse

Bughtlin

2

Turnhouse Farm Road

Golf Course

Cammo Walk

Crumblands

Lennie
Park

74

A902

MAYBU

Bu

Bugh

Almond Gn

3

Turnhouse
Business Park

Turnhouse
Golf Club

Craigs Road

24

MAYBURY

East Craigs

West
Craigs

4

Cr

Gogar
Mains

Turnhouse Road

Meadowfield Road

Meadowfield
Farm

West Craigs
Industrial
Estate

W Craigs

W
Craigs
AV

W Craigs
N Cyle

Grove

A90

MAYBURY ROAD

North

Turnhouse Road

West Craigs AV

S Mv

Trnh's Rd

West Craigs
Ind Est

5

Marriott Hotel

P

GOGAR
ROUNDABOUT

A8

GOGAR

The South Gyle
Shopping Centre

16
17

E

F

Gogar

39

ar Park

G

THE CITY OF E

H

Cyle

18

e
Broadwy

Lochside V

Edbh
Pk

GLASGOW ROAD

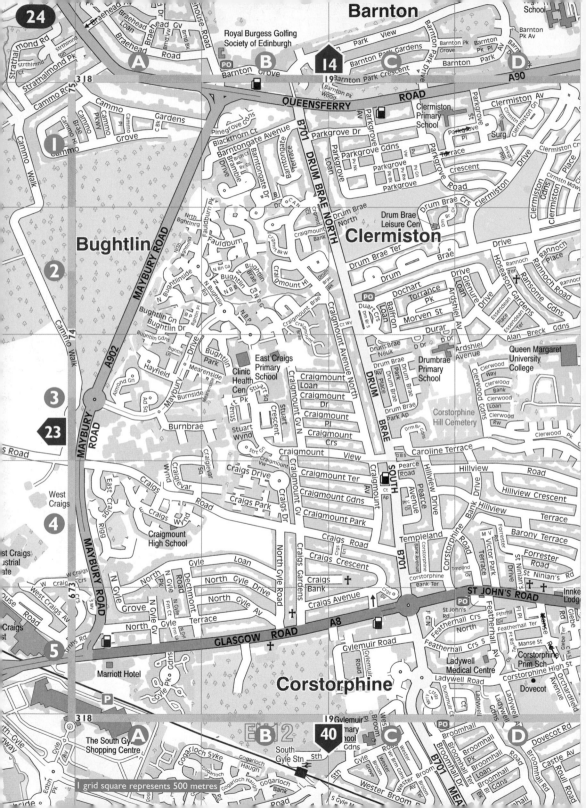

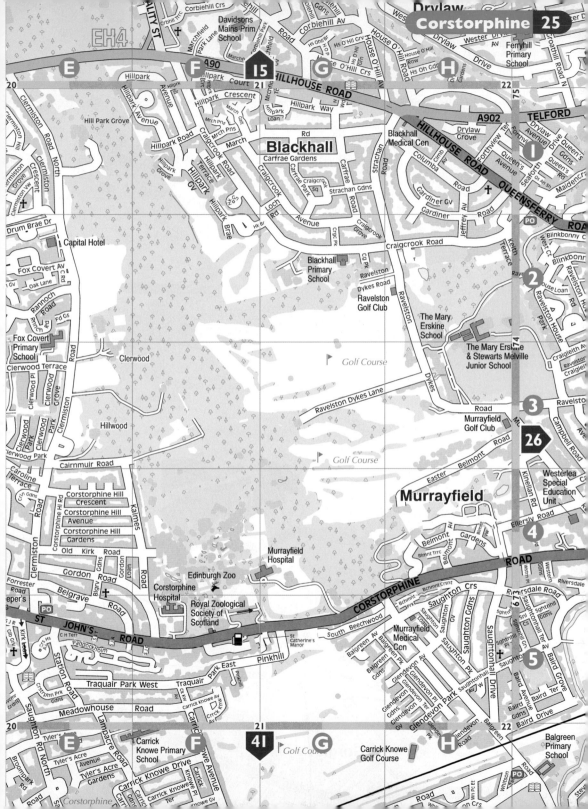

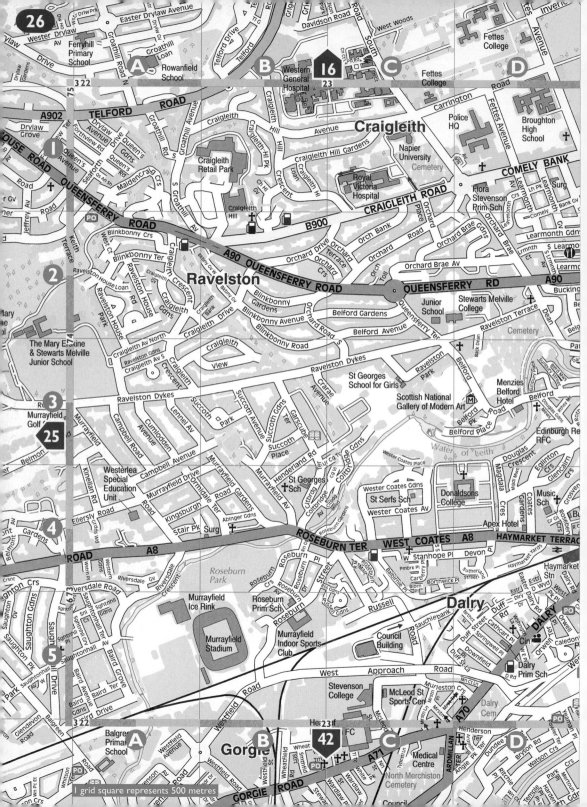

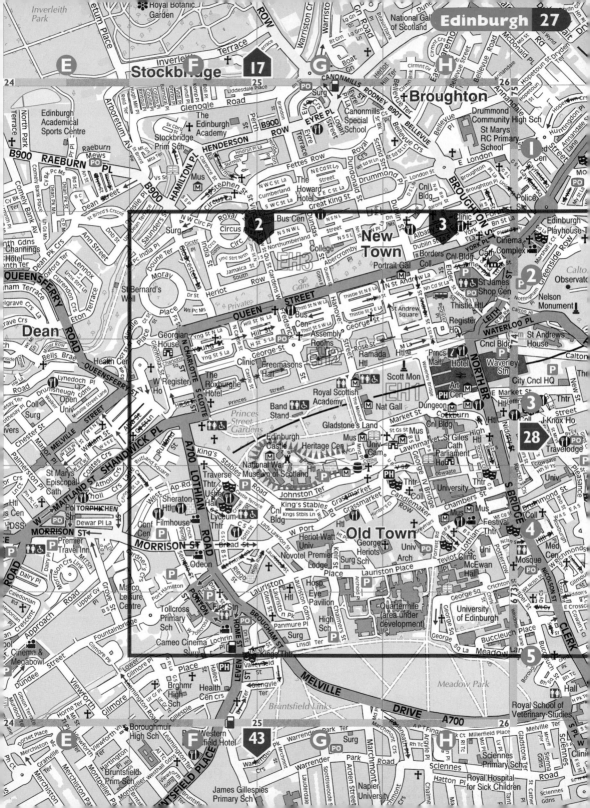

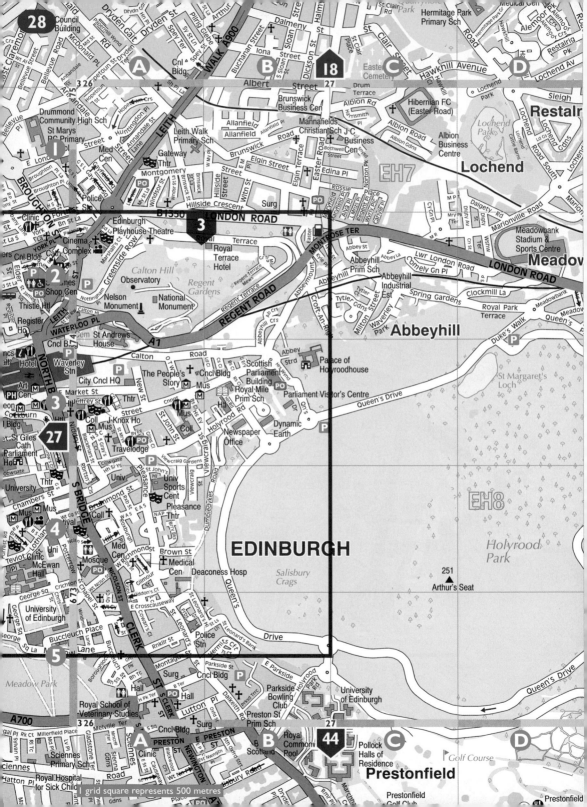

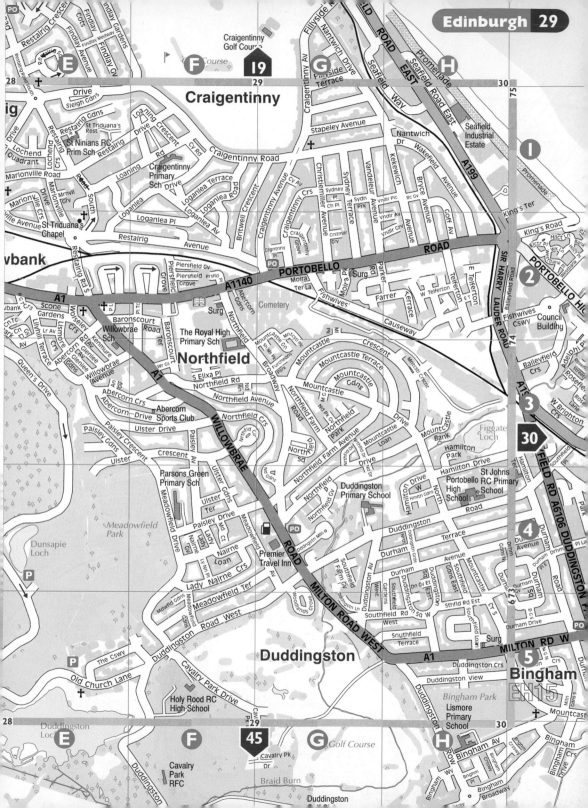

E F G H

32 33 34

75

1

2

74

3

32 ▶ ...erow
...nds

4

Firth of Forth

MUSSELBURGH ROAD

Council
Building
...esdene
...ctisun
EAST A199
Milton Gln

Crs
Milton Ter
Av
Eastfield
Gdns
Milton
Cv
Eastfield Pl
Brnstn
Mil Rd
MUSSELBURGH RD

EDINBURGH ROAD A199

Fisherrow

Promenade Beach La Links Av
Crs Rd Bush
B St Fishers
Links Vw 673
Links
New Street
...ownie Pl
Ladywell

Portobello
Cemetery

Newhailes
Newhailes
Maitland Pk Rd
Maitland
Av
Crs
Dalrymple Crs

New St
Lgt Rd N
NORTH HIGH ST
Market
Campie La
Hrcs Ln
Hercus Loan

Watt's Ct
Ct
Cnct
Bldg
Links Gal
N High
Health
Cen PO
South
Street

Eskvale
BRI...
Ladywell Wk

Medical
Cen
5
Eskbridge
Medical
Cen

Newhailes

Newhailes Av
Newhailes RD

Bogpark Rd

Olivebank
Retail
Park

Fisherrow
Industrial
Estate

Musselburgh
RFC

Campie
Gdns
Campie
Street
Campie Gdns

Olivebank
Farm Rd
Campie Rd

W Holmes Gdns
Belfield Av

Bellfield Av W
Eskside West

Mountjoy Ter

MALL AV
A6095
Station Rd
Inveravon

St Mic...
Avenu...

Newhailes
NEWHAIL...
NEWHAILES
ROAD

E F 47 G

33

Stoneyhill
Dr
Stoneyhill Ter
Stnyhl Rse
Stnyhl Wynd
Claykhowes Crs
Claykn...
Stoneybank
Claykhowes Pl

Stoneyhill
Ct
Stoneyhill Av

The Orch

Eskview Ter
Eskview Av
Eskview Crs
Eskview Rd

OLIVEBANK ROAD
34
OLI...BANK ROAD
...VIEW TER

Inverest Rd
Rive...

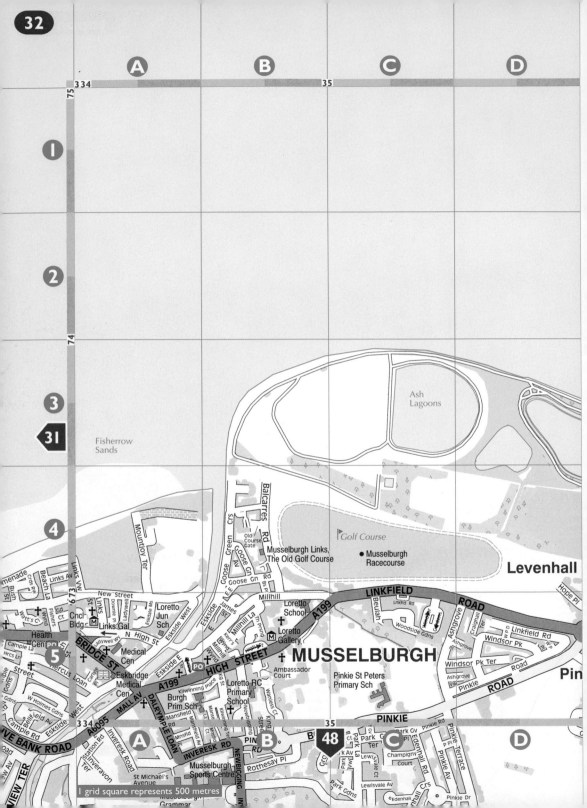

A B C D

334 35

75

74

73

I

2

3

31

4

5

48

Fisherrow
Sands

Ash
Lagoons

Levenhall

Golf Course

Musselburgh
Racecourse

Musselburgh Links,
The Old Golf Course

Balcarres Rd

Goose Green Crs

Goose Gn

Goose Gn Rd

Old Course Gate

Mountjoy Ter

Links VW

Links AV

Beach La

New Street

Eskdale Ms

Loretto
Jun
Sch

Links Gal

N High St

Eskside West

Downie Pl

Eskside West

James

Millhill La

Millhill

Kerr's

Loretto
School

Loretto
Gallery

Millhill

Linkfield Rd

LINKFIELD   ROAD

Beulah

Woodside Gdns

Ashgrove

Craighall

Linkfield Rd

Windsor Pk

Ashgrove

Windsor Pk Ter

Windsor
Road

Ashgrove Vw

Pinkie

ROAD

Pin

Hope Pl

MUSSELBURGH

Pinkie St Peters
Primary Sch

Ambassador
Court

A199

Cncl
Bldg

Health
Cen

Medical
Cen

Eskbridge
Medical
Cen

BRIDGE ST

Eskside E

Mall AV

Dalrymple Loan

West

Percus Loan

Campie La

Hrcs Ln

W Holmes Gdns

Balfield AV

Campie Rd

Eskside

HIGH STREET

PO

A199

Kilwinning Place

Burgh
Prim Sch

Wanless Ct

Newbigging

King Street

Loretto RC
Primary
School

Mansfield Rd

Manse

Mnsfld
Ct

334

A6095

INVERESK RD

Station Rd

Inveravon
Ter

Inveresk Road

NEWBIGGING

35

Pinkie
Rd

PINKIE

Rothesay Pl

Cross

Park La

Park Av

Lewisvale Ct

Lewisvale Av

Park Gdns

Park Gv

Champigny
Court

Edenhall Rd

Pinkie Rd

Pinkie Ter

Pinkie Terrace

Edenhall Crs

Pinkie AV

Pinkie Dr

St Michael's
Avenue

Musselburgh
Sports Centre

Musselburgh
Grammar

VIEW TER

IVE BANK ROAD

1 grid square represents 500 metres

E   F   G   H

36   37   38   75

I

PRESTO

34 Ox Roc

Cuthill
Rocks

Inchvie   2 B1348

The
tery

Bankfoot

Summerlee

Prestongrange
Ter

North

74

Cuthill

Prestongrange Rd

Drummore
Drive

Bank

3

Royal Musselburgh
Golf Club

M Prestongrange
Industrial Heritage
Museum

Golf Course

4

Drum Mohr
Caravan Park

Drummohr

B1361

B1348

RAVENSHAUGH ROAD

Mayville Bk

Ravens

673 50

Dolphingstone

PO

Goshen

A199

A199

5

Haddington
Rd

HADDINGTON ROAD

Moir Crs

St Anns Wy
Moir Ter
Moir
Place

Moir Av

Moir

Moir

Rd

kie Braes

Macbeth

Delta
Drive

Delta Dr

Delta
Rd

Delta vw

Delta Dr

Delta Cons

36   37   38

E   Galt Road   Wallyford ⇌
Station   F   49   G   H

Galt
Avenue

Galt Crs

Delta Rd

Delta Av

Galt Terrace

RTS ROAD

Moir Ter

Wemyss
Gdns

Inchview Road

Oliphant
Cns

Inchview Crs

Dury

mmohr

carlett

Walkford

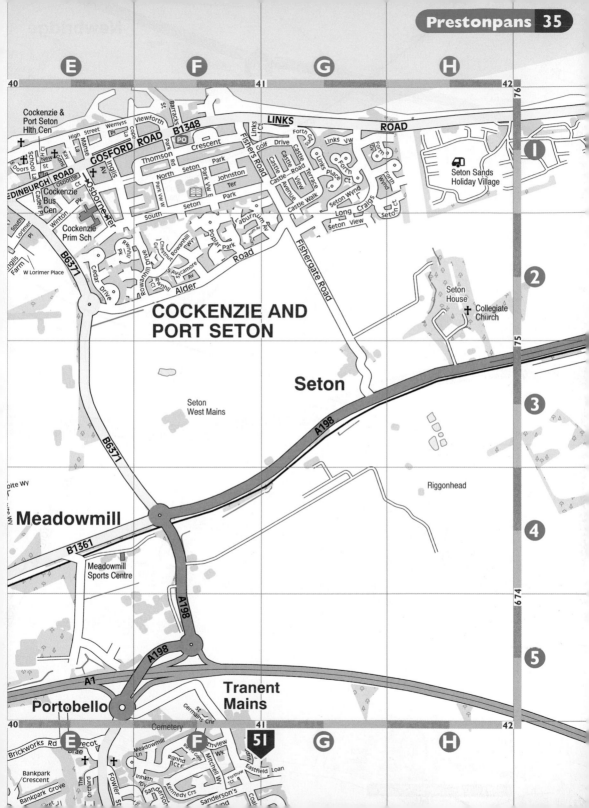

Newbridge

A **B** **20** **C** **D**

310

1

A89

Road

Haugh

River Almond

Newbridge
Industrial
Estate

City of Edinburgh

West Lothian

Ratho
Viaduct

CLIFTONHALL

2

72

punt

Clifton
Trading
Estate

Newbridge
Industrial
Estate

Claylands

3

71

Birdsmill
House

Loup-o-Lees

Clifton
Trading
Estate

M8

Clifton Road

B7030

CLIFTONHALL

4

end

Clifton
Hall School

Clifton Hall

Clifton
Mains

ROAD

Clifton Road

5

670

310

A **B** **C** **D**

West
Clifton

Linwater

1 grid square represents 500 metres

Rural
Centre

Royal Highland
Showground

A   B   C   D

314

P+

22 s
15

A8

Gogar
Stone

Cogarstone Road

Gogar
Mount

Middle Norton

1

ton
se Hotel

72

Norton Mains

Easter
Norton

Freelands Road

2

M8

Ratho
Byres

Freelands Road

Ashley

3

Baird Rd

Rd

37

71

Union Canal

Ratho Park
Golf Club

+

PH

Baird Road Baird Rd

Baird Road
Health Ce

West
Croft

East Cft

Park

Road

Golf Course

4

treet

Dalmahoy Rd

Ratho

Lidgate
shot

ottages

Ransfield

5

Brampton
Lodge

Addiston Farm Road

670

314

15

A   B   C   D

Addiston
Mai

A71

1 grid square represents 500 metres

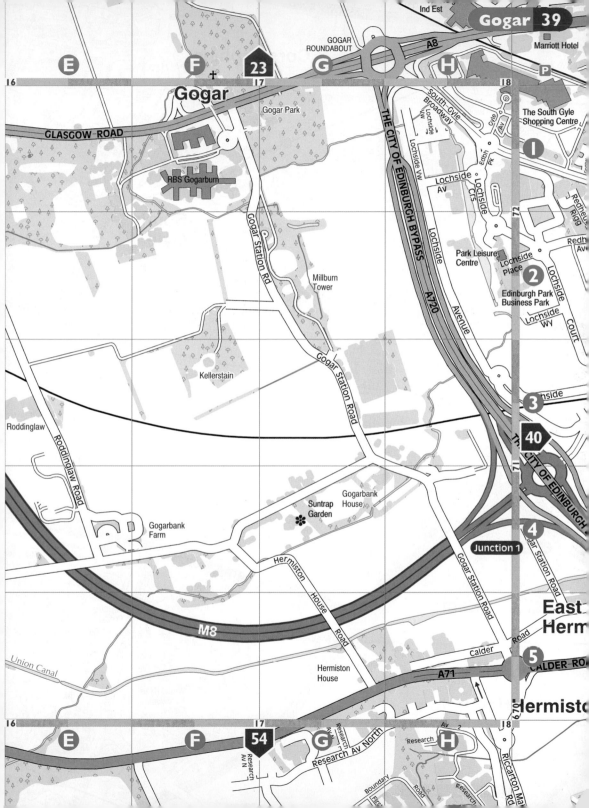

Ind Est

A8

GOGAR
ROUNDABOUT

■ Marriott Hotel

P

E + **F** **23** **G** **H**

16 17 18

Gogar

Gogar Park

The South Gyle
Shopping Centre

South Gyle
Broadway

GLASGOW ROAD

RBS Gogarburn

Lochside VW

Lochside
AV

Lochside
Crs

Lochside
Place

I

Edbh
Pk

Gyle
AV

Redheus
Rigg

Redh
Av

THE CITY OF EDINBURGH BYPASS

Gogar Station Rd

Millburn
Tower

Park Leisure
Centre

Lochside

72

2

A720

Edinburgh Park
Business Park

Lochside
Wy

Lochside
Court

Kellerstain

Gogar Station Road

Avenue

nside

3

Roddinglaw

40

THE CITY OF EDINBURGH

Roddinglaw Road

Gogarbank
House

Suntrap
Garden

4

Gogarbank
Farm

Junction 1

Gogar Station Road

**East
Herm**

M8

Hermiston House Road

Road

Calder

5

CALDER-RO

Union Canal

Hermiston
House

A71

Hermisto

16 17 18

E **F** **54** **G** **H**

Research Av North

Research
AV N

Research

Riccarton Ma

Boundary
Road

Research

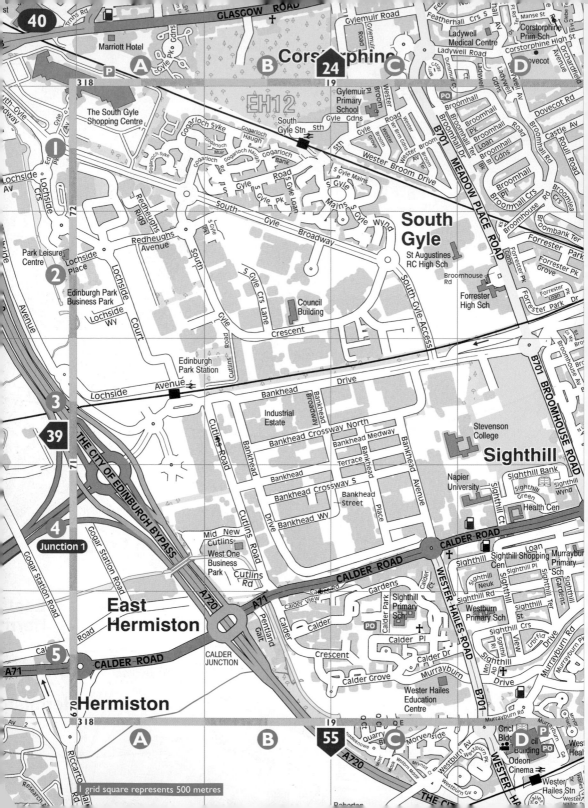

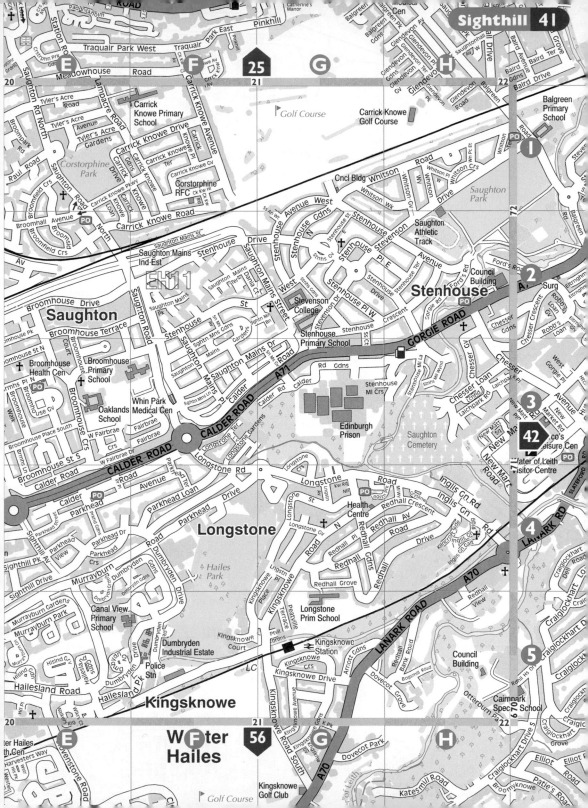

Golf Course

Carrick Knowe Golf Course

Traquair Park West

Traquair

Meadowhouse Road

Pinkhill

Catherine's Manor

Balgreen Cen

Glendevon Av

Glendevon Pl

Glendevon Ter

Glendevon Gdns

Glendevon Gv

Glendevon Road

Baird Drive

Baird Avenue

Baird Ter

Baird Grove

Balgreen Primary School

PO

Whitson Ter

Balgreen Road

Baird Drive

I

Tyler's Acre Road

Tyler's Acre Avenue

Tyler's Acre Gardens

Carrick Knowe Primary School

Carrick Knowe Drive

Carrick Knowe Avenue

Carrick Knowe Gdns

Carrick Knowe Pl

Carrick Knowe Ter

Corstorphine RFC

Ck Kw Hl

Ck Kw Rd

Corstorphine Park

Saughton Road North

Raul Road

Broompark Rd

Broomfield Crs

Broomhall Avenue

Broomside

Broomfield Crs

PO

Carrick Knowe Road

Carrick Knowe Loan

Carrick Knowe Pkwy

Carrick Knowe

Whitson Road

Cncl Bldg

Whitson

Whitson Wk

Whitson Gv

Whitson Cres

Whitson Pl

Whitson Wy

Whitson Dr

Wn Pl

Wn Pce

Saughton Park

2

A

Surg

Chesser Crescent

Chesser Gdns

Robb's Loan Gv

Robb's Loan

Stenhouse Avenue West

Stenhouse N Gdns

Stenhouse St E

Stenhouse St W

Stenhouse Ter

Stenhouse Stevenson Avenue

Saughton Athletic Track

Ford's Rd

Council Building

Ford's Rd

Stenhouse

Gorgie Rd

PO

Chesser Loan

Chesser Gv

West Gorgie Rd

Chesser Avenue

New Market Rd

New Mkt Rd

Broomhouse Drive

Saughton

Broomhouse Terrace

Broomhouse Pk

Saughton Mains St

Saughton Mains Ind Est

EH11

Saughton Mains Pk

Saughton Mains

Saughton Mains Ter

Stenhouse Drive

Stenhouse Drive

Stenhouse Pl E

Stenhouse Cres

Stenhouse Pl W

Stevenson College

Stenhouse Primary School

Rd Gdns

Stenhouse Ml La

Stenhouse Ml Crs

Stnhs Ml Wynd

Stnns

GORGIE ROAD

Broomhouse St N

Court

Broomhouse Health Cen

PO

Broomhouse Primary School

Oaklands School

Whin Park Medical Cen

Saughton Road

Saughton Mains Dr

Saughton Mains Gdns

Sghtn Mns Ln

Calder Road

Calder Ter

Calder Gardens

Calder Rd Gdns

Calder

A71

A71 Road

Edinburgh Prison

Saughton Cemetery

3

Tesco's

New Market Rd

Water of Leith Visitor Centre

42

PO

New Mart Road

Slatef Rd

Broomhouse St S

Broomhouse Crs

Bmhs Pl S

Bmhs Ln

W Fairbrae Crs

W Fairbrae Dr

Fairbrae

Fairbrae

CALDER ROAD

Longstone Ter

Longstone Gardens

Longstone Rd

Longstone Crs

Longstone St

Longstone Gv

Kw Rd

Kw Pl

Redhall Crescent

Redhall Pl

Redhall Gdns

Redhall Av

Redhall Road

Inglis Gn.Rd

Inglis Gn

Inglis Gn Cotts

Wincorge Side

Inglis Gn Rigg

LANARK RD

4

A70

Broomhouse Road

Calder Road

PO

Parkhead

Parkhead Loan

Parkhead Drive

Parkhead Ter

Parkhead Pl

Parkhead Gdns

Parkhead View

Parkhead Crs

Parkhead Dr

W Fairbrae Dr

Longstone

Longstone Road

Health Centre

PO

Redhall Grove

Redhall Dr

Redhall Drive

Redhall View

Redhall

A70

LANARK ROAD

Leisure Cen

5

Sighthill Pk Av

Sighthill Drive

Murrayburn

Murrayburn Park

Murrayburn Gardens

Hlsind Gdns

Hlsind Gv

Dumbryden Drive

Dumbryden Gdns

Dmbrydn Gdns

Hailes Park

Kingsknowe Place

Kingsknowe Road

Kingsknowe Gardens

Peatville Ter

Lngstn Gv

Lngstn Pl

Longstone Prim School

Kingsknowe Court

Kingsknowe Cres

Bank Road

Bogsmill Road

Redhall

Dovecot Grove

Council Building

Cairnmuir Spec School

Otterburn Pk

A70

A70

Craiglockhart Dell Road

Craiglockhart

Canal View Primary School

Dumbryden Industrial Estate

Police Stn

Hailesland Road

Hailesland Pk

Walker's Rig

Hislop Gdns

LC

Kingsknowe Station

Kingsknowe Drive

Ptvll Gdns

Arrott Gdns

Dovecot Park

Katesmill Road

Broomyknowe

Elliot Road

Patie's Rd

Craiglockhart Grove

Craiglock

Craigl

Kingsknowe

W   ter Hailes

Water Hailes

th.Cen

Harvesters Way

venstone Road

Golf Course

Kingsknowe Golf Club

Dovecot Park

Water of Leith

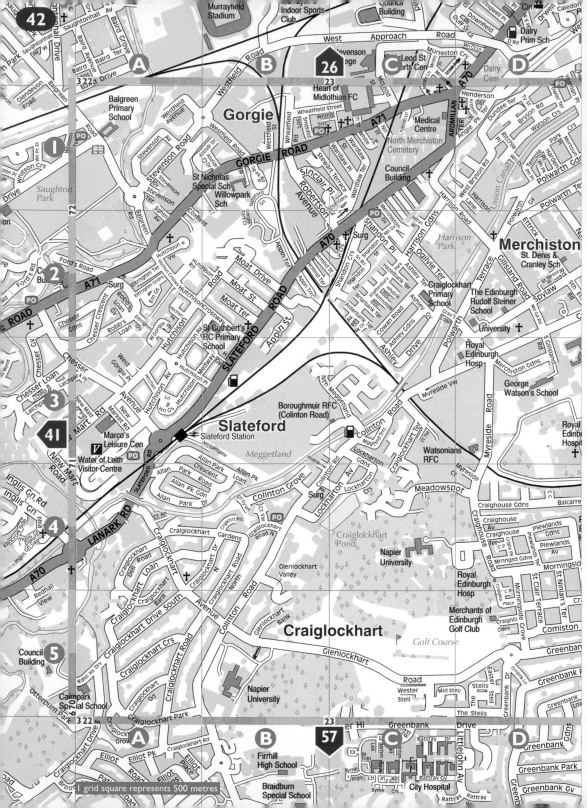

P Cinema & Megabowl

Cameo Cinema

Kings Thtr

Meadow Park

Royal School of Veterinary Studies

Hall

E

Boroughmuir High Sch

Best Western Bruntsfield Hotel

F

Brghmr High Sch

Health Cen

27

G

H

I

Royal Hospital for Sick Children

Sciennes Primary Sch

Sciennes

PO

Warrender Park Ter

Surg

Warrender Park Road

Marchmont Road

Napier University

James Gillespies Primary Sch

Bruntsfield Prim Sch

Bruntsfield Health Cen

James Gillespies High School

Warrender Baths Swimming Pool

Hatton Pl

Grange

Newingto

Grange Cemetery

2

Napier University

Chamberlain Rd

Greenhill Pk

St Margaret's Rd

Strathearn Road

EH9

Carlton CC

Dairymple Crescent

Church Hill

Clinton Road

Hope Terrace

Hospital

Blackford Road

Whitehouse Terrace

3

44

Health Cen

Dominion Cinema

Newbattle Terrace

Royal Blind Sch

Astley Ainsley Hospital

Royal College of Nursing

Oswald Road

Oswald Road

W Relugas

Morningside

Falcon Av

St Peters RC Prim Sch

George Watson's College

Cncl Bldg

Morningside Place

Steel's Pl

Canaan Lane

Blackford Gate

Mortonhall Road

Charterhall Gv

4

Jordan Lane

Cluny Pl

Charterhall Road

Avenue

Blackford Hill Gv

Blackford Hill Vw

Craigmillar Golf Club

Nile Grove

Surg

Cluny

Cluny

Gardens

Midmar Drive

Blackford Pond

Ladysmith Rd

Royal Edinburgh Hospital

Morningside Cemetery

Belhaven Ter

Comiston Pl

Cluny

Drive

Royal Observatory Visitor Centre V

Blackford Hill

Observatory Road

5

Golf Co

South Morningside Primary Sch

Cmstn Ter

Correnie Dr

Braid Crescent

Midmar Gdns

Council Building

Hermitage of Braid

Greenbank Av

Greenbank Crs

Hermitage

Braid Hills Drive

Farm Road

Braid Hills Road

E

F

58

Braid Hills Golf Cours

G

H

Hills Drive

Braidburn Valley Park

Braid Hills

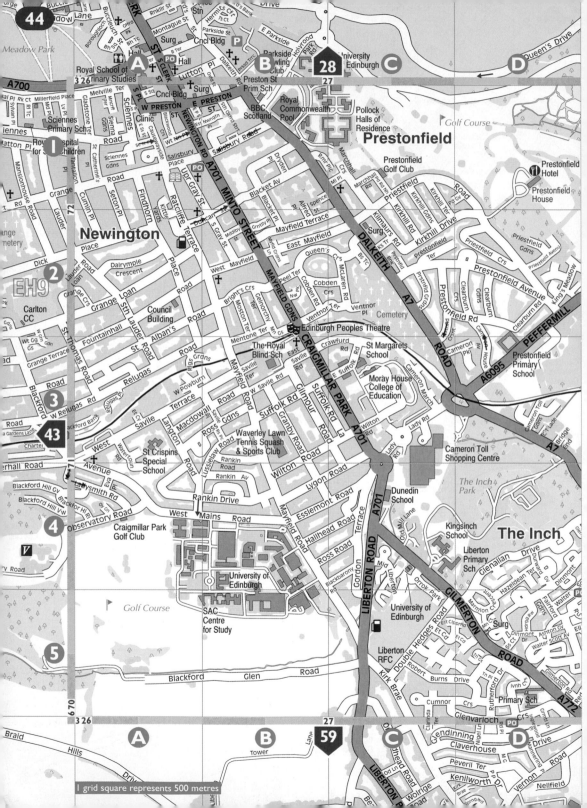

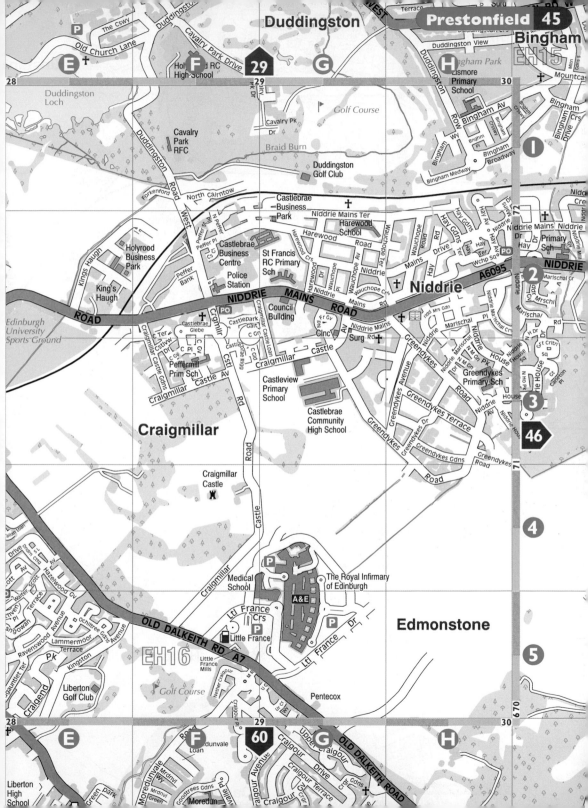

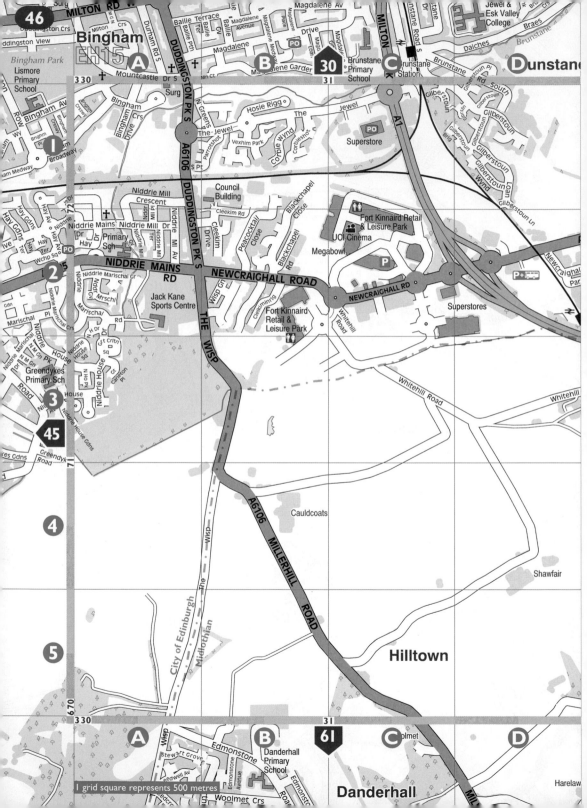

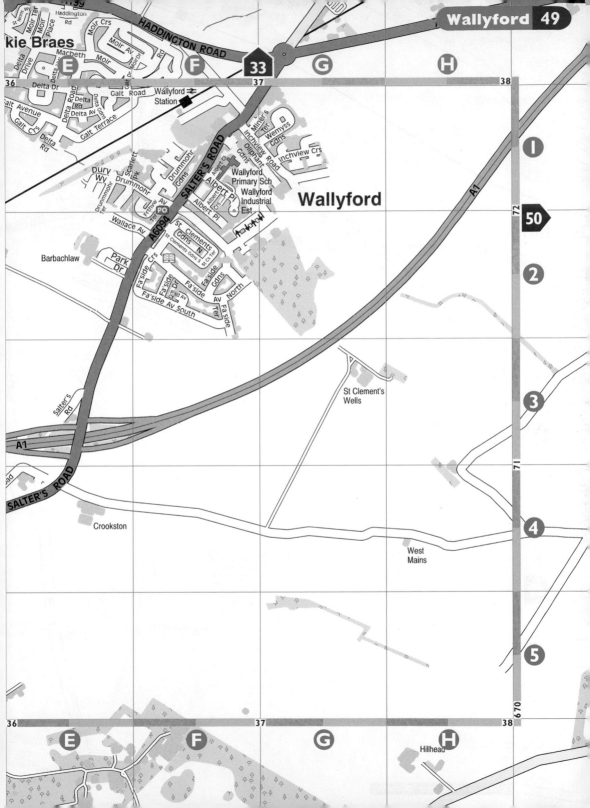

kie Braes

Haddington Rd

HADDINGTON ROAD

E **F** **33** **G** **H**

36 37 38

St Ninian's Wy
Moir Ter
Moir
Moir
Place
Macbeth
Moir Crs
Moir Av
Moir Rd
Delta Drive

Delta Dr
Galt Road
Wallyford Station
Delta Road
Delta Gdns
Galt Av
Galt Avenue
Galt Cr's
Delta Rd
Delta Av
Galt Terrace
Delta Rd

I

72

Miner's Ter
Wemyss Gdns
Inchview Road
Oliphant Gdns
Inchview Crs
Dury Wy
Scarlett Pk
Drummohr
Drummohr
SALTER'S ROAD
Albert Ct
Albert Pl
Wallyford Primary Sch
Drummohr Ter
Fr Stw Av
PO
Albert Pl
Albert Crs
Wallyford Industrial Est
Wallyford

50

A6094
Wallace Av
St. Clements Gdns N
St Clements Gdns S SC Ter
St Clements Gdns S C's Ter

2

Barbachlaw
Park Dr
Fa'side Crs
Fa'side Av
Fa'side Dr
Fa'side Gdns
Fa'side Av North
Fa'side Ter
Fa'side
Fa'side Av South

A1
A1

Salter's Rd

St Clement's Wells

3

71

SALTER'S ROAD

Crookston

4

West Mains

5

670

36 37 38

E **F** **G** **H**

Hillhead

50

Royal Musselburgh
Golf Club

Golf Course

Jimmore
Rigley Ter
Rd
B1361

Prestonpans
Industrial Estate

Mid Road
Industrial Estate

34
39

Prestonpans
Station

Johnnie

Bankton

Cope's

A **B** **C** **D**

3 38

A1

Road

Bankpark
Brae

Bankpark
Crs

I

Stair Pk

33
73

Dolphingstone

A1

Bankhead

A199

EDIN

Polson
Gdns

A199

2

Lammermoor Gdns

Lammermoor
Ter

B6414

3

A1

72

4

49

Myles
Farm

W Wm
Gdns

B6414

5

671

3 38

39

A **B** **C** **D**

North
Elphinstone

Waterloo

1 grid square represents 500 metres

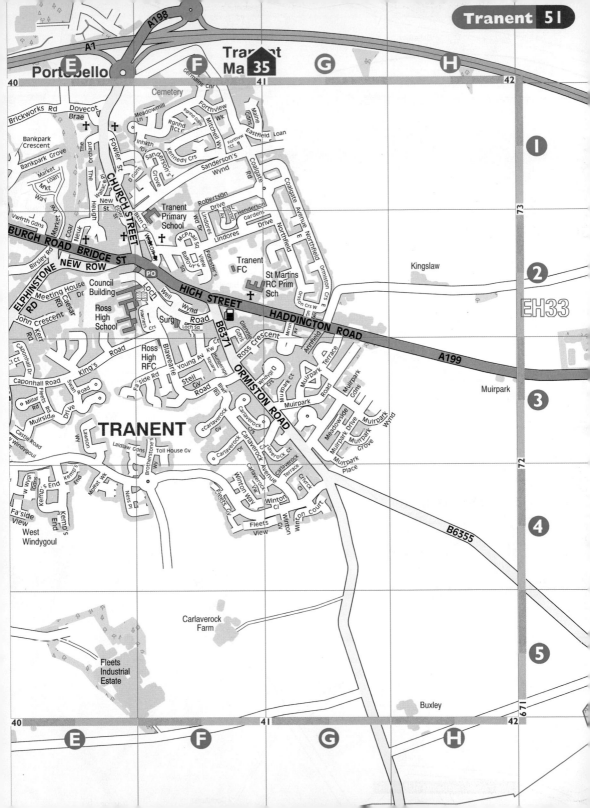

Dalmahoy
Mains

A **B** **C** **D**

314 15

67

1

Lanark Rd
West

LANARK ROAD WEST

Ravelrig Rd

Ravelrig PK

Ravelrig Ct

Ravelrig Dr

Tur
Av

2

Hannahfield

Ravelrig
Hill

A70

3

Larch
Grove

Lovec
AV

Johnsburn

Clayhills

Lovecale
Cv

PK

Clayhills
Cv

Glenpark

Bankhead
House

Johnsburn
Haugh

Rd

Glenbrook Road

Dd

66

Whelpside

Johnsburn
Rd

Deanpark
Ct.

Glenbrook

Crosswood
AV

Crosswood
Cv

De
Pr

4

House of
Cockburn

Goodtrees

Crosswood
Crs

Cairns Drive

Cairns
Gdns

Cockburn

Highlea
Rd

5

Cockburn

Cockburnhill Road

Highlea
Circle

Cr

665

314 15

A **B** **C** **D**

Cockdurno

Calder

Union Canal

A71

Hermiston House

Research Av North

A

B

39
17

C

D

316
70

Riccar... K...

Research Av N

Research Av N

A71

Research

Av 2

Histon ns

Research

Research AV S

The Avenue

Meadow Rd

Research East

1

North

First Gait

Boundary

Road

Fourth Gait

Second Gait

Third Gait

Heriot Watt University

2

69

Warriston

Road

Farm

Warriston

Cameron

Small Road

3

Long Dalmahoy Road

Malcolmstone

Cocklaw

Curr

Curriehill

Weaver...

N

Currievale

Curriehill Station

4

Gowanhill

Gowanhill

Farm

Road

Forth Vw Crs

Palmer Rd

Palmer Pl

Curriehill

Ric Pri

Cu Pri

316

Stevenson College

Drive

Currievale

Dolphin Gdns East

Forth Vw Pl

Portland Rd

Pentland Rd

Curriehill Health Cen

5

Newmills

LC

Currievale Pk Gv

Currievale Pk

Dolphin Av

Dolphin Rd

rig Road

Road

Currievale Dr

Cherry Tree Park

Rowan Tree Av

Dolphin Gdns W

Stewart Cres

Curriehill Castle Drive

Newmills Crs

Cherry Tree Gdns

Rowan Tree Av

Stewart Rd

A70

Old Newmills Rd

Cherry Tree Loan

Cherry Tree Cres

A

B

53
17

C

Stewart Gv

D

Addiston Gv

Horsburgh B...

Iston ...

Cherry Tree Pl

Cherry Tree Gdns

ow Tree Pl

Waulkmill Loan

Dalmaho...

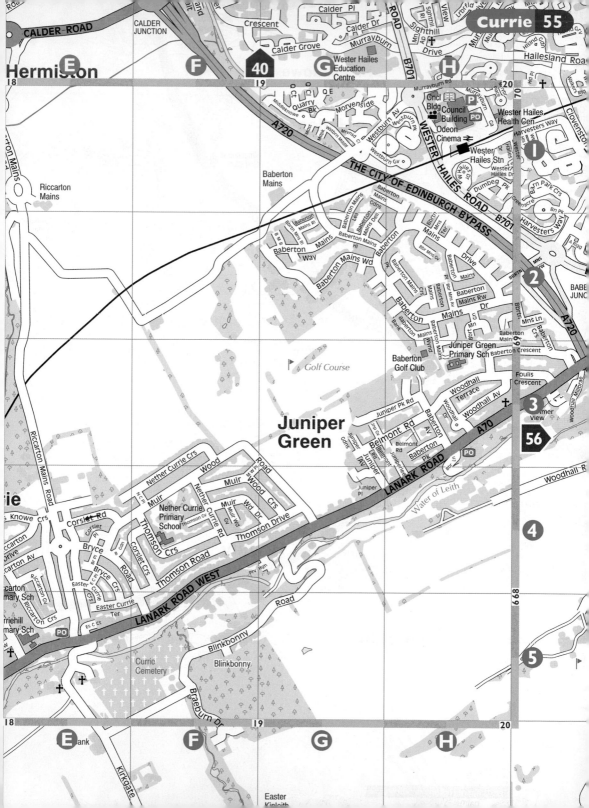

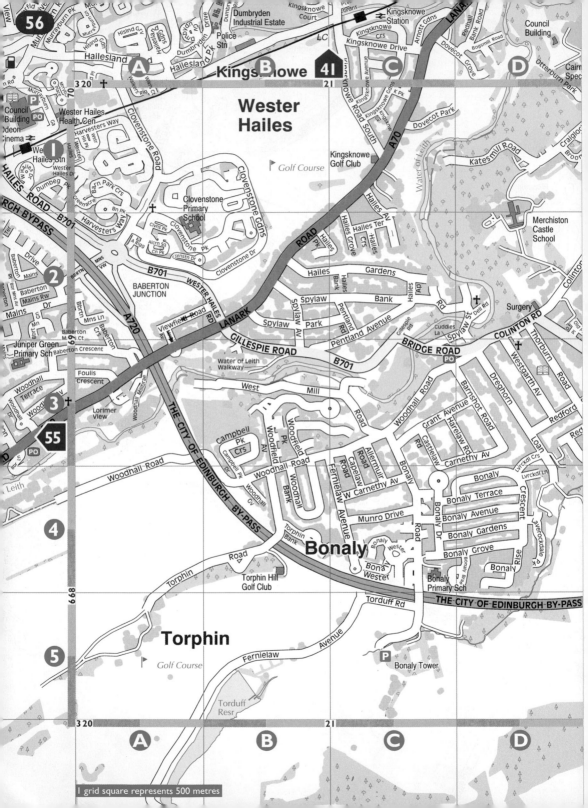

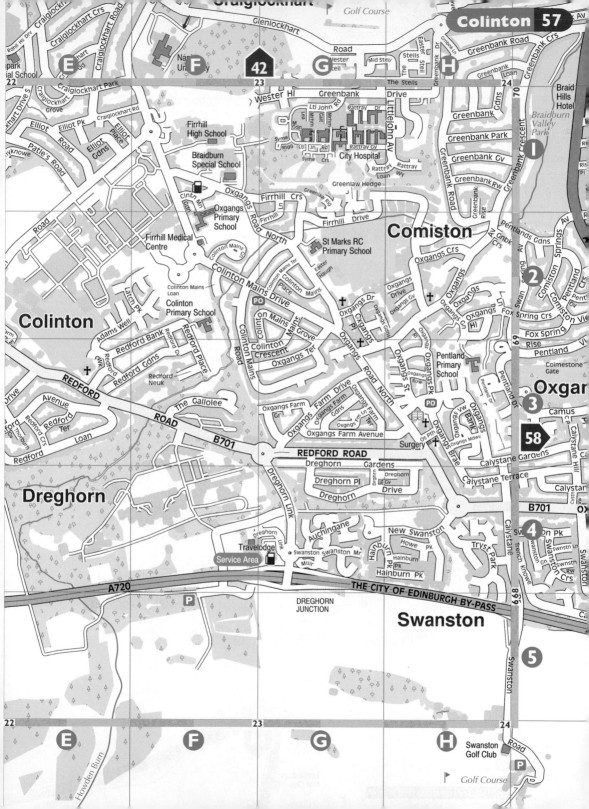

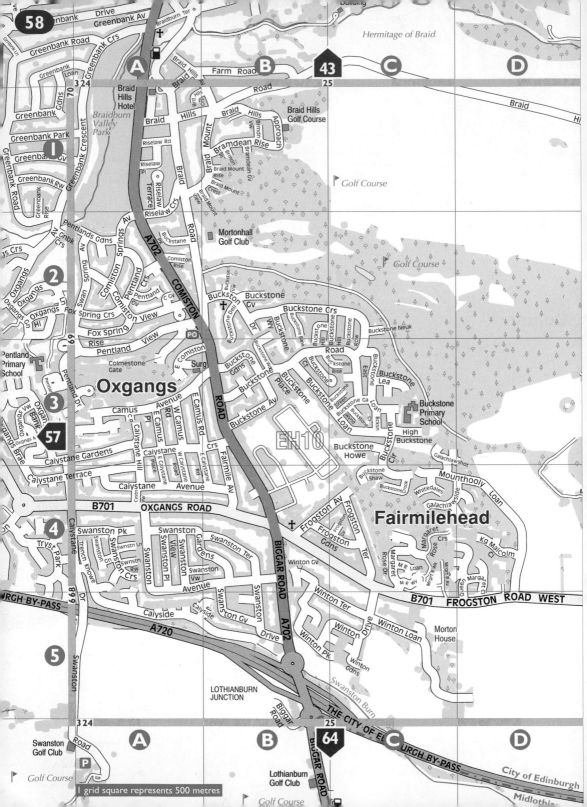

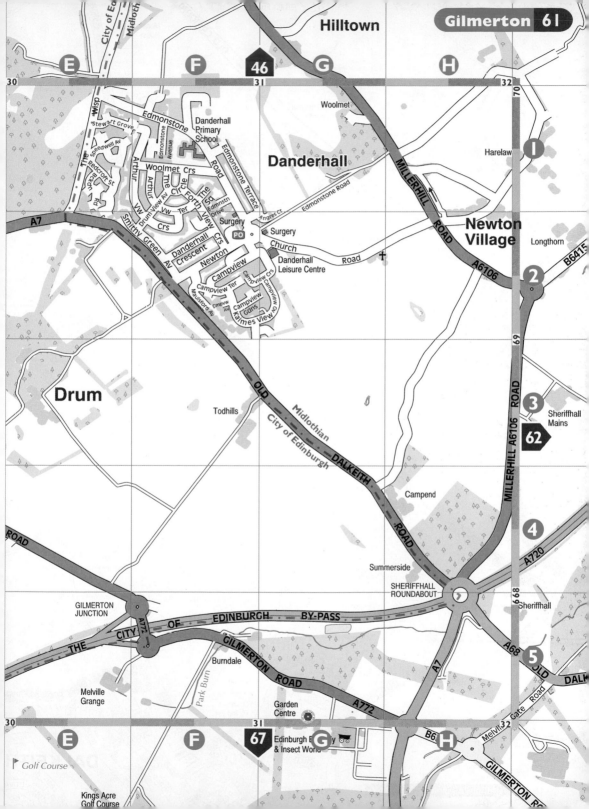

E   F   46   G   H

30   31   32

City of Ed
Midloth

Woolmet

The Wisp
Stewart Grove
Speedwell Av
Redcroft St
Edmonstone Avenue
Edmonstone
Arthur
Woolmet Crs
Arthur
The Circle
Forth View
The Sq
VW Drum View Av
Crs
VW Ter
Edmnstn Drive
Surgery
PO
Danderhall Crescent
Crs
Newton
Campview
Campview Ter
Cmpvw Av
Maulsford Av
Campview Crs
Campvw
Cmpvw
Kaimes View
Campview Gdns

Danderhall Primary School
Edmonstone Terrace
Edmonstone Road

Danderhall

Harelaw
ngres Ct
Edmonstone Road
Surgery
Church
Danderhall Leisure Centre
Road

MILLERHILL ROAD

Newton Village
Longthorn

A7
Smithy Green Av

Drum

OLD DALKEITH ROAD
Midlothian
City of Edinburgh

Todhills

A6106

2

B6415

69

3
Sheriffhall Mains

62

Campend

4
A720

Summerside

SHERIFFHALL ROUNDABOUT

MILLERHILL A6106 ROAD

668
Sheriffhall

A68
OLD DALK

5

GILMERTON JUNCTION
A772
THE CITY OF EDINBURGH BY-PASS

GILMERTON ROAD
A772
A7
Melvil Gate Road

Burndale
Park Burn

Melville Grange

Garden Centre

E   F   67   G   H

30   31   32

Edinburgh B   y & Insect World
B6
B6
GILMERTON R

Golf Course

Kings Acre Golf Course

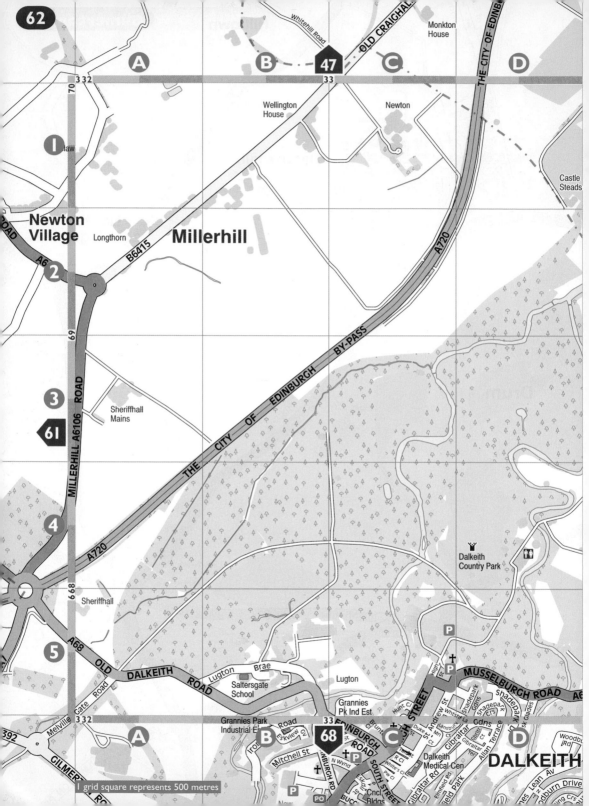

A **B** **47** **C** **D**

33

Whitehill Road

OLD CRAIGHALL

THE CITY OF EDINBURGH

Monkton House

I law

Castle Steads

Wellington House

Newton

Newton Village

Longthorn **Millerhill**

B6415

A6

2

A720

69

3

61

Sheriffhall Mains

MILLERHILL A6106 ROAD

THE CITY OF EDINBURGH BY-PASS

Dalkeith Country Park

4

A720

668

Sheriffhall

5

A68 OLD DALKEITH ROAD

Lugton Brae

Saltersgate School

Lugton

Grannies Pk Ind Est

MUSSELBURGH ROAD A6

P

HIGH STREET

SOUTH STREET

P

P

Melville Gate Road

332

A **B** **68** **C** **D**

Grannies Park Industrial E

Mitchell St

Road

kview Cl

33 EDINBURGH ROAD

Hunt La

Duke St

St Andrew St

Whst

Lansbu

Shadepa Gdns

Shadepa CRS

Shadepark Glades

Allan Terrace

Gibraltar Gdns

Gibraltar Ter

Dalkeith Medical Cen

DALKEITH

Woodbu Rd

Woodbu Drive

Cncl Bldgs

N Wynd

P

PO

GILMERTON RD

392

E   F   48   G   H

Carberry Mains

WHITECRAIG

Whitecraig Rd
Whitecraig Rd

A6094

Whitecraig Primary School

Whitecraig Gdns

Deantown Dr

PO

The La

La

Deantown Av

Carberry Ct

Whitecraig Av

34   35   36

70

I

A6124

Home Farm

SALTERS ROAD

A6094

Smeaton

2

69

Newfarm

Smeaton Shaw

3

East Lothian
Midlothian

Langside

4

Dalkeith Schools
Community Campus –
Dalkeith High School
St Davids RC High School
Saltersgate School

SALTERS ROAD A6094

Langside
Head

68

5

Thornyhall

Thorny Bank

B6414

Thornybank Industrial Estate

A6094

SALTERS ROAD

34

E   F   69   G   H   EH22

Wilson Av

Salters

Gilson

Drive

Woodburn Primary School

Cowden Park

Cowden Crs

Cwdn Gv

Cowden

Cowden Ter

Wester
Cowden

35   36

Woodburn Road

Woodburn

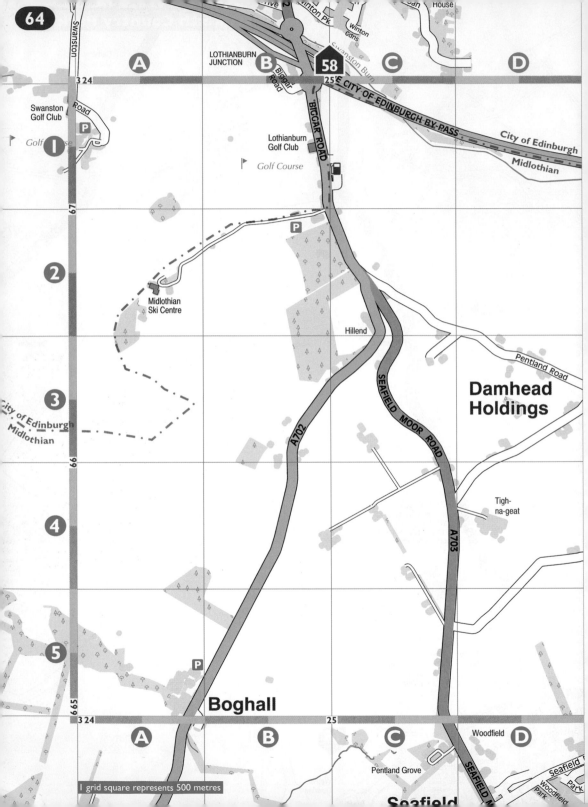

64

A B **58** C D

LOTHIANBURN
JUNCTION

3 24

25

E CITY OF EDINBURGH BY-PASS

City of Edinburgh

Midlothian

Swanston
Golf Club

P

Golf Course

1

Lothianburn
Golf Club

Golf Course

67

P

2

Midlothian
Ski Centre

Hillend

Pentland Road

**Damhead
Holdings**

City of Edinburgh

Midlothian

3

69

A702

SEAFIELD MOOR ROAD

Tigh-
na-geat

4

A703

5

665

P

3 24

Boghall

25

A B C D

Woodfield

Pentland Grove

SEAFIELD

Seafield
Park

Woodfield
Park

Seafield

1 grid square represents 500 metres

Burdiehouse
Primary
School

The Mun

B Crs

Burdiehouse Drive

A

B

Lasswade

60
29

C

Gilmerton Station

D

West Edge
Farm

Road

A720

THE CITY OF EDINBURGH BY-PASS

LASSWADE
JUNCTION

1

Lang Loan

67

2

raiton

Eldin
Industrial
Estate

Wester
Melville

Edgefield Road
Industrial Estate

328

3

65

HAWTHORN

Mays Road

Gdns

Edgefield Road

The Green

Avon Rd

Edgefield

Foundry Lane

Wadingburn
Lane

LASSWADE R

Glebe Place
Church Rd

Green Lane

St Margarets
RC Primary
School

Edgefield Pl

FOUNTAIN PL

Loanhead
Hospital

Cemetery

A768

WADINGBURN ROAD

Kevock Road

EH18

GDNS

Clayburn Road

Myorn St

M B Pl

George Av

Surgery

4

Loanhead
Leisure
Centre

CLERK ST

Engine Rd

Town
Hall

Hunter Crs

Hunter Ter

Hunter Av

LASSWADE RD

Braeside Road

Clinic

George Ter

George Drive

Loanhead
Primary Sch

Fowler

Linden PL

HIGH ST

PO

LINDEN PL

on Av

THE LOAN

A768

High St

Mayfield Crs

Arbuthnot

Burghlee Ter

Police Station

Caprain Ter

LOANHEAD

Park View

5

Burghlee

Mavisbank

Cemetery

Mavisbank
House

Polton Rd

Polton
House

Polton
Vale

665

328

A

B

74
29

C

Bank

Polton

Polton
Bank
Terrace

Mavisbank PL

Quincey Road

Methven Ter

McLean Pl

West

Rd

Farm Av

Pentland Road

Dalno Place

Argyle Pl

Polton Road

D

Seaforth
Terrace

Hawthornden
Primary
School

Gordon Av

Polton

1 grid square represents 500 metres

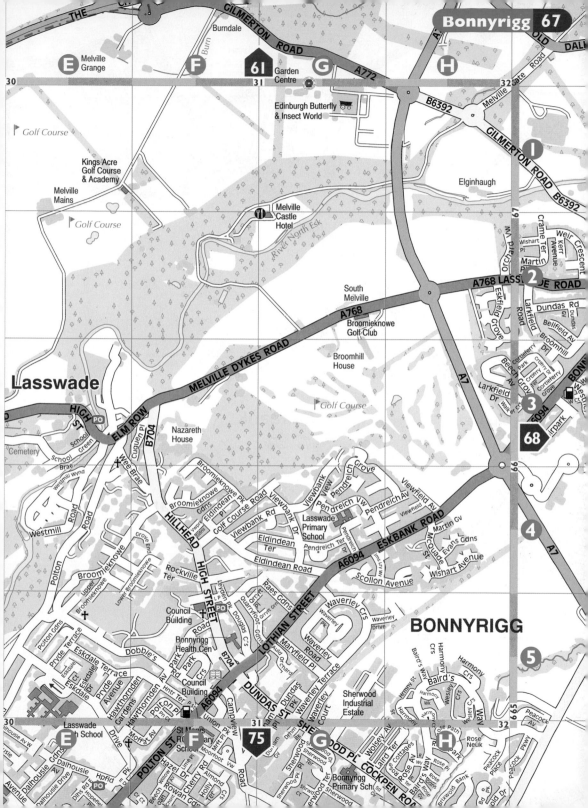

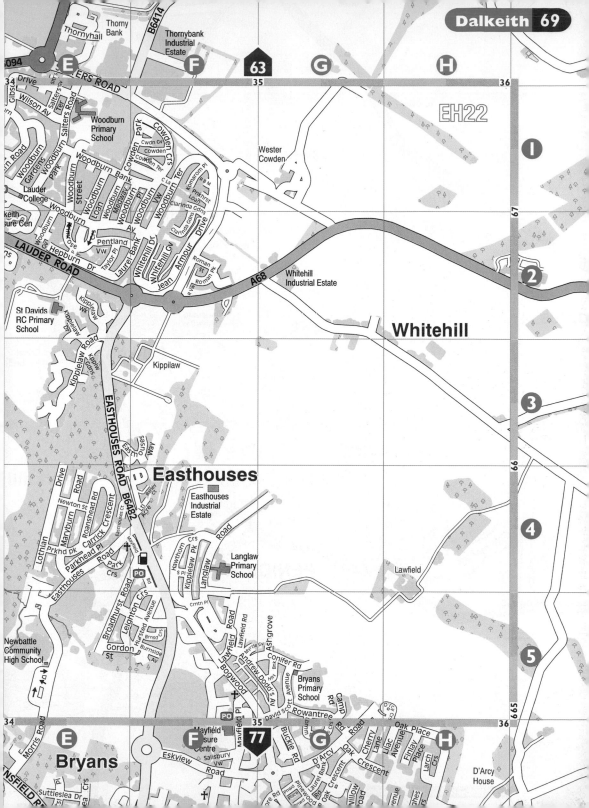

A6094

B6414

Thornyhall

Thorny Bank

Thornybank Industrial Estate

E SALTERS ROAD **F** **63** 35 **G** **H**

EH22

36

Gibson Road

Drive

Salters Ter

Salters Road

Wilson Av

Woodburn Primary School

Cowden Park

Cwdn Gv

Cowden Crs

Cowden Pl

Cowden Ter

Wester Cowden

67

I

Woodburn Gardens

Woodburn Park

Woodburn Bank

Woodburn Street

Woodburn Loan

Woodburn Pl

Medway

Woodburn Av

Woodburn Ter

Kinnaird Pk

R P M

PnkHrst

Loan

Clarinda Gdns

Clarinda Gdns

Lauder College

Keith Leisure Cen

Woodburn

G Hepburn Dr

Pentland Vw

Taylor Pl

Laurel Bank

Jean Armour Drive

Whitehill Dr

Whitehill Gv

Roman St

Roman Pk

R Vw

A68

Whitehill Industrial Estate

LAUDER ROAD **2**

St Davids RC Primary School

Kipplelaw Wk

Kipplelaw Dr

Kipplelaw Road

Kpplw Gdns

Kippilaw

Whitehill

3

EASTHOUSES ROAD B6482

Easthouses Way

Kippilaw

66

Easthouses

Drive

Maryburn Road

Newton St

Roanshead Rd

Carrick Crescent

Parkhead Pl

Parkhead Pk

Lothian

Easthouses Ct

Mayfield

Saffer Rd

Acre Rd

Easthouses Industrial Estate

Easthouses

Road

Hawthorn Crs

H S Pl

Kipplelaw Pk

Langlaw Road

Langlaw Primary School

Lawfield

4

Broadhurst Road

Leighton Crs

Hufsted Avenue

Brnsd

Crs

Brnsd Crs

Lawfield Road

Lawfield Rd

Whytle S Pl

Crmtn Pl

Ashgrove

Lawfield

5

Newbattle Community High School

Park Crs

Gordon St

Burnside Av

Bogwood Road

Andrew Dodd's Av

Conifer Rd

Camp Rd

Bryans Primary School

665

E **F** **G** **H**

Morris Road

MANSFIELD R

PO

Mayfield Leisure Centre

Salisbury Vw

77 35

Mayfield Pl

Buckie Rd

David Scott Av

Rowantree

Camp Road

D'Arcy

Cherry Lane

Oak Place

Lilac Avenue

Finlay Place

Larch Crs

Oak Crescent

D'Arcy House

36

Bryans

Eskview Road

Suttieslea Dr

Laurel Bank

Oak Crescent

Willow

enue

PO

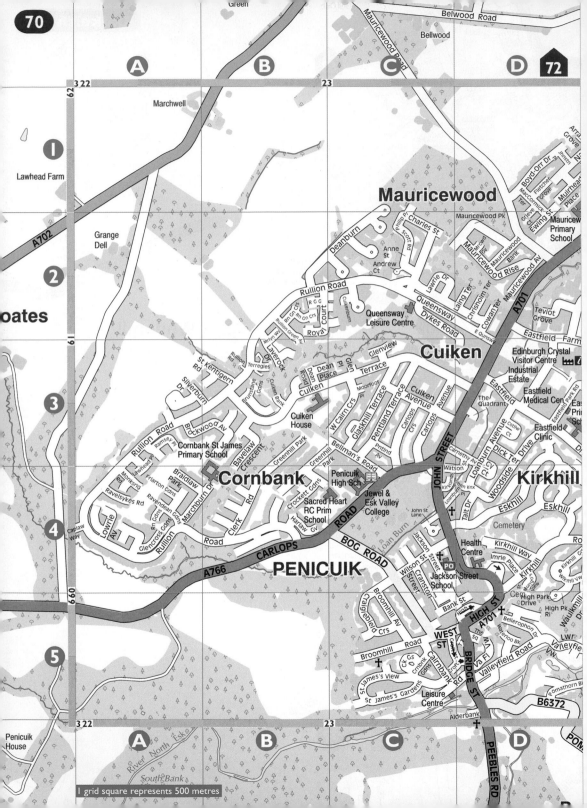

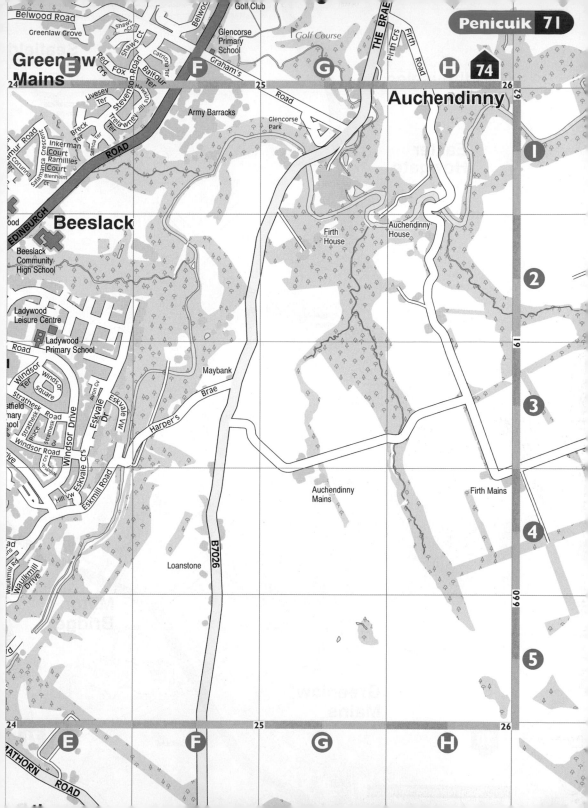

74

Belwood Road
Greenlaw Grove
Golf Club
Glencorse Primary School
Golf Course
THE BRAE
Firth Crs
Firth Road

Greenlaw Mains
Graham's Road
Shaws Cres
Shaws Ct
Catriona Ter
Red Fox
Balfour Ter
Livesey Ter
Breck Ter
Samoa Ter
Trela wney
Stevenson Road
Wilson Road
Hawking Ct

Auchendinny

Army Barracks
Glencorse Park

Inkerman Court
Corunna Crescent
Ramillies Court
Salamanca
Blenheim Ct

EDINBURGH ROAD

Beeslack

Beeslack Community High School

Firth House

Auchendinny House

Ladywood Leisure Centre
Ladywood Primary School
Road

Maybank

Windsor Ter
Winds of square
Strathesk Road
Strathesk Place
Strathesk
Eskvale Dr
Eskvale VW
Harper's Brae
Avon Gv

estfield mary chool
Windsor Drive
Windsor Road
Eskvale Crs
Eskmill Road
Hill VW

Auchendinny Mains

Firth Mains

B7026

Loanstone

Waulkmill Rd
Waulkmill Drive

MATHORN ROAD

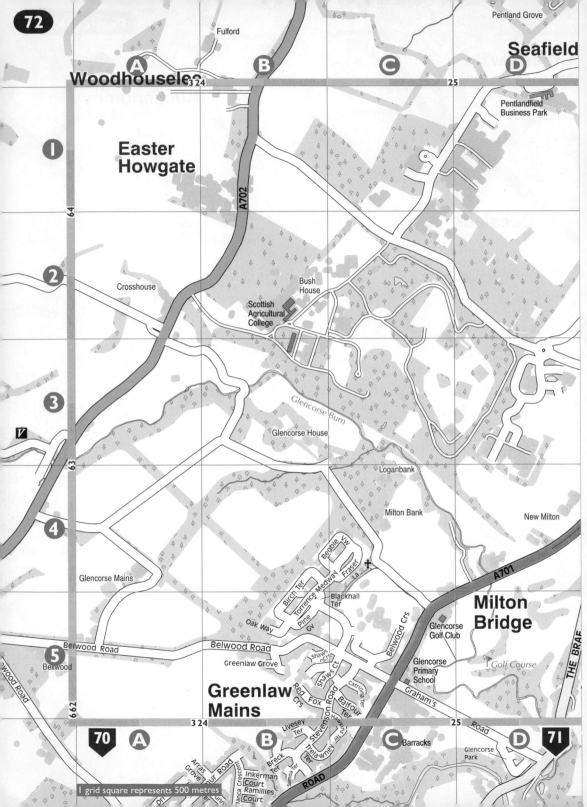

Pentland Grove

Fulford

A Woodhouselee 3 24

B

C 25

D **Seafield**

Pentlandfield
Business Park

I Easter
Howgate

64

A702

2 Crosshouse

Bush House

Scottish
Agricultural
College

63

V

3 Glencorse Burn

Glencorse House

Loganbank

Milton Bank

New Milton

4 Glencorse Mains

Begbie Vw
Fraser La
Birch Ter
Torrence Medway
Pine Gv
Blackhall Ter

Belwood Crs

**Milton
Bridge**

A701

Glencorse
Golf Club

Belwood Road

Belwood Road

Oak Way

Greenlaw Grove

Glencorse
Primary
School

Golf Course

5 Bellwood

Shaws Crs
Shaws Ct
Red Fox Crs
Shaws Road
Catriona Ter
Balfour Ter

Graham's

662

**Greenlaw
Mains**

3 24

25

Road

Stevenson Road

Livesey Ter
Breck Ter
Samoa Ter
Trefawney
Hawley Ter

Barracks

THE BRAE

Glencorse
Park

Arras Grove
Balfour Road
Inkerman Court
Ramillies Court
Bianca Crescent

ROAD

Woodwood Road

I grid square represents 500 metres

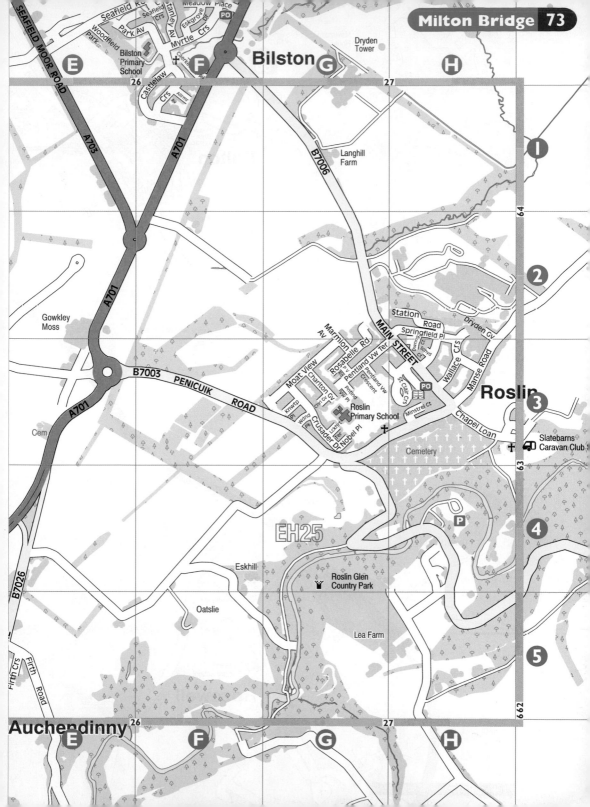

Seafield Rd
Stanley Av
Meadow Place
PO
Seafield Crs
Eskgrove Dr
Myrtle Crs
Woodfield Park
Seafield Park
Park Av
Bilston Primary School
Castlelaw Crs
Allmr Av
Clarke

Bilston

E F G H

26 27

Dryden Tower

A703
A701

B7006

Langhill Farm

I

64

2

Gowkley Moss

station
Road
Springfield Pl
Dryden Gv
Marmion Av
Rosabelle Rd
Pentland Vw Ter
Pentland Vw Crescent
MAIN STREET
Wallace Crs
Manse Road

B7003 PENICUIK ROAD

Moat View
Charlton Gv
Knwtp Pl
Wdnd Gv
Crusader Dr
Lcktht Pl
Lohr Gv
Tee
Nobel Pl
Roslin Primary School
Minstrel Ct
St Clair Crs
PO

Roslin

3

A701

Cem

Chapel Loan
Slatebarns Caravan Club

Cemetery

63

P

4

EH25

Eskhill

Oatslie

Roslin Glen Country Park

5

B7026

Firth Crs
Firth Road

Lea Farm

662

Auchendinny 26

E F G H

27

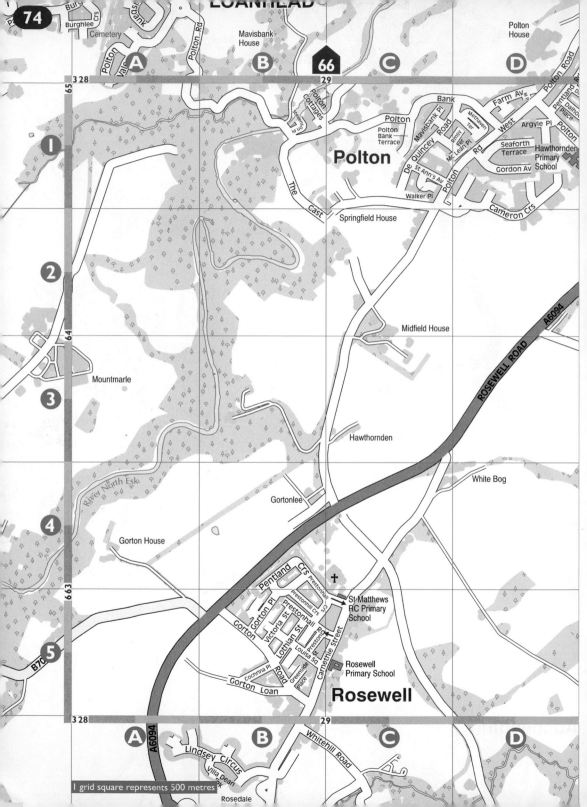

LOANHEAD

Burghlee Cemetery

Polton Vale **A**

Mavisbank House **B**

66 **C**

Polton House

Polton Rd

Polton Road

Pentland Place

Dalmoir

Polton

D

Polton Cottages

Stewing

Polton

Bank

Farm Av

West

Polton Bank Terrace

Mavisbank Pl

Methaven Ter

Ramsy

McLean Pl

Seaforth Terrace

Argyle Pl

Polton

De Quincey

St Ann's Av

Polton

Gordon Av

Hawthornden Primary School

Walker Pl

Cameron Crs

I

The Cast

Springfield House

2

Midfield House

ROSEWELL ROAD

A6094

3

Mountmarle

Hawthornden

4

River North Esk

Gortonlee

White Bog

Gorton House

Pentland Crs

Prestonhall Crs

St Matthews RC Primary School

Prestonhall St

Gorton Pl

Victoria St

Prestonhall

Gorton

Lothian St

Louisa Sq

Preston

Carnethie Street

5

B70

Cochrina Pl

Greenside Place

Rosewell Primary School

Gorton Loan

Road

Rosewell

A

A6094

Lindsey Circus

B

Whitehill Road

C

D

Villa Dean

Rosedale

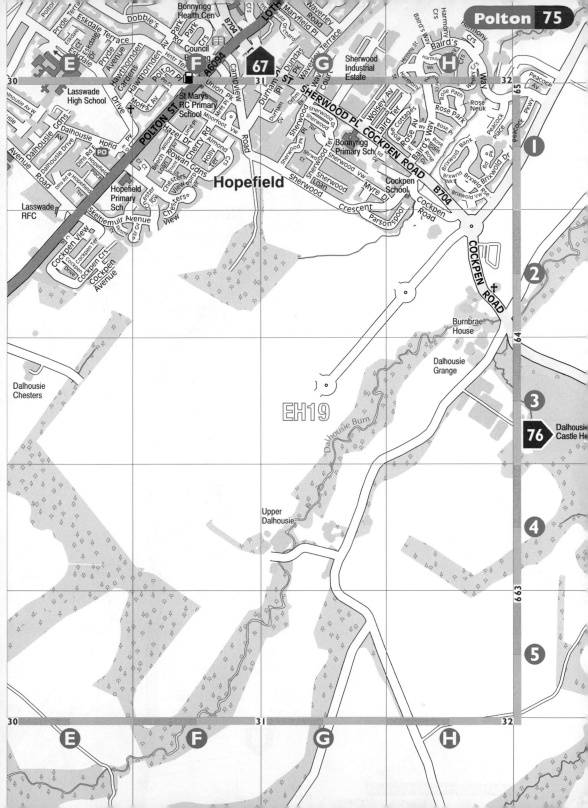

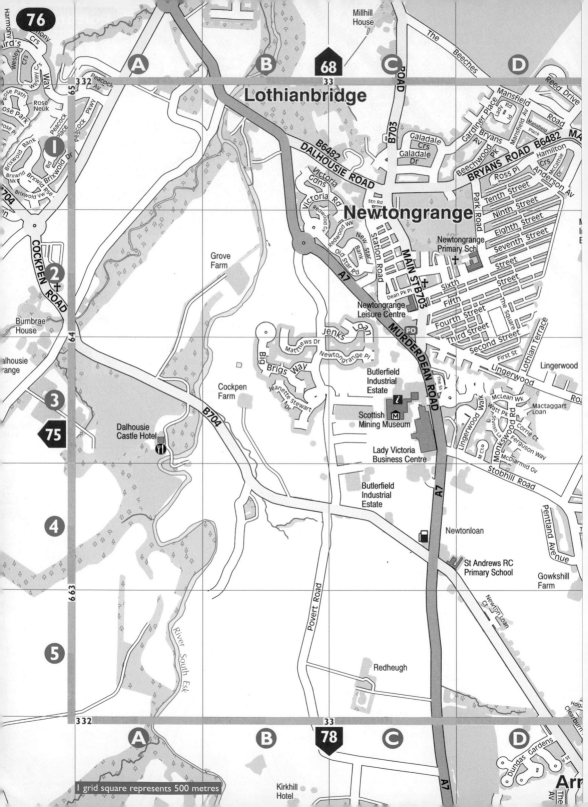

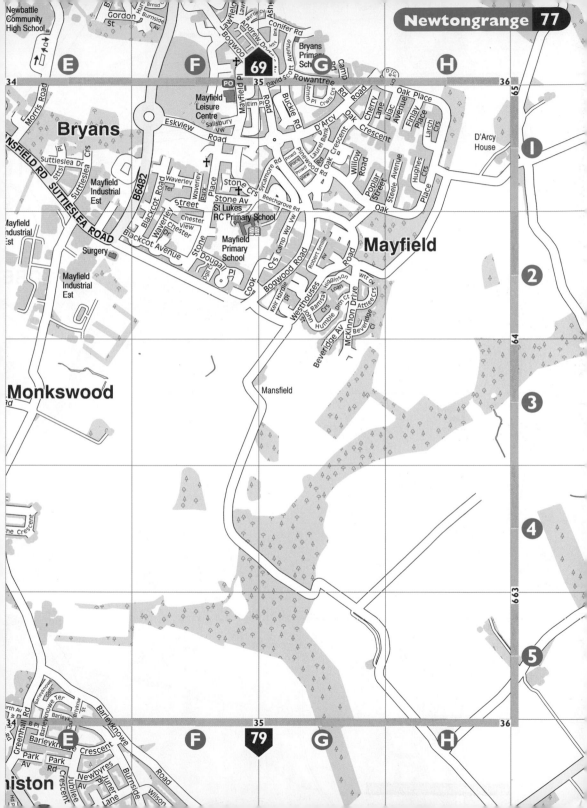

River South Esk

A
B
76
33
C
D

Redheugh

Hogar

Clearburn

Dundas Gardens

Arr

The Av

3 32

62

I

Kirkhill
Hotel

A7

Engine Road

Park H

Aikendean

Millbank
House

Arniston Ra

GORE

2

3

61

Whitehill
Aisle

Carrington
Barns

Shank
Bridge

A7

4

Primrose Gdns

PO

Arniston
Mains

B63

5

660

3 32

33

A
B
C
D

1 grid square represents 500 metres

Carrington

E **F** 77 **G** **H**

I

Greenhall Rd
Barleyknowe Gdns
North Av
B Pl
Barleyknowe Pl
Barleyknowe
Park Av
Park Rd
Newbyres Av
Jubilee Crescent
Glen View Rd
Barleyknowe Crescent
Barleyknowe Lane
Burnside
Wilson Road
Road

niston

PO

B704

Gorebridge
Primary
School

Glen Vw Rd
Glen Vw Ct

angers Junior FC

BRIDGE

River Gore Rd
River Gore
R G Vw
Emily J W
J W

Millbank
Gv

Moorfoot
View

Kirkhill
Castle Ct
Castle Place
Castle Av
Castle W

HUNTERFIELD ROAD

Gore Crs
Gore Av
Newbyres Crs
Newbyres Av
Newbyrs Wy
Newbyrs Gdns
R G Wy

Emily
Swan
Crescent
Gore
Av
Hillside Crescent N
Bonnybank Ct
Hunter Square
Hunting Ct
Dnbnk
Pl
Springfield
Hn Villas
Vogrie
Pl

McLean Place
Carlowrie Place
Bonnybank
Brad Rd
Armorfoor Rd
Braeside
Vogrie Rd
Crs Sth
Braeside Rd
Crs S
Hillside Crs S

Stobhill

Stobhill
Primary
School

Monteith
Houses

Barleyknowe Road

LADY BRAE

Mossend

B6372

Stobs

Health
Cen

Cncl Bldg

PO

MAIN ST

STATION RD

B6372

LADY
Vogrie Road

Glenview Pl

John Bernard Way

Robertsons Bank

Harvieston
Mains

Roseberry Crs

POWDERMILL BRAE

Bells
Mains

Bellsmains

Cemetery

Harvieston
House

Harvieston
Mains

A7

Wright's
Houses

2

3

4

5

E **F** Eastwood **G** **H** Catcune

A7

Abbeyhill	28 C2	Currie	54 D4	Hilltown	46 C5	Muirhouse	15 G2	Ratho Station	37 H1
Arniston	78 D1	Cuthill	33 H3	Hopefield	75 F1	Murrayfield	25 H4	Ravelston	26 A2
Auchendinny	71 G1	Dalkeith	68 D1	The Inch	44 D4	Musselburgh	32 B5	Restalrig	28 D1
Balerno	53 F3	Dalmeny	12 B1	Inveresk	48 A2	Newbattle	68 C4	Rosewell	74 C5
Barnton	14 C5	Damhead Holdings	64 D5	Inverleith	16 D4	Newbigging	11 E1	Roslin	73 H3
Beeslack	71 E2	Danderhall	61 G1	Joppa	30 C4	Newcraighall	20 D5	Saughton	41 E2
Bingham	30 A5	Davidson's Mains	15 E4	Juniper Green	55 G3	Newcraighall	47 E2	Seton	35 G3
Blackhall	25 G1	Dean	27 E2	Kaimes	59 F4	Newhailes	31 F5	Sighthill	40 D3
Boghall	64 B5	Dolphingstone	33 H5	Kingsknowe	41 F5	Newhaven	18 A1	Silverknowes	15 E3
Bonaly	56 B1	Dreghorn	57 E4	Kirkhill	70 D4	Newington	44 A2	Slateford	42 B5
Bonnyrigg & Lasswade	67 H5	Drum	61 E3	Kirkliston	21 E1	Newliston	20 C4	South Gyle	40 C2
Braepark	14 A5	Drylaw	15 H5	Lasswade	67 E3	Newtongrange	76 C2	South Queensferry	6 A5
Broughton	27 H1	Duddingston	29 G5	Leith	19 E2	Newton Village	61 H2	Stenhouse	41 H2
Brunstane	30 D5	Easter Howgate	72 A1	Levenhall	32 D4	New Town	3 H1	Stockbridge	17 F5
Bryans	77 E1	East Hermiston	40 A5	Liberton	59 G2	Niddrie	45 H2	Stoneybank	31 G2
Bughtlin	24 A2	Easthouses	69 F4	Loanhead	66 B5	Northfield	29 F3	Straiton	65 H2
Burdiehouse	59 G5	Edinburgh	3 J5	Lochend	28 D1	North Queensferry	4 C3	Swanston	57 H5
Clermiston	24 C2	Edmonstone	45 H5	Longstone	41 F4	Old Town	2 E5	Torphin	56 A5
Cockenzie & Port Seton	35 F2	Esknank	68 B3	Lothianbridge	76 B1	Oxgangs	58 A3	Tranent	51 E3
Colinton	57 E2	Fairmilehead	58 C4	Mauricewood	71 F4	Penicuik	70 B4	Tranent Mains	35 F5
Comiston	57 H2	Fisherrow	31 H4	Mauricewood	70 C1	Pilrig	18 A5	Trinity	17 G2
Cornbank	70 B4	Gilmerton	60 D3	Mayfield	77 G2	Pilton	16 D5	Turnhouse	23 E2
Corstorphine	24 B5	Glenbrook	52 A4	Meadowbank	28 D2	Pinkie Braes	32 D5	Wallyford	49 G1
Craigentinny	29 F1	Gogar	39 F1	Meadowmill	35 E4	Polton	74 C1	Warriston	17 G4
Craighall	13 F4	Gorebridge	78 D2	Merchiston	42 D2	Port Edgar	6 A3	Wester Hailes	56 B1
Craigleith	26 C1	Gorgie	42 B1	Millerhill	62 A2	Portobello	30 A3	Whitecraig	48 C5
Craiglockhart	42 B5	Gracemount	59 H3	Milton Bridge	72 D5	Portobello	35 E5	Whitehill	69 H2
Craigmillar	45 F3	Granton	16 B2	Monkswood	77 E3	Preston	34 C4	
Cramond	14 C3	Greenlaw Mains	72 B5	Monktonhall	47 H3	Prestonfield	44 C1	
Cramond Bridge	13 G5	Hermiston	39 H5	Moredun	60 C2	Prestonpans	34 A3	
Culken	70 C3			Morningside	43 F3	Ratho	37 H5	

USING THE STREET INDEX

Street names are listed alphabetically. Each street name is followed by its postal town or area locality, the Postcode District, the page number, and the reference to the square in which the name is found.

Standard index entries are shown as follows:

Abbeyhill *HLYRPK/NF* EH8............**3** K3

Street names and selected addresses not shown on the map due to scale restrictions are shown in the index with an asterisk:

Leamington La
MCH/MOR/FMHD EH10 *.........**43** F1

GENERAL ABBREVIATIONS

ACC	ACCESS	CTYD	COURTYARD	HLS	HILLS	MWY	MOTORWAY	SE	SOUTH EAST
ALY	ALLEY	CUTT	CUTTINGS	HO	HOUSE	N	NORTH	SER	SERVICE AREA
AP	APPROACH	CV	COVE	HOL	HOLLOW	NE	NORTH EAST	SH	SHORE
AR	ARCADE	CYN	CANYON	HOSP	HOSPITAL	NW	NORTH WEST	SHOP	SHOPPING
ASS	ASSOCIATION	DEPT	DEPARTMENT	HRB	HARBOUR	O/P	OVERPASS	SKWY	SKYWAY
AV	AVENUE	DL	DALE	HTH	HEATH	OFF	OFFICE	SMT	SUMMIT
BCH	BEACH	DM	DAM	HTS	HEIGHTS	ORCH	ORCHARD	SOC	SOCIETY
BLDS	BUILDINGS	DR	DRIVE	HVN	HAVEN	OV	OVAL	SP	SPUR
BND	BEND	DRO	DROVE	HWY	HIGHWAY	PAL	PALACE	SPR	SPRING
BNK	BANK	DRY	DRIVEWAY	IMP	IMPERIAL	PAS	PASSAGE	SQ	SQUARE
BR	BRIDGE	DWGS	DWELLINGS	IN	INLET	PAV	PAVILION	ST	STREET
BRK	BROOK	E	EAST	IND EST	INDUSTRIAL ESTATE	PDE	PARADE	STN	STATION
BTM	BOTTOM	EMB	EMBANKMENT	INF	INFIRMARY	PH	PUBLIC HOUSE	STR	STREAM
BUS	BUSINESS	EMBY	EMBASSY	INFO	INFORMATION	PK	PARK	STRD	STRAND
BVD	BOULEVARD	ESP	ESPLANADE	INT	INTERCHANGE	PKWY	PARKWAY	SW	SOUTH WEST
BY	BYPASS	EST	ESTATE	IS	ISLAND	PL	PLACE	TDG	TRADING
CATH	CATHEDRAL	EX	EXCHANGE	JCT	JUNCTION	PLN	PLAIN	TER	TERRACE
CEM	CEMETERY	EXPY	EXPRESSWAY	JTY	JETTY	PLNS	PLAINS	THWY	THROUGHWAY
CEN	CENTRE	EXT	EXTENSION	KG	KING	PLZ	PLAZA	TNL	TUNNEL
CFT	CROFT	F/O	FLYOVER	KNL	KNOLL	POL	POLICE STATION	TOLL	TOLLWAY
CH	CHURCH	FC	FOOTBALL CLUB	L	LAKE	PR	PRINCE	TPK	TURNPIKE
CHA	CHASE	FK	FORK	LA	LANE	PREC	PRECINCT	TR	TRACK
CHYD	CHURCHYARD	FLD	FIELD	LDG	LODGE	PREP	PREPARATORY	TRL	TRAIL
CIR	CIRCLE	FLDS	FIELDS	LGT	LIGHT	PRIM	PRIMARY	TWR	TOWER
CIRC	CIRCUS	FLS	FALLS	LK	LOCK	PROM	PROMENADE	U/P	UNDERPASS
CL	CLOSE	FM	FARM	LKS	LAKES	PRS	PRINCESS	UNI	UNIVERSITY
CLFS	CLIFFS	FT	FORT	LNDG	LANDING	PRT	PORT	UPR	UPPER
CMP	CAMP	FTS	FLATS	LTL	LITTLE	PT	POINT	V	VALE
CNR	CORNER	FWY	FREEWAY	LWR	LOWER	PTH	PATH	VA	VALLEY
CO	COUNTY	FY	FERRY	MAG	MAGISTRATE	PZ	PIAZZA	VIAD	VIADUCT
COLL	COLLEGE	GA	GATE	MAN	MANSIONS	QD	QUADRANT	VIL	VILLA
COM	COMMON	GAL	GALLERY	MD	MEAD	QU	QUEEN	VIS	VISTA
COMM	COMMISSION	GDN	GARDEN	MDW	MEADOWS	QY	QUAY	VLG	VILLAGE
CON	CONVENT	GDNS	GARDENS	MEM	MEMORIAL	R	RIVER	VLS	VILLAS
COT	COTTAGE	GLD	GLADE	MI	MILL	RBT	ROUNDABOUT	VW	VIEW
COTS	COTTAGES	GLN	GLEN	MKT	MARKET	RD	ROAD	W	WEST
CP	CAPE	GN	GREEN	MKTS	MARKETS	RDG	RIDGE	WD	WOOD
CPS	COPSE	GND	GROUND	ML	MALL	REP	REPUBLIC	WHF	WHARF
CR	CREEK	GRA	GRANGE	MNR	MANOR	RES	RESERVOIR	WK	WALK
CREM	CREMATORIUM	GRG	GARAGE	MS	MEWS	RFC	RUGBY FOOTBALL CLUB	WLS	WALKS
CRS	CRESCENT	GT	GREAT	MSN	MISSION	RI	RISE	WLS	WELLS
CSWY	CAUSEWAY	GTWY	GATEWAY	MT	MOUNT	RP	RAMP	WY	WAY
CT	COURT	GV	GROVE	MTN	MOUNTAIN	RW	ROW	YD	YARD
CTRL	CENTRAL	HGR	HIGHER	MTS	MOUNTAINS	S	SOUTH	YHA	YOUTH HOSTEL
CTS	COURTS	HL	HILL	MUS	MUSEUM	SCH	SCHOOL		

POSTCODE TOWNS AND AREA ABBREVIATIONS

BAL/CUR	Balerno/Currie	DAL/STH/STNH	Prestonpans Dairy/Sighthill/ Stenhouse	EDOT	Edinburgh Old Town	LIB/NID	Liberton/Niddrie	NWGTN	Newington
BNYRG	Bonnyrigg			GIL/MOR	Gilmerton/Moredun	LNHD	Loanhead	PBLO/DUD	Portobello/ Duddingston
BROX/UP	Broxburn/ Uphall	DFLS	Dunfermline south	GNTN	Granton	LSWD	Lasswade	PNCK	Penicuik
CED/PRST	Central Edinburgh/ Princes Street	DLKTH	Dalkeith	GORBR	Gorebridge	MCH/MOR/FMHD	Merchiston/ Morningside/ Fairmilehead	QFRY	Queensferry
COLIN	Colinton	ECALD	East Calder	HLYRPK/NF	Holyrood Park/ Northfield			RATHO	Ratho
CPS/PPNS	Cockenzie and Port Seton/	EDNT/CEDW	Edinburgh New Town/ Central Edinburgh west	KLSTN	Kirkliston	MRYFD/COR	Murrayfield/ Corstorphine	ROSLIN	Roslin
		EDNW	Edinburgh northwest	KNWTN	Kirknewton	MUS	Musselburgh	RSTRG	Restalrig
				LEITH	Leith			RSWL	Rosewell

A

Abbeyhill HLYRPK/NF EH8....3 K3
Abbeyhill Crs HLYRPK/NF EH8...3 J3
Abbey La HLYRPK/NF EH8....28 C2
Abbeymount HLYRPK/NF EH8...3 J3
Abbey Rd DLKTH EH22....68 B2
Abbey Strd HLYRPK/NF EH8....3 K3
Abbey St RSTRG EH7....28 C2
Abbotsford Crs
  MCH/MOR/FMHD EH10....43 E2
Abbotsford Pk
  MCH/MOR/FMHD EH10....43 E2
Abercorn Crs HLYRPK/NF EH8...29 E3
Abercorn Dr HLYRPK/NF EH8...29 E3
Abercorn Gdns
  HLYRPK/NF EH8....29 F2
Abercorn Rd HLYRPK/NF EH8...29 E3
Abercorn Rd HLYRPK/NF EH8...29 E3
Abercorn Ter PBLO/DUD EH15...30 B3
Abercromby Pl
  EDNT/CEDW EH3....2 D1
Abinger Gdns
  MRYFD/COR EH12....26 B4
Academy La LNHD EH20....65 H5
Academy Pk LEITH EH6....18 C4
Academy St LEITH EH6....18 C4
Acheson Dr CPS/PPNS EH32....34 A5
Adams Well COLIN EH13....57 E3
Addiston Crs BAL/CUR EH14....53 E1
Addiston Farm Rd RATHO EH28...38 D5
Addiston Gv BAL/CUR EH14....53 E1
Addiston Pk BAL/CUR EH14....52 D1
Adelphi Gv PBLO/DUD EH15...30 A3
Adelphi Pl PBLO/DUD EH15...30 A3
Admiral Ter
  MCH/MOR/FMHD EH10....43 F1
Admiralty St LEITH EH6....18 B2
Afton Pl GNTN EH5....17 E3
Afton Ter GNTN EH5....17 E3
Agnew Ter LEITH EH6....17 H3
Ainslie Pl EQWI/QLNE EH3...2 C5
Aird's Cl EDOT EH1....2 D5
Alan Breck Gdns EDNW EH4....24 D5
Albany La LNHD EH20....27 H1
Albany St EDOT EH1....2 E1
Albert Crs MUS EH21....49 F1
Albert Crs MUS EH21....49 F1
Albert Pl MUS EH21....49 F1
Albert Rd LEITH EH6....18 B5
Albert Ter
  MCH/MOR/FMHD EH10....43 F1
Albion Gdns RSTRG EH7....28 C1
Albion Rd RSTRG EH7....28 C1
Alcorn Rigg BAL/CUR EH14....56 A2
Alcorn Sq BAL/CUR EH14....56 A2
Alderbank Gdns
  DAL/STH/STNH EH11....42 C2
Alderbank Pl
  DAL/STH/STNH EH11....42 C2
Alderbank Ter
  DAL/STH/STNH EH11....42 C2
Alder Rd CPS/PPNS EH32....35 F2
Alemoor Crs RSTRG EH7....18 D5
Alemoor Pk RSTRG EH7....18 D5
Alexander Dr CPS/PPNS EH32...34 A5
Alfred Pl NWGTN EH9....44 B1
Allanfield RSTRG EH7....28 B1
Allanfield Pl RSTRG EH7....28 B1
Allan Pk KLSTN EH29....21 E1
Allan Park Crs BAL/CUR EH14...42 A3
Allan Park Dr BAL/CUR EH14...42 A4
Allan Park Gdns BAL/CUR EH14...42 A4
Allan Park Loan BAL/CUR EH14...42 B4
Allan Park Rd BAL/CUR EH14...42 A4
Allan St EDNW EH4....27 E1
Allan Ter DLKTH EH22....68 D1
Allermuir Av ROSLIN EH25...73 F1
Allermuir Rd COLIN EH13....56 C3
Allison Pl KLSTN EH29....21 F1
Almond Av MRYFD/COR EH12...22 B4
Almondbank Ter
  DAL/STH/STNH EH11....42 C2
Almond Crs BNYRG EH19....75 F1
Almond Gn MRYFD/COR EH12...24 A3
Almond Gv QFRY EH30....6 D5
Almondhill Rd KLSTN EH29....21 F1
Almond Rd MRYFD/COR EH12...22 B4
Almondside KLSTN EH29....21 F2
Almond Sq MRYFD/COR EH12...22 B4
Alnwickhill Ct LIB/NID EH16...59 F3
Alnwickhill Crs LIB/NID EH16...59 F3
Alnwickhill Dr LIB/NID EH16...59 F3
Alnwickhill Gdns LIB/NID EH16...59 F3
Alnwickhill Gv LIB/NID EH16...59 F3
Alnwickhill Loan LIB/NID EH16...59 F3
Alnwickhill Pk LIB/NID EH16...59 G2
Alnwickhill Rd LIB/NID EH16...59 F3
Alnwickhill Ter LIB/NID EH16...59 F3
Alnwickhill Vw LIB/NID EH16...59 F3
Alva Pl RSTRG EH7....28 C2
Alva St CED/PRST EH2....27 E3
Ambassador Ct MUS EH21....32 B5
Amos Pth LNHD EH20....6 D5
Ancrum Bank DLKTH EH22....68 B3
Ancrum Rd DLKTH EH22....68 B3
Anderson Av DLKTH EH22....76 D1
Anderson Pl LEITH EH6....18 A3
Andrew Ct PNCK EH26....70 C2
Andrew Dodd's Av
  DLKTH EH22....69 G5
Andrew Wood Ct LEITH EH6...17 G2
Angle Park Ter
  DAL/STH/STNH EH11....42 D1
Angres Ct DLKTH EH22....61 F2
Annandale St RSTRG EH7....27 H1
Annandale Street La
  RSTRG EH7....28 A1
Anne St PNCK EH26....70 C2
Annfield LEITH EH6....17 H2
  TRNT EH33....51 G3
Annfield St LEITH EH6....17 H2
Ann St EDNW EH4....27 E2
Appin Dr CPS/PPNS EH32....34 C3
Appin Sq BAL/CUR EH14....42 B3
Appin Ter BAL/CUR EH14....42 B3

Arboretum Av
  EDNT/CEDW EH3....27 E1
Arboretum Pl EDNT/CEDW EH3..17 E5
Arboretum Rd
  EDNT/CEDW EH3....17 E4
Archibald Pl EDNT/CEDW EH3...2 C6
Arden St NWGTN EH9....43 G1
Ardmillan Pl
  DAL/STH/STNH EH11....42 D1
Ardmillan Ter
  DAL/STH/STNH EH11....42 D1
Ardshiel Av EDNW EH4....24 B5
Argyle Crs PBLO/DUD EH15...30 B3
Argyle Park Ter NWGTN EH9...43 H1
Argyle Pl BNYRG EH19....74 D1
Argyle St LEITH EH6....18 B5
Arnott Gdns BAL/CUR EH14...41 G5
Arnprior Rd GORBR EH23....79 F2
Arran Pl PBLO/DUD EH15...30 C3
Arras Gv PNCK EH26....70 D1
Arrol Pl QFRY EH30....6 D5
Arthur St LEITH EH6....18 B5
Arthur Street La LEITH EH6...18 B5
Arthur View Crs DLKTH EH22...61 F2
Arthur View Ter DLKTH EH22...61 F1
Ashburnham Gdns QFRY EH30...7 E5
Ashburnham Loan QFRY EH30...7 E4
Ashgrove DLKTH EH22....69 G5
  MUS EH21....32 C5
Ashgrove Gv MUS EH21....32 C5
Ashgrove Vw MUS EH21....32 C5
Ashley Gdns
  DAL/STH/STNH EH11....43 E2
Ashley Gra BAL/CUR EH14....53 E2
Ashley Gv DAL/STH/STNH EH11...42 C2
Ashley Pl LEITH EH6....18 A4
Ashley Ter DAL/STH/STNH EH11...42 C2
Ashton Gv LIB/NID EH16....44 D5
Assembly St LEITH EH6....18 C3
Atheling Gv QFRY EH30....6 D5
Atholl Crs EDNT/CEDW EH3...27 E4
Atholl Crescent La
  EDNT/CEDW EH3....27 E4
Atholl Vw CPS/PPNS EH32...34 C3
Attlee Crs DLKTH EH22....68 D1
Auchingane
  MCH/MOR/FMHD EH10...57 G4
Auldgate KLSTN EH29....21 F2
Auld Orch BNYRG EH19....74 D1
Avenel EDNW EH4....14 A4
Avenue Rd DLKTH EH22....68 B2
The Avenue BAL/CUR EH14...54 D2
  GORBR EH23....78 D1
Avenue Vls EDNW EH4....26 D1
Avondale Pl EDNT/CEDW EH3...17 F5
Avon Gv EDNW EH4....14 A4
  PNCK EH26....71 E5
Avon Pl EDNW EH4....14 A4
Avon Rd EDNW EH4....14 A4
Ayres Wynd CPS/PPNS EH32...34 B4

B

Baberton Av BAL/CUR EH14...55 H3
Baberton Crs BAL/CUR EH14...56 A3
Baberton Jct BAL/CUR EH14...56 A2
Baberton Loan BAL/CUR EH14...55 H4
Baberton Mains Av
  BAL/CUR EH14....55 H2
Baberton Mains Bank
  BAL/CUR EH14....55 H2
Baberton Mains Brae
  BAL/CUR EH14....55 G2
Baberton Mains Ct
  BAL/CUR EH14....55 H2
Baberton Mains Crs
  BAL/CUR EH14....55 H2
Baberton Mains Dell
  BAL/CUR EH14....55 G2
Baberton Mains Dr
  BAL/CUR EH14....55 H2
Baberton Mains Gdns
  BAL/CUR EH14....55 G1
Baberton Mains Gn
  BAL/CUR EH14....55 H2
Baberton Mains Gv
  BAL/CUR EH14....55 H2
Baberton Mains Hl
  BAL/CUR EH14....55 H2
Baberton Mains Lea
  BAL/CUR EH14....55 G2
Baberton Mains Loan
  BAL/CUR EH14....56 A2
Baberton Mains Pk
  BAL/CUR EH14....55 H2
Baberton Mains Rw
  BAL/CUR EH14....55 H2
Baberton Mains Ter
  BAL/CUR EH14....55 H2
Baberton Mains Vw
  BAL/CUR EH14....55 H2
Baberton Mains Wy
  BAL/CUR EH14....55 G2
Baberton Mains Wd
  BAL/CUR EH14....55 G2
Baberton Mains Wynd
  BAL/CUR EH14....55 H2
Baberton Pk BAL/CUR EH14...55 H3
Back Dean EDNW EH4....26 D3
Backdean Rd DLKTH EH22....61 F1
Backlee LIB/NID EH16....59 F3
Baileyfield Crs PBLO/DUD EH15...30 A3
Baileyfield Rd PBLO/DUD EH15...30 A3
Baillie Gv PBLO/DUD EH15...30 D5
Baillie Pth PBLO/DUD EH15...30 B5
Baillie Rd PBLO/DUD EH15...30 B5
Baillie Ter PBLO/DUD EH15...30 B5
Baird Av MRYFD/COR EH12...26 A5
Baird Dr MRYFD/COR EH12...42 A1

Baird Gdns MRYFD/COR EH12...25 H5
Baird Gv MRYFD/COR EH12...26 A5
Baird Rd RATHO EH28....38 H4
Baird's Wy BNYRG EH19....75 H1
Baird Ter MRYFD/COR EH12...25 H5
Bakehouse Ct HLYRPK/NF EH8...3 H5
Balbirnie Pl MRYFD/COR EH12...26 C4
Balcarres Pl MUS EH21....32 B4
Balcarres Rd MUS EH21....32 B4
Balcarres St
  MCH/MOR/FMHD EH10...42 D4
Balfour Pl LEITH EH6....18 A5
Balfour's Sq TRNT EH33....51 F2
Balfour St LEITH EH6....18 A5
Balfour Ter PNCK EH26....72 C5
Balfron Loan EDNW EH4....24 C2
Balgreen Av MRYFD/COR EH12...25 G5
Balgreen Gdns
  MRYFD/COR EH12....25 G5
Balgreen Pk MRYFD/COR EH12...25 G5
Balgreen Rd
  DAL/STH/STNH EH11....42 A1
  MRYFD/COR EH12....25 H5
Ballantyne Rd LEITH EH6....18 B3
Balmoral Pl EDNT/CEDW EH3...17 F5
Balmoral Av LIB/NID EH16...59 H4
Balmwell Av LIB/NID EH16...59 G4
Balmwell Ter LIB/NID EH16...59 G4
Baltic St LEITH EH6....18 C3
Bangholm Av EDNW EH4....17 E4
Bangholm Bower Av GNTN EH5...17 F3
Bangholm Gv GNTN EH5....17 G3
Bangholm Ln GNTN EH5....17 G3
Bangholm Pl GNTN EH5....17 F3
Bangholm Ter
  EDNT/CEDW EH3....17 F4
Bangholm Vw GNTN EH5....17 G3
Bangholm Vls GNTN EH5....17 G3
Bangor Rd LEITH EH6....18 B3
Bankfoot CPS/PPNS EH32....33 H5
Bankhead Av
  DAL/STH/STNH EH11....40 C3
Bankhead Broadway
  DAL/STH/STNH EH11....40 B3
Bankhead Crossway North
  DAL/STH/STNH EH11....40 B3
Bankhead Crossway South
  DAL/STH/STNH EH11....40 B4
Bankhead Dr
  DAL/STH/STNH EH11....40 C3
Bankhead Gv QFRY EH30....7 E4
Bankhead Medway
  DAL/STH/STNH EH11....40 B4
Bankhead Pl
  DAL/STH/STNH EH11....40 C3
Bankhead Rd QFRY EH30....7 F4
Bankhead St
  DAL/STH/STNH EH11....40 C4
Bankhead Ter
  DAL/STH/STNH EH11....40 C4
Bankhead Wy
  DAL/STH/STNH EH11....40 B4
Bankpark Brae TRNT EH33....50 D1
Bankpark Crs TRNT EH33....50 D1
Bankpark Gv TRNT EH33....51 E1
Bank St EDOT EH1....2 E4
Bankton Ct TRNT EH33....51 E2
Barclay Ter
  MCH/MOR/FMHD EH10...27 F5
Barley Ct DLKTH EH22....69 F4
Barleyknowe Crs GORBR EH23...79 F1
Barleyknowe Gdns
  GORBR EH23....77 E5
Barleyknowe La GORBR EH23...79 E1
Barleyknowe Pl GORBR EH23...79 E1
Barleyknowe St GORBR EH23...79 E1
Barleyknowe Ter GORBR EH23...79 E1
Barnbougle Ride QFRY EH30...13 F1
Barn Pk BAL/CUR EH14....56 A1
Barn Park Crs BAL/CUR EH14...56 A1
Barnshot Rd COLIN EH13....56 B4
Barnton Av EDNW EH4....14 D5
Barnton Av West EDNW EH4...14 B4
Barnton Brae EDNW EH4....14 B4
Barntongate Av EDNW EH4...24 B1
Barntongate Dr EDNW EH4...24 B2
Barntongate Ter EDNW EH4...24 B1
Barnton Gv EDNW EH4....14 D5
Barnton Pk EDNW EH4....15 E4
Barnton Park Av EDNW EH4...14 D5
Barnton Park Crs EDNW EH4...14 C5
Barnton Park Dell EDNW EH4...14 C5
Barnton Park Dr EDNW EH4...14 C5
Barnton Park Gdns EDNW EH4...14 C5
Barnton Park Gv EDNW EH4...14 C5
Barnton Park Pl EDNW EH4...14 C5
Barnton Park Vw EDNW EH4...14 C5
Barnton Park Wd EDNW EH4...24 B1
Baronscourt Rd
  HLYRPK/NF EH8....29 E2
Baronscourt Ter
  HLYRPK/NF EH8....29 F2
Barony Pl EDNT/CEDW EH3...27 H1
Barony St EDNT/CEDW EH3...27 H1
Barony Ter MRYFD/COR EH12...25 F3
Barracks St CPS/PPNS EH32...35 F1
Bath Rd LEITH EH6....18 A2
Bath St PBLO/DUD EH15...30 B3
Bath Street La PBLO/DUD EH15...30 B3
Battery Rd DFLS KY11....4 D5
Bavelaw Crs PNCK EH26....70 B4
Bavelaw Gdns BAL/CUR EH14...53 G2
Bavelaw Gn BAL/CUR EH14...53 G2
Bavelaw Rd BAL/CUR EH14...53 G2
Beach La MUS EH21....31 H4
  PBLO/DUD EH15....30 B2
Beauchamp Gv LIB/NID EH16...59 G1
Beauchamp Rd LIB/NID EH16...59 G1
Beaufort Rd NWGTN EH9...43 H2
Beaverbank Pl RSTRG EH7...17 G5
Beaverhall Rd RSTRG EH7...17 H5
Bedford Ct EDNW EH4....27 E1
Bedford St EDNW EH4....27 E1
Bedford Ter PBLO/DUD EH15...30 D3
The Beeches DLKTH EH22....68 C5
Beech Grove Av DLKTH EH22...67 H3
Beechgrove Rd DLKTH EH22...67 H3
Beech Loan BNYRG EH19....75 F1

Beechmount Crs
  MRYFD/COR EH12....25 H4
Beechmount Pk
  MRYFD/COR EH12....25 H5
Beechwood Pk DLKTH EH22...76 D1
Beechwood Ter LEITH EH6...18 C5
Begbie Vw MRYFD/COR EH12...72 B4
Belford Av EDNW EH4....26 C5
Belford Gdns EDNW EH4....26 C5
Belford Ms EDNW EH4....26 D5
Belford Pk EDNW EH4....26 C5
Belford Pl EDNW EH4....26 C5
Belford Rd EDNW EH4....26 D5
Belgrave Crs EDNW EH4....26 D2
Belgrave Crescent La
  EDNW EH4....26 D2
Belgrave Gdns
  MRYFD/COR EH12....25 E4
Belgrave Rd
  MRYFD/COR EH12....25 E4
Belhaven Pl
  MCH/MOR/FMHD EH10...43 E4
Belhaven Ter
  MCH/MOR/FMHD EH10...43 E4
Bellerophon Dr PNCK EH26...70 D5
Bellevue EDNT/CEDW EH3...27 H1
Bellevue Crs EDNT/CEDW EH3...27 G1
Bellevue Gdns RSTRG EH7...17 H5
Bellevue Gv RSTRG EH7....17 H5
Bellevue La RSTRG EH7....17 H5
Bellevue Pl RSTRG EH7....17 H5
Bellevue Rd RSTRG EH7....17 H5
Bellevue St RSTRG EH7....17 H5
Bellevue Ter RSTRG EH7....17 H5
Bellfield Av DLKTH EH22....68 A2
Bellfield La PBLO/DUD EH15...30 B3
Bellfield St PBLO/DUD EH15...30 B3
Bellfield Ter PBLO/DUD EH15...30 B3
Bellman's Rd PNCK EH26....70 C5
Bell Pl EDNT/CEDW EH3....17 F5
Bells Brae EDNW EH4....27 E3
Bellsmains GORBR EH23....77 E5
Bell Stane QFRY EH30....6 C4
Belmont Av MRYFD/COR EH12...25 H4
Belmont Gdns
  MRYFD/COR EH12....25 H4
Belmont Rd BAL/CUR EH14...55 H3
Belmont Ter MRYFD/COR EH12...25 H4
Belmont Vw MRYFD/COR EH12...25 H4
Belwood Crs PNCK EH26....72 C5
Belwood Rd PNCK EH26....72 B5
Beresford Av LEITH EH6....17 G2
Beresford Gdns GNTN EH5...17 G3
Beresford Pl GNTN EH5....17 G3
Bernard St LEITH EH6....18 C2
Bernard Ter HLYRPK/NF EH8...28 A5
Beveridge Av DLKTH EH22....77 G5
Beveridge Cl DLKTH EH22....77 G2
Big Brigs Wy DLKTH EH22....76 B3
Biggar Rd
  MCH/MOR/FMHD EH10...64 B1
Bingham Av PBLO/DUD EH15...45 H1
Bingham Broadway
  PBLO/DUD EH15....45 H1
Bingham Crs PBLO/DUD EH15...46 A1
Bingham Crossway
  PBLO/DUD EH15....46 A1
Bingham Medway
  PBLO/DUD EH15....45 H1
Bingham Pl PBLO/DUD EH15...45 H1
Bingham Wy PBLO/DUD EH15...45 H1
Birch Cl EDNW EH4....24 A3
Birch Crs LNHD EH20....65 F5
Birch Ter PNCK EH26....70 D5
Birsley Rd TRNT EH33....51 E2
Blackbarony Rd LIB/NID EH16...44 B4
Blackchapel Cl LIB/NID EH16...46 B4
Blackchapel Rd PBLO/DUD EH15...46 B2
Blackcot Av DLKTH EH22....77 F2
Blackcot Dr DLKTH EH22....77 F2
Blacket Av NWGTN EH9....44 B1
Blacket Pl NWGTN EH9....44 B1
Blackford Av NWGTN EH9...43 H3
Blackford Bank NWGTN EH9...43 H3
Blackford Gv NWGTN EH9...43 H3
Blackford Hill Gv NWGTN EH9...43 H4
Blackford Hill Ri NWGTN EH9...43 H4
Blackford Hill Vw NWGTN EH9...43 H4
Blackford Glen Rd
  LIB/NID EH16....44 A5
Blackford Ga NWGTN EH9...43 H3
Blackfriars St EDOT EH1....3 G4
Blackhall Ter PNCK EH26....72 C5
Blackie Rd LEITH EH6....18 D4
Blackthorn Ct PNCK EH26....70 C5
Blackwood Crs HLYRPK/NF EH8...44 A1
Blaeberry Gdns EDNW EH4...24 B1
Blair St EDOT EH1....3 F4
Blantyre Ter
  MCH/MOR/FMHD EH10...43 E2
Blawearie Rd TRNT EH33....51 E3
Bleinheim Ct PNCK EH26....71 E1
Blenheim Pl RSTRG EH7....28 A2
Blinkbonny Av EDNW EH4....26 B2
Blinkbonny Crs EDNW EH4...26 A2
Blinkbonny Gdns EDNW EH4...26 B2
Blinkbonny Gv EDNW EH4...26 B2
Blinkbonny Gv West
  EDNW EH4....26 A2
Blinkbonny Rd BAL/CUR EH14...55 F5
Blinkbonny Rd West
  EDNW EH4....26 A2
Boat Gn EDNT/CEDW EH3...17 H4
Boathouse Br KLSTN EH29...22 A2
Bogpark Rd MUS EH21....31 G5
Bog Rd PNCK EH26....70 C4
Bogsmill Rd BAL/CUR EH14...41 H5
Bogwood Rd DLKTH EH22....69 F5
Bonaly Av COLIN EH13....56 C4
Bonaly Brae COLIN EH13....56 C4
Bonaly Crs COLIN EH13....56 C4
Bonaly Dr COLIN EH13....56 C4
Bonaly Gdns COLIN EH13....56 C4
Bonaly Gv COLIN EH13....56 C4
Bonaly Ri COLIN EH13....56 C4
Bonaly Rd COLIN EH13....56 C4
Bonaly Ter COLIN EH13....56 C4
Bonaly Wester COLIN EH13...56 C4
Bonar Pl LEITH EH6....17 H3

Bo'ness Rd QFRY EH30....6 A4
Bonnington Av LEITH EH6...17 H3
Bonnington Gait LEITH EH6...18 A4
Bonnington Gv LEITH EH6...17 H3
Bonnington Road La LEITH EH6...18 A4
Bonnington Road La LEITH EH6...18 A4
Bonnybank Ct GORBR EH23...79 F2
Bonnybank Rd GORBR EH23...79 F2
Bonnyhaugh LEITH EH6....17 H4
Bonnyhaugh La RSTRG EH7...17 H4
Bonnyrigg Rd DLKTH EH22...68 A3
Boothacre La LEITH EH6....18 D4
Boroughloch HLYRPK/NF EH8...28 A5
Boroughloch Sq
  HLYRPK/NF EH8....28 A5
Borthwick Pl
  MRYFD/COR EH12....26 C4
Borthwick Vw LNHD EH20....65 F5
Boswall Av GNTN EH5....16 D3
Boswall Crs GNTN EH5....16 D3
Boswall Dr GNTN EH5....16 D3
Boswall Gdns GNTN EH5....16 D3
Boswall Gn GNTN EH5....16 D3
Boswall Gv GNTN EH5....16 D3
Boswall Loan GNTN EH5....16 D2
Boswall Pkwy GNTN EH5....16 D3
Boswall Pl GNTN EH5....16 D3
Boswall Qd GNTN EH5....16 D3
Boswall Rd GNTN EH5....17 E2
Boswall Sq GNTN EH5....16 D3
Boswall Ter GNTN EH5....16 D3
Bothwell St RSTRG EH7....28 C1
Boundary Rd East
  BAL/CUR EH14....54 D1
Boundary Rd North
  BAL/CUR EH14....54 B2
Bowling Green Rd KLSTN EH29...21 E2
The Bowling Grn LEITH EH6...18 B4
Bowmont Pl HLYRPK/NF EH8...3 H7
Boyd-Orr Dr PNCK EH26....70 D5
Boyd's Entry EDOT EH1....3 G4
Braeburn Dr BAL/CUR EH14...55 F5
Braehead Av EDNW EH4....14 A5
Braehead Bank EDNW EH4...14 A5
Braehead Crs EDNW EH4....14 A5
Braehead Dr EDNW EH4....14 A5
Braehead Gv EDNW EH4....14 A5
Braehead Loan EDNW EH4...14 A5
Braehead Pk EDNW EH4....14 A5
Braehead Rd EDNW EH4....14 A5
Braehead Rw EDNW EH4....14 A5
Brae Pk EDNW EH4....14 A4
Braepark Rd EDNW EH4....14 A4
Braeside Rd GORBR EH23....79 F2
Braeside Rd North
  GORBR EH23....79 F2
Braeside Rd South
  GORBR EH23....79 F3
The Brae PNCK EH26....72 D5
Braid Av
  MCH/MOR/FMHD EH10...43 F5
Braidburn Crs
  MCH/MOR/FMHD EH10...43 E5
Braidburn Ter
  MCH/MOR/FMHD EH10...43 E5
Braid Crs
  MCH/MOR/FMHD EH10...43 E5
Braid Farm Rd
  MCH/MOR/FMHD EH10...58 A1
Braid Hills Ap
  MCH/MOR/ ...58 B1
Braid Hills Av
  MCH/MOR/FMHD EH10...43 E5
Braid Hills Crs
  MCH/MOR/FMHD EH10...58 A1
Braid Hills Dr LIB/NID EH16...58 D1
Braid Hills Rd
  MCH/MOR/FMHD EH10...58 A1
Braidlaw Pk PNCK EH26....70 A4
Braid Mt
  MCH/MOR/FMHD EH10...58 B1
Braid Mount Crest
  MCH/MOR/ ...58 B1
Braid Mount Ri
  MCH/MOR/ ...58 B1
Braid Mount Vw
  MCH/MOR/ ...58 B1
Braid Rd
  MCH/MOR/FMHD EH10...58 A1
Bramble Dr EDNW EH4....24 B1
Bramdean Gv
  MCH/MOR/FMHD EH10...58 B1
Bramdean Pl
  MCH/MOR/FMHD EH10...58 B1
Bramdean Ri
  MCH/MOR/FMHD EH10...58 B1
Bramdean Vw
  MCH/MOR/FMHD EH10...58 B1
Brand Dr PBLO/DUD EH15...30 B5
Brandfield St EDNT/CEDW EH3...27 F4
Brand Gdns PBLO/DUD EH15...30 D4
Brandon St EDNT/CEDW EH3...27 G1
Brandon Ter EDNT/CEDW EH3...27 F1
Breadalbane St LEITH EH6...18 A3
Bread St EDNT/CEDW EH3...2 B6
Bread Street La
  EDNT/CEDW EH3....2 B6
Breck Ter PNCK EH26....71 E1
Brewery Cl QFRY EH30....6 C4
Briarbank Ter
  DAL/STH/STNH EH11....42 C2
Brickworks Rd TRNT EH33....51 E1
Bridge End LIB/NID EH16....44 D3
Bridge Rd BAL/CUR EH14....53 E2
  COLIN EH13....56 C3
The Bridges DFLS KY11....5 H1
Bridge St MUS EH21....31 H5
  PBLO/DUD EH15....30 A2
  PNCK EH26....70 D5
  RATHO EH28....20 D5
  TRNT EH33....51 E2
Bridge Street La
  MUS EH21....30 A2
Bridge Vw QFLS KY11....4 D4
Briery Bauks HLYRPK/NF EH8...3 H6
Brighouse Park Gait EDNW EH4...14 C2
Brighouse Park Rd EDNW EH4...14 C2
Brighton Pl PBLO/DUD EH15...30 A3
Brighton St EDOT EH1....3 F6
Bright's Crs NWGTN EH9...44 B2

Bristo Pl *EDOT* EH1 .... 3 F6
Bristo Port *EDOT* EH1 .... 3 F6
Britwell Crs *RSTRG* EH7 .... 29 F2
Brixwold Bank *BNYRG* EH19 .... 75 H1
Brixwold Dr *BNYRG* EH19 .... 75 H1
Brixwold Neuk *BNYRG* EH19 .... 75 H1
Brixwold Pk *BNYRG* EH19 .... 75 H1
Brixwold Ri *BNYRG* EH19 .... 75 H1
Brixwold Vw *BNYRG* EH19 .... 75 H1
Broadhurst Rd *DLKTH* EH22 .... 69 E5
Broad Wynd *LEITH* EH6 .... 18 C5
Brock St *DFLS* KY11 .... 4 C4
Brockwood Av *PNCK* EH26 .... 70 A3
Broombank Ter
　　MRYFD/COR EH12 .... 40 D2
Broomfield Crs
　　MRYFD/COR EH12 .... 41 E2
Broomhall Av
　　MRYFD/COR EH12 .... 41 E2
Broomhall Bank
　　MRYFD/COR EH12 .... 40 D1
Broomhall Crs
　　MRYFD/COR EH12 .... 40 D1
Broomhall Dr
　　MRYFD/COR EH12 .... 40 D1
Broomhall Gdns
　　MRYFD/COR EH12 .... 40 D1
Broomhall Loan
　　MRYFD/COR EH12 .... 40 D1
Broomhall Pk
　　MRYFD/COR EH12 .... 40 D1
Broomhall Pl
　　MRYFD/COR EH12 .... 40 D1
Broomhall Rd
　　MRYFD/COR EH12 .... 40 D1
Broomhall Ter
　　MRYFD/COR EH12 .... 40 C1
Broomhill Av *PNCK* EH26 .... 70 C4
Broomhill Dr *DLKTH* EH22 .... 68 A2
Broomhill Rd *PNCK* EH26 .... 70 C5
Broomhouse Av
　　DAL/STH/STNH EH11 .... 40 D3
Broomhouse Ct
　　DAL/STH/STNH EH11 .... 41 E2
Broomhouse Crs
　　DAL/STH/STNH EH11 .... 41 E3
Broomhouse Dr
　　DAL/STH/STNH EH11 .... 41 E2
Broomhouse Gdns West
　　DAL/STH/STNH EH11 .... 40 D2
Broomhouse Gv
　　DAL/STH/STNH EH11 .... 41 E3
Broomhouse Loan
　　DAL/STH/STNH EH11 .... 41 E3
Broomhouse Pk
　　DAL/STH/STNH EH11 .... 40 D3
Broomhouse Pl North
　　DAL/STH/STNH EH11 .... 40 D3
Broomhouse Pl South
　　DAL/STH/STNH EH11 .... 41 E3
Broomhouse Rd
　　DAL/STH/STNH EH11 .... 40 D2
Broomhouse St North
　　DAL/STH/STNH EH11 .... 40 D3
Broomhouse St South
　　DAL/STH/STNH EH11 .... 41 E4
Broomhouse Ter
　　DAL/STH/STNH EH11 .... 41 E2
Broomhouse Wk
　　DAL/STH/STNH EH11 .... 41 E3
Broomieknowe *LSWD* EH18 .... 67 E4
Broomieknowe Gdns
　　BNYRG EH19 .... 67 F4
Broomieknowe Pk
　　BNYRG EH19 .... 67 F3
Broomlea Crs
　　MRYFD/COR EH12 .... 40 D1
Broompark Rd
　　RSTRG EH7 .... 29 E2
Broomside Ter
　　MRYFD/COR EH12 .... 41 E2
Broomyknowe *BAL/CUR* EH14 .... 56 D1
Brotherstone's Wy *TRNT* EH33 .... 51 F4
Brougham St *EDNT/CEDW* EH3 .... 2 B7
Broughton Market
　　EDNT/CEDW EH3 .... 2 E1
Broughton Pl *EDOT* EH1 .... 27 H1
Broughton Place La *EDOT* EH1 .... 27 H1
Broughton Rd *RSTRG* EH7 .... 17 H5
Broughton St *EDOT* EH1 .... 27 H1
Broughton Street La *EDOT* EH1 .... 3 F1
Brown's Cl *HLYRPK/NF* EH8 .... 3 J3
Brown St *HLYRPK/NF* EH8 .... 3 H6
Bruce Gdns *DLKTH* EH22 .... 68 D2
Bruce St
　　MCH/MOR/FMHD EH10 .... 43 E4
Brunstane Bank
　　PBLO/DUD EH15 .... 30 D5
Brunstane Crs *PBLO/DUD* EH15 .... 30 C5
Brunstane Dr *PBLO/DUD* EH15 .... 30 C5
Brunstane Gdns
　　PBLO/DUD EH15 .... 30 C4
　　PNCK EH26 .... 70 B3
Brunstane Mill Rd
　　PBLO/DUD EH15 .... 31 F4
Brunstane Rd *PBLO/DUD* EH15 .... 30 C4
Brunstane Rd North
　　PBLO/DUD EH15 .... 30 C3
Brunstane Rd South
　　PBLO/DUD EH15 .... 30 C5
Brunswick Rd *RSTRG* EH7 .... 28 B1
Brunswick Street La
　　RSTRG EH7 .... 28 A1
Brunton's Cl *DLKTH* EH22 .... 68 C1
Brunton Ter *RSTRG* EH7 .... 3 K1
Bruntsfield Av
　　MCH/MOR/FMHD EH10 .... 43 F1
Bruntsfield Crs
　　MCH/MOR/FMHD EH10 .... 43 F2
Bruntsfield Gdns
　　MCH/MOR/FMHD EH10 .... 43 F2
Bruntsfield Pl
　　MCH/MOR/FMHD EH10 .... 43 F1
Bruntsfield Ter
　　MCH/MOR/FMHD EH10 .... 43 F1
Bryans Av *DLKTH* EH22 .... 76 D1
Bryans Rd *DLKTH* EH22 .... 76 D1
Bryce Av *RSTRG* EH7 .... 29 H1
Bryce Crs *BAL/CUR* EH14 .... 55 E4

Bryce Gdns *BAL/CUR* EH14 .... 55 E4
Bryce Gv *RSTRG* EH7 .... 29 H1
Bryce Pl *BAL/CUR* EH14 .... 55 E4
Bryce Rd *BAL/CUR* EH14 .... 55 E4
Bryson Rd *DAL/STH/STNH* EH11 .... 42 D1
Buccleuch Pl *HLYRPK/NF* EH8 .... 3 F7
Buccleuch St *DLKTH* EH22 .... 68 C1
　　HLYRPK/NF EH8 .... 3 G7
Buccleuch Ter *LEITH* EH6 .... 18 B5
Buchan St *DLKTH* EH22 .... 77 G1
Buckingham Ter *EDNW* EH4 .... 26 D2
Buckstane Pk
　　MCH/MOR/FMHD EH10 .... 58 A2
Buckstone Av
　　MCH/MOR/FMHD EH10 .... 58 B3
Buckstone Bank
　　MCH/MOR/FMHD EH10 .... 58 B2
Buckstone Cir
　　MCH/MOR/FMHD EH10 .... 58 C2
Buckstone Cl
　　MCH/MOR/FMHD EH10 .... 58 C3
Buckstone Ct
　　MCH/MOR/FMHD EH10 .... 58 B3
Buckstone Crs
　　MCH/MOR/FMHD EH10 .... 58 B2
Buckstone Crook
　　MCH/MOR/FMHD EH10 .... 58 C4
Buckstone Dell
　　MCH/MOR/FMHD EH10 .... 58 C3
Buckstone Dr
　　MCH/MOR/FMHD EH10 .... 58 B2
Buckstone Gdns
　　MCH/MOR/FMHD EH10 .... 58 B3
Buckstone Ga
　　MCH/MOR/FMHD EH10 .... 58 C3
Buckstone Gn
　　MCH/MOR/FMHD EH10 .... 58 C3
Buckstone Gv
　　MCH/MOR/FMHD EH10 .... 58 B3
Buckstone Hl
　　MCH/MOR/FMHD EH10 .... 58 C3
Buckstone Howe
　　MCH/MOR/FMHD EH10 .... 58 C3
Buckstone Lea
　　MCH/MOR/FMHD EH10 .... 58 C3
Buckstone Loan
　　MCH/MOR/FMHD EH10 .... 58 B3
Buckstone Loan East
　　MCH/MOR/FMHD EH10 .... 58 C3
Buckstone Neuk
　　MCH/MOR/FMHD EH10 .... 58 C2
Buckstone Pl
　　MCH/MOR/FMHD EH10 .... 58 B3
Buckstone Ri
　　MCH/MOR/FMHD EH10 .... 58 C3
Buckstone Rd
　　MCH/MOR/FMHD EH10 .... 58 B3
Buckstone Rw
　　MCH/MOR/FMHD EH10 .... 58 C3
Buckstone Shaw
　　MCH/MOR/FMHD EH10 .... 58 C3
Buckstone Vw
　　MCH/MOR/FMHD EH10 .... 58 B2
Buckstone Wy
　　MCH/MOR/FMHD EH10 .... 58 B2
Buckstone Wd
　　MCH/MOR/FMHD EH10 .... 58 B3
Buckstone Wynd
　　MCH/MOR/FMHD EH10 .... 58 C3
Bughtlin Dr *MRYFD/COR* EH12 .... 24 A2
Bughtlin Gdns
　　MRYFD/COR EH12 .... 24 A2
Bughtlin Gn *MRYFD/COR* EH12 .... 24 A2
Bughtlin Loan
　　MRYFD/COR EH12 .... 24 A3
Bughtlin Pk *MRYFD/COR* EH12 .... 34 C3
Bughtlin Pl *MRYFD/COR* EH12 .... 24 A2
Buie Rigg *KLSTN* EH29 .... 20 D1
Builyeon Rd *QFRY* EH30 .... 6 A5
Burdiehouse Av *MCH/MOR/FMHD* EH10 .... 59 H5
Burdiehouse Crs
　　GIL/MOR EH17 .... 59 H5
Burdiehouse Crossway
　　GIL/MOR EH17 .... 59 H5
Burdiehouse Dr *GIL/MOR* EH17 .... 65 H1
Burdiehouse Medway
　　GIL/MOR EH17 .... 59 H5
Burdiehouse Sq *GIL/MOR* EH17 .... 65 G1
Burdiehouse St *GIL/MOR* EH17 .... 65 H1
Burdiehouse Ter *GIL/MOR* EH17 .... 59 H5
Burgess Rd *QFRY* EH30 .... 6 C5
Burgess St *LEITH* EH6 .... 18 C5
Burgess Ter *NWGTN* EH9 .... 44 C2
Burghlee Crs *LNHD* EH20 .... 65 H5
Burghlee Ter *LNHD* EH20 .... 65 H5
Burghtoft *GIL/MOR* EH17 .... 60 C4
Burlington St *LEITH* EH6 .... 18 B3
Burnbank *LNHD* EH20 .... 65 G3
Burnbank Crs *LNHD* EH20 .... 65 G3
Burnbank Gv *LNHD* EH20 .... 65 G3
Burnbrae *MRYFD/COR* EH12 .... 24 A3
Burnhead Crs *LIB/NID* EH16 .... 59 H3
Burnhead Gv *LIB/NID* EH16 .... 59 H3
Burnhead Loan *LIB/NID* EH16 .... 59 H3
Burnhead Pth East
　　LIB/NID EH16 .... 59 H3
Burnside *MRYFD/COR* EH12 .... 24 A3
Burnside Av *DLKTH* EH22 .... 69 F5
Burnside Crs *DLKTH* EH22 .... 69 F5
Burnside Pk *BAL/CUR* EH14 .... 53 E3
Burnside Rd *GORBR* EH23 .... 79 E1
　　MRYFD/COR EH12 .... 24 A3
Burns St *LEITH* EH6 .... 18 C4
Bush St *MUS* EH21 .... 31 H4
Bush Ter *MUS* EH21 .... 31 H5

C

Cables Wynd *LEITH* EH6 .... 18 B4
Cadell Pl *CPS/PPNS* EH32 .... 35 E1
Cadiz St *LEITH* EH6 .... 18 C5
Cadogan Rd *LIB/NID* EH16 .... 59 G2
Caesar Rd *TRNT* EH33 .... 51 E2
Cairds Rw *MUS* EH21 .... 31 H4
Cairnbank Gdns *PNCK* EH26 .... 70 C5

Cairnbank Rd *PNCK* EH26 .... 70 C5
Cairnmuir Rd
　　MRYFD/COR EH12 .... 25 E3
Cairns Dr *BAL/CUR* EH14 .... 52 D4
Cairns Gdns *BAL/CUR* EH14 .... 52 D4
Cairntows Cl *LIB/NID* EH16 .... 45 F2
Caiyside
　　MCH/MOR/FMHD EH10 .... 58 A5
Caiystane Av
　　MCH/MOR/FMHD EH10 .... 58 A4
Caiystane Crs
　　MCH/MOR/FMHD EH10 .... 58 A3
Caiystane Dr
　　MCH/MOR/FMHD EH10 .... 57 H4
Caiystane Gdns
　　MCH/MOR/FMHD EH10 .... 57 H3
Caiystane Hl
　　MCH/MOR/FMHD EH10 .... 58 A3
Caiystane Ter
　　MCH/MOR/FMHD EH10 .... 57 H4
Caiystane Vw
　　MCH/MOR/FMHD EH10 .... 58 A4
Calder Cl *DAL/STH/STNH* EH11 .... 40 B5
Calder Crs *DAL/STH/STNH* EH11 .... 40 B5
Calder Dr *DAL/STH/STNH* EH11 .... 40 C5
Calder Gdns
　　DAL/STH/STNH EH11 .... 40 B5
Calder Gv *DAL/STH/STNH* EH11 .... 40 B5
Calder Jct *DAL/STH/STNH* EH11 .... 40 C5
Calder Pk *DAL/STH/STNH* EH11 .... 40 B5
Calder Pl *DAL/STH/STNH* EH11 .... 40 C5
Calder Road Gdns
　　DAL/STH/STNH EH11 .... 39 H5
Calder Rd
　　DAL/STH/STNH EH11 .... 41 G3
Calder Vw *DAL/STH/STNH* EH11 .... 40 B5
Caledonian Crs
　　DAL/STH/STNH EH11 .... 26 D5
Caledonian Pl
　　DAL/STH/STNH EH11 .... 26 D5
Caledonian Rd
　　DAL/STH/STNH EH11 .... 27 E5
Calton Hl *EDOT* EH1 .... 3 F2
Calton Rd *EDOT* EH1 .... 3 G3
Cambridge Av *LEITH* EH6 .... 18 A5
Cambridge Gdns *LEITH* EH6 .... 18 A5
Cambusnethan St *RSTRG* EH7 .... 28 D2
Cameron House Av
　　LIB/NID EH16 .... 44 D2
Cameron March *LIB/NID* EH16 .... 44 C3
Cameron Pk *LIB/NID* EH16 .... 44 C3
Cameron Smaill Rd
　　BAL/CUR EH14 .... 54 C2
Cameron Toll Gdns
　　LIB/NID EH16 .... 44 D3
Cameron Toll Lade
　　LIB/NID EH16 .... 44 D3
Cammo Av *MRYFD/COR* EH12 .... 23 H1
Cammo Bank *EDNW* EH4 .... 24 A1
Cammo Brae *EDNW* EH4 .... 24 A1
Cammo Gdns *EDNW* EH4 .... 24 A1
Cammo Hl *EDNW* EH4 .... 23 H1
Cammo Pkwy *EDNW* EH4 .... 24 A1
Cammo Pl *EDNW* EH4 .... 24 A1
Cammo Rd *MRYFD/COR* EH12 .... 23 E2
Cammo Wk *EDNW* EH4 .... 23 H1
Campbell Av *MRYFD/COR* EH12 .... 25 H5
Campbell Park Crs *COLIN* EH13 .... 56 B5
Campbell Park Dr *COLIN* EH13 .... 56 B5
Campbell's Cl *HLYRPK/NF* EH8 .... 3 J3
Campie Gdns *MUS* EH21 .... 31 H5
Campie La *MUS* EH21 .... 31 H5
Campie Rd *MUS* EH21 .... 31 H5
Camp Rd *DLKTH* EH22 .... 69 C5
Campview *DLKTH* EH22 .... 61 F2
Campview Av *DLKTH* EH22 .... 61 F2
Campview Crs *DLKTH* EH22 .... 61 F2
Campview Gdns *DLKTH* EH22 .... 61 F2
Campview Gv *DLKTH* EH22 .... 61 G2
Campview Rd *BNYRG* EH19 .... 67 F5
Campview Ter *DLKTH* EH22 .... 61 F2
Camp Wood Vw *DLKTH* EH22 .... 77 G2
Camus Av
　　MCH/MOR/FMHD EH10 .... 58 A3
Camus Pk
　　MCH/MOR/FMHD EH10 .... 58 A3
Canaan La
　　MCH/MOR/FMHD EH10 .... 43 F3
Candlemaker Rw *EDOT* EH1 .... 2 E5
Candlemaker's Crs
　　GIL/MOR EH17 .... 60 D3
Candlemaker's Pk
　　GIL/MOR EH17 .... 60 D3
Canmore St *QFRY* EH30 .... 6 C5
Canning Street La
　　EDNT/CEDW EH3 .... 27 E4
Canongate *HLYRPK/NF* EH8 .... 3 H4
Canonmills *EDNT/CEDW* EH3 .... 17 G5
Capelaw Rd *COLIN* EH13 .... 56 C5
Caponhall Ct *TRNT* EH33 .... 51 E5
Caponhall Dr *TRNT* EH33 .... 51 E5
Caponhall Rd *TRNT* EH33 .... 51 E5
Captain's Dr *LIB/NID* EH16 .... 59 G3
Captain's Rd *GIL/MOR* EH17 .... 59 G4
Carberry Ct *LNHD* EH20 .... 65 G5
Carberry Pl *MRYFD/COR* EH12 .... 26 C4
Carberry Rd *MUS* EH21 .... 48 B3
Carfrae Gdns *EDNW* EH4 .... 25 G1
Carfrae Pk *EDNW* EH4 .... 25 G1
Carfrae Rd *EDNW* EH4 .... 25 G1
Cargilfield Vw *EDNW* EH4 .... 14 B3
Cargil Ter *GNTN* EH5 .... 17 F5
Carlaverock Av *TRNT* EH33 .... 51 F5
Carlaverock Ct *TRNT* EH33 .... 51 G4
Carlaverock Crs *TRNT* EH33 .... 51 F5
Carlaverock Dr *TRNT* EH33 .... 51 F5
Carlaverock Gv *TRNT* EH33 .... 51 F5
Carlaverock Ter *TRNT* EH33 .... 51 G5
Carlaverock Vw *TRNT* EH33 .... 51 F4
Carlingnose Ct *DFLS* KY11 .... 4 D4
Carlingnose Pk *DFLS* KY11 .... 4 D4
Carlingnose Point *DFLS* KY11 .... 4 D4
Carlingnose Vw *DFLS* KY11 .... 4 D4
Carlingnose Wy *DFLS* KY11 .... 4 D4

Carlops Av *PNCK* EH26 .... 70 C3
Carlops Crs *PNCK* EH26 .... 70 C3
Carlops Rd *PNCK* EH26 .... 70 B4
Carlowrie Av *QFRY* EH30 .... 12 A1
Carlowrie Crs *QFRY* EH30 .... 12 A1
Carlowrie Pl *GORBR* EH23 .... 79 E1
Carlton St *EDNW* EH4 .... 27 E2
Carlton Ter *RSTRG* EH7 .... 3 J1
Carlton Terrace La *RSTRG* EH7 .... 3 J1
Carlton Terrace Ms *RSTRG* EH7 .... 3 J1
Carlyle Pl *MUS* EH21 .... 32 A5
　　RSTRG EH7 .... 28 C2
Carmel Av *KLSTN* EH29 .... 21 E1
Carmelite Rd *QFRY* EH30 .... 6 C5
Carmel Rd *KLSTN* EH29 .... 21 E2
Carnbee Av *LIB/NID* EH16 .... 60 A3
Carnbee Crs *LIB/NID* EH16 .... 60 A3
Carnbee Dell *LIB/NID* EH16 .... 60 A3
Carnbee End *LIB/NID* EH16 .... 60 A3
Carnbee Pk *LIB/NID* EH16 .... 60 A3
Carnegie St *HLYRPK/NF* EH8 .... 3 H6
Carnethie St *RSWL* EH24 .... 74 B5
Carnethy Av *COLIN* EH13 .... 56 C4
　　PNCK EH26 .... 70 C3
Carnethy Ct *PNCK* EH26 .... 70 D4
Caroline Gdns
　　MRYFD/COR EH12 .... 25 E4
Caroline Park Gv *GNTN* EH5 .... 16 B2
Caroline Ter *MRYFD/COR* EH12 .... 24 C3
Carpet La *LEITH* EH6 .... 18 C3
Carrick Crs *DLKTH* EH22 .... 69 E4
Carrick Knowe Av
　　MRYFD/COR EH12 .... 25 F5
Carrick Knowe Dr
　　MRYFD/COR EH12 .... 41 F1
Carrick Knowe Gdns
　　MRYFD/COR EH12 .... 41 F1
Carrick Knowe Gv
　　MRYFD/COR EH12 .... 41 F1
Carrick Knowe Hl
　　MRYFD/COR EH12 .... 41 F1
Carrick Knowe Loan
　　MRYFD/COR EH12 .... 41 E1
Carrick Knowe Pkwy
　　MRYFD/COR EH12 .... 25 E5
Carrick Knowe Pl
　　MRYFD/COR EH12 .... 41 F1
Carrick Knowe Rd
　　MRYFD/COR EH12 .... 41 F1
Carrick Knowe Ter
　　MRYFD/COR EH12 .... 41 F1
Carrington Crs *EDNW* EH4 .... 16 C5
Carrington Rd *EDNW* EH4 .... 26 C1
Carron Pl *LEITH* EH6 .... 18 D5
Casselbank St *LEITH* EH6 .... 18 B4
Cassel's La *LEITH* EH6 .... 18 B4
Castland Hill Rd *DFLS* KY11 .... 4 B1
Castle Av *CPS/PPNS* EH32 .... 35 G1
　　GORBR EH23 .... 79 G2
　　MRYFD/COR EH12 .... 40 D1
Castlebrae Glebe *LIB/NID* EH16 .... 45 F3
Castlebrae Pl *LIB/NID* EH16 .... 45 F3
Castlebrae Rigg *LIB/NID* EH16 .... 45 F3
Castlehill *EDOT* EH1 .... 2 D4
Castlelaw Ct *PNCK* EH26 .... 70 D5
Castlelaw Crs *ROSLIN* EH25 .... 73 F1
Castlelaw Rd *COLIN* EH13 .... 56 C3
Castlepark Gait *LIB/NID* EH16 .... 45 F2
Castlepark Gld *LIB/NID* EH16 .... 45 F2
Castlepark Gn *LIB/NID* EH16 .... 45 F2
Castle Pl *GORBR* EH23 .... 79 E2
Castlelaw Rd *LIB/NID* EH16 .... 45 F2
Castle St *EDNT/CEDW* EH3 .... 2 C5
Castle Ter *CPS/PPNS* EH32 .... 35 G1
　　EDNT/CEDW EH3 .... 2 C5
Castle Vw *CPS/PPNS* EH32 .... 35 G1
　　GORBR EH23 .... 79 E3
Castleview Dr *LIB/NID* EH16 .... 45 F3
Castleview Gv *LIB/NID* EH16 .... 45 F3
Castleview Ter *LIB/NID* EH16 .... 45 F3
Castle Wk *CPS/PPNS* EH32 .... 35 G1
Castle Wynd South *EDOT* EH1 .... 2 D5
The Cast *LSWD* EH18 .... 74 B1
Cathcart Pl
　　DAL/STH/STNH EH11 .... 26 D5
Cathedral La *EDOT* EH1 .... 3 F1
Catriona Ter *PNCK* EH26 .... 72 C5
Causewayside *NWGTN* EH9 .... 44 A1
Causeway *PBLO/DUD* EH15 .... 29 F5
Cavalry Park Dr
　　PBLO/DUD EH15 .... 29 F5
Cedar Dr *CPS/PPNS* EH32 .... 35 E2
Cedar Rd *LNHD* EH20 .... 65 F5
Cemetery Rd *CPS/PPNS* EH32 .... 34 B3
　　DLKTH EH22 .... 68 B2
Chalmers Crs *NWGTN* EH9 .... 43 H1
Chalmers St *EDNT/CEDW* EH3 .... 2 D7
Chamberlain Rd
　　MCH/MOR/FMHD EH10 .... 43 F2
Chambers St *EDOT* EH1 .... 3 F5
Champigny Ct *MUS* EH21 .... 48 C1
Chancelot Crs *GNTN* EH5 .... 17 G3
Chancelot Gv *GNTN* EH5 .... 17 G3
Chapel La *LEITH* EH6 .... 18 C3
Chapel Loan *ROSLIN* EH25 .... 73 H5
Chapel Pl *DFLS* KY11 .... 4 D5
Chapel St *HLYRPK/NF* EH8 .... 3 G6
Chariot Av *RATHO* EH28 .... 37 E1
Charles St *HLYRPK/NF* EH8 .... 3 F6
　　PNCK EH26 .... 70 C2
Charlotte La *CPS/PPNS* EH32 .... 2 A3
Charlotte Sq *EDNT/CEDW* EH3 .... 2 B4
Charlton Gv *ROSLIN* EH25 .... 73 G3
Charterhall Gv *NWGTN* EH9 .... 43 H3
Charterhall Rd *NWGTN* EH9 .... 43 H4
Cherry Av *BNYRG* EH19 .... 75 F1
Cherry Tree Av *BAL/CUR* EH14 .... 53 G1
Cherry Tree Crs *BAL/CUR* EH14 .... 53 F1
Cherry Tree Gdns
　　BAL/CUR EH14 .... 53 F1
Cherry Tree Loan
　　BAL/CUR EH14 .... 53 G1
Cherry Tree Pk *BAL/CUR* EH14 .... 53 F1
Cherry Tree Pl *BAL/CUR* EH14 .... 53 G1
Cherry Tree Vw *BAL/CUR* EH14 .... 53 G1
Chesser Av *BAL/CUR* EH14 .... 41 H5

Chesser Crs *BAL/CUR* EH14 .... 42 A3
Chesser Gdns *BAL/CUR* EH14 .... 41 H2
Chesser Gv *BAL/CUR* EH14 .... 41 H3
Chesser Loan *BAL/CUR* EH14 .... 41 H3
Chester St *BNYRG* EH19 .... 75 F1
Chester Ct *DLKTH* EH22 .... 77 F2
Chester Gv *BNYRG* EH19 .... 75 F1
Chester St *EDNT/CEDW* EH3 .... 27 E3
Chesters Vw *BNYRG* EH19 .... 75 F2
Chester Vw *DLKTH* EH22 .... 77 F2
Chestnut Gv *BNYRG* EH19 .... 75 F2
Chestnut St *GNTN* EH5 .... 16 C1
Cheyne St *EDNW* EH4 .... 27 E1
Chisholm Ter *PNCK* EH26 .... 70 D2
Christian Crs *PBLO/DUD* EH15 .... 30 B4
Christian Gv *PBLO/DUD* EH15 .... 30 B4
Christiemiller Av *RSTRG* EH7 .... 29 G1
Christiemiller Gv *RSTRG* EH7 .... 29 G1
Christiemiller Pl *RSTRG* EH7 .... 29 G1
Chuckie Pend *EDNT/CEDW* EH3 .... 2 A5
Church Hl
　　MCH/MOR/FMHD EH10 .... 43 F2
Churchill Dr
　　MCH/MOR/FMHD EH10 .... 43 F2
Church Hill Pl
　　MCH/MOR/FMHD EH10 .... 43 F2
Church Rd *LSWD* EH18 .... 66 D3
Church St *TRNT* EH33 .... 51 E1
The Circle *DLKTH* EH22 .... 61 F1
Circus Gdns *EDNT/CEDW* EH3 .... 2 B1
Circus La *EDNT/CEDW* EH3 .... 27 F1
Circus Pl *EDNT/CEDW* EH3 .... 27 F1
Citadel Pl *LEITH* EH6 .... 18 B2
The City of Edinburgh By-Pass
　　BAL/CUR EH14 .... 55 G1
　　GIL/MOR EH17 .... 61 E5
　　LSWD EH18 .... 61 E5
　　MRYFD/COR EH12 .... 39 G1
Clackmae Rd *LIB/NID* EH16 .... 59 F1
Clarebank Crs *LEITH* EH6 .... 18 D4
Claremont Bank *RSTRG* EH7 .... 27 H1
Claremont Crs *RSTRG* EH7 .... 17 H5
Claremont Gdns *LEITH* EH6 .... 18 D4
Claremont Gv *RSTRG* EH7 .... 17 H5
Claremont Pk *LEITH* EH6 .... 18 D4
Claremont Rd *LEITH* EH6 .... 18 D4
Clarence St *EDNT/CEDW* EH3 .... 27 F1
Clarendon Crs *EDNW* EH4 .... 27 E2
Clarinda Gdns *DLKTH* EH22 .... 69 F2
Clarinda Ter *LIB/NID* EH16 .... 59 G1
Clark Av *GNTN* EH5 .... 17 G3
Clark Pl *GNTN* EH5 .... 17 F3
Claverhouse Dr *LIB/NID* EH16 .... 59 C1
Clayhills Gv *BAL/CUR* EH14 .... 52 D3
Clayhills Pk *BAL/CUR* EH14 .... 52 D3
Clayknowes Av *MUS* EH21 .... 47 G1
Clayknowes Ct *MUS* EH21 .... 47 G2
Clayknowes Crs *MUS* EH21 .... 47 G1
Clayknowes Dr *MUS* EH21 .... 47 F1
Clayknowes Pl *MUS* EH21 .... 47 F1
Clayknowes Wy *MUS* EH21 .... 47 G1
Claylands Rd *RATHO* EH28 .... 36 D3
Clearburn Crs *LIB/NID* EH16 .... 44 D2
Clearburn Gdns *LIB/NID* EH16 .... 44 D2
Clearburn Rd *GORBR* EH23 .... 76 D5
　　LIB/NID EH16 .... 44 D2
Cleekim Dr *PBLO/DUD* EH15 .... 46 B2
Cleekim Rd *PBLO/DUD* EH15 .... 46 B2
Cleikiminrig *PBLO/DUD* EH15 .... 46 B2
Clerk Rd *PNCK* EH26 .... 70 B4
Clerk St *HLYRPK/NF* EH8 .... 3 G7
　　LNHD EH20 .... 66 A4
Clermiston Av *EDNW* EH4 .... 24 D1
Clermiston Crs *EDNW* EH4 .... 24 D2
Clermiston Dr *EDNW* EH4 .... 24 D2
Clermiston Gdns *EDNW* EH4 .... 24 D2
Clermiston Gn *EDNW* EH4 .... 24 D1
Clermiston Gv *EDNW* EH4 .... 24 D2
Clermiston Loan *EDNW* EH4 .... 24 D1
Clermiston Medway
　　EDNW EH4 .... 24 D1
Clermiston Pl *EDNW* EH4 .... 24 D2
Clermiston Rd
　　MRYFD/COR EH12 .... 25 E4
Clermiston Rd North
　　EDNW EH4 .... 25 E1
Clermiston Vw *EDNW* EH4 .... 25 E2
Clerwood Bank
　　MRYFD/COR EH12 .... 24 D3
Clerwood Gdns
　　MRYFD/COR EH12 .... 24 D3
Clerwood Gv *MRYFD/COR* EH12 .... 25 E3
Clerwood Loan
　　MRYFD/COR EH12 .... 24 D3
Clerwood Pk *MRYFD/COR* EH12 .... 25 E3
Clerwood Pl M
　　RYFD/COR EH12 .... 25 E3
Clerwood Rw
　　MRYFD/COR EH12 .... 24 D3
Clerwood Ter
　　MRYFD/COR EH12 .... 25 E3
Clerwood Wy
　　MRYFD/COR EH12 .... 24 D3
Cliftonhall Rd
　　RATHO EH28 .... 36 D4
Clifton Rd *RATHO* EH28 .... 36 B5
Clinton Rd
　　MCH/MOR/FMHD EH10 .... 43 F2
Clockmill La *HLYRPK/NF* EH8 .... 28 D2
Clovenstone Dr *BAL/CUR* EH14 .... 56 B2
Clovenstone Gdns
　　BAL/CUR EH14 .... 56 B1
Clovenstone Pk *BAL/CUR* EH14 .... 56 B1
Clovenstone Rd *BAL/CUR* EH14 .... 56 A1
Clufflat *QFRY* EH30 .... 6 A3
Clufflat Brae *QFRY* EH30 .... 6 A4
Cluny Av
　　MCH/MOR/FMHD EH10 .... 43 F4
Cluny Dr
　　MCH/MOR/FMHD EH10 .... 43 F4
Cluny Gdns
　　MCH/MOR/FMHD EH10 .... 43 F4
Cluny Pl
　　MCH/MOR/FMHD EH10 .... 43 G3
Cluny Ter
　　MCH/MOR/FMHD EH10 .... 43 F4
Clyde St *EDOT* EH1 .... 2 E2

Coalgate Av TRNT EH33 .... 51 G1
Coalgate Rd TRNT EH33 .... 51 F1
Coal Neuk TRNT EH33 .... 51 F1
Coates Crs EDNT/CEDW EH3 .... 27 E4
Coates Gdns MRYFD/COR EH12 .... 26 D4
Coatfield La LEITH EH6 .... 18 C3
Cobden Crs NWGTN EH9 .... 44 B2
Cobden Rd NWGTN EH9 .... 44 B2
Coburg St LEITH EH6 .... 18 B3
Cochrane Pl LEITH EH6 .... 18 D4
Cochrina Pl RSWL EH24 .... 74 B5
Cockburn Crs BAL/CUR EH14 .... 52 D4
Cockburnhill Rd BAL/CUR EH14 .... 52 D4
Cockburn St EDOT EH1 .... 2 E4
Cockpen Av BNYRG EH19 .... 75 E2
Cockpen Crs BNYRG EH19 .... 75 E2
Cockpen Dr BNYRG EH19 .... 75 E2
Cockpen Pl BNYRG EH19 .... 75 H2
Cockpen Rd BNYRG EH19 .... 75 H2
Cockpen Ter BNYRG EH19 .... 75 E2
Cockpen Vw BNYRG EH19 .... 75 E2
Coillesdene Av PBLO/DUD EH15 .... 30 D4
Coillesdene Crs PBLO/DUD EH15 .... 30 D4
Coillesdene Dr PBLO/DUD EH15 .... 30 D4
Coillesdene Gdns PBLO/DUD EH15 .... 30 D4
Coillesdene Loan PBLO/DUD EH15 .... 31 E4
Coillesdene Ter PBLO/DUD EH15 .... 30 D4
Coillesdene Gv PBLO/DUD EH15 .... 30 D4
Colinton Gv EH13 .... 57 F1
Colinton Gv West BAL/CUR EH14 .... 42 B4
Colinton Mains Crs COLIN EH13 .... 57 F3
Colinton Mains Dr COLIN EH13 .... 57 F2
Colinton Mains Gdn COLIN EH13 .... 57 F1
Colinton Mains Gn COLIN EH13 .... 57 F2
Colinton Mains Gv COLIN EH13 .... 57 G2
Colinton Mains Loan COLIN EH13 .... 57 F2
Colinton Mains Pl COLIN EH13 .... 57 G2
Colinton Mains Rd COLIN EH13 .... 57 G2
Colinton Rd BAL/CUR EH14 .... 42 B5
COLIN EH13 .... 56 D5
College Wynd EDOT EH1 .... 3 F5
Collins Pl EDNT/CEDW EH3 .... 27 F1
Colmestone Ga MCH/MOR/FMHD EH10 .... 58 A3
Coltbridge Av MRYFD/COR EH12 .... 26 B4
Coltbridge Gdns MRYFD/COR EH12 .... 26 C4
Coltbridge Millside MRYFD/COR EH12 .... 26 C4
Coltbridge Ter MRYFD/COR EH12 .... 26 B4
Coltbridge V MRYFD/COR EH12 .... 26 C4
Columba Rd EDNW EH4 .... 25 H1
Colvin Rd EDNW EH4 .... 24 B5
Colville Pl EDNT/CEDW EH3 .... 27 F1
Comely Bank EDNW EH4 .... 26 D1
Comely Bank Av EDNW EH4 .... 27 E1
Comely Bank Gv EDNW EH4 .... 26 D2
Comely Bank Pl EDNW EH4 .... 27 E1
Comely Bank Place Ms 27 E1
Comely Bank Ter EDNW EH4 .... 27 E1
Comely Green Pl RSTRG EH7 .... 28 C2
Comiston Dr MCH/MOR/FMHD EH10 .... 58 A2
Comiston Gdns MCH/MOR/FMHD EH10 .... 43 E4
Comiston Gv MCH/MOR/FMHD EH10 .... 58 A2
Comiston Pl MCH/MOR/FMHD EH10 .... 43 E4
Comiston Ri MCH/MOR/FMHD EH10 .... 58 A2
Comiston Rd MCH/MOR/FMHD EH10 .... 58 A2
Comiston Springs Av MCH/MOR/FMHD EH10 .... 58 A2
Comiston Ter MCH/MOR/FMHD EH10 .... 43 E4
Comiston Vw MCH/MOR/FMHD EH10 .... 58 A2
Commercial St LEITH EH6 .... 18 B2
Conifer Rd DLKTH EH22 .... 69 G5
Connaught Pl LEITH EH6 .... 17 H3
Considine Gdns HLYRPK/NF EH8 .... 29 E2
Considine Ter HLYRPK/NF EH8 .... 29 E2
Constitution Pl LEITH EH6 .... 18 C2
Constitution St LEITH EH6 .... 18 C4
Cook Crs DLKTH EH22 .... 77 F2
Cope La CPS/PPNS EH32 .... 35 E1
Corbiehill Av EDNW EH4 .... 15 G5
Corbiehill Crs EDNW EH4 .... 15 F5
Corbiehill Gdns EDNW EH4 .... 15 G5
Corbiehill Pk EDNW EH4 .... 15 F5
Corbiehill Pl EDNW EH4 .... 15 F5
Corbiehill Rd EDNW EH4 .... 15 F5
Corbiehill Ter EDNW EH4 .... 15 F5
Corbieshot PBLO/DUD EH15 .... 46 B1
Corbie Wynd PBLO/DUD EH15 .... 46 B1
Cornhill Ter LEITH EH6 .... 18 D4
Cornwallis Pl EDNT/CEDW EH3 .... 27 F1
Cornwall St EDOT EH1 .... 2 B5
Coronation Pl DLKTH EH22 .... 69 F5
Corrennie Dr MCH/MOR/FMHD EH10 .... 43 F4
Corrennie Gdns MCH/MOR/FMHD EH10 .... 43 F5
Corrie Ter DLKTH EH22 .... 76 D3
Corslet Crs BAL/CUR EH14 .... 55 G4
Corslet Pl BAL/CUR EH14 .... 55 G4
Corslet Rd BAL/CUR EH14 .... 55 G4
Corstorphine Bank Av MRYFD/COR EH12 .... 24 C4
Corstorphine Bank Dr MRYFD/COR EH12 .... 24 C4
Corstorphine Bank Ter MRYFD/COR EH12 .... 24 C4

Corstorphine High St MRYFD/COR EH12 .... 24 D5
Corstorphine Hill Av MRYFD/COR EH12 .... 25 E4
Corstorphine Hill Crs MRYFD/COR EH12 .... 25 E4
Corstorphine Hill Gdns MRYFD/COR EH12 .... 25 E4
Corstorphine Hill Rd MRYFD/COR EH12 .... 25 E4
Corstorphine House Av MRYFD/COR EH12 .... 25 E5
Corstorphine House Ter MRYFD/COR EH12 .... 25 E5
Corstorphine Park Gdns MRYFD/COR EH12 .... 25 E5
Corstorphine Rd MRYFD/COR EH12 .... 25 E5
Cortleferry Dr DLKTH EH22 .... 68 A3
Cortleferry Gv DLKTH EH22 .... 68 A3
Cortleferry Pk DLKTH EH22 .... 68 A3
Cortleferry Ter DLKTH EH22 .... 68 A3
Corunna Pl LEITH EH6 .... 18 B3
Corunna Ter PNCK EH26 .... 71 E1
Cottage Gn EDNW EH4 .... 25 G2
Cottage Pk EDNW EH4 .... 25 G2
County Rd CPS/PPNS EH32 .... 34 A4
County Sq CPS/PPNS EH32 .... 34 A4
Couperfield LEITH EH6 .... 18 B2
Couper St LEITH EH6 .... 18 B2
Covenanters La QFRY EH30 .... 6 C4
Cowan Rd DAL/STH/STNH EH11 .... 42 C2
Cowan's Cl HLYRPK/NF EH8 .... 3 G7
Cowan Ter PNCK EH26 .... 70 D2
Cowden Crs DLKTH EH22 .... 69 F1
Cowden Gv DLKTH EH22 .... 69 F1
Cowden La DLKTH EH22 .... 69 F1
Cowden Pk DLKTH EH22 .... 69 F1
Cowden Ter DLKTH EH22 .... 69 F1
Cowden Vw DLKTH EH22 .... 69 F1
Cowgate EDOT EH1 .... 2 E5
Cowgatehead EDOT EH1 .... 2 E5
Cowpits Ford Rd MUS EH21 .... 48 A3
Cowpits Rd MUS EH21 .... 48 B5
Coxfield DAL/STH/STNH EH11 .... 42 A2
Craigcrook Av EDNW EH4 .... 25 F1
Craigcrook Gdns EDNW EH4 .... 25 G2
Craigcrook Pk EDNW EH4 .... 25 G2
Craigcrook Rd EDNW EH4 .... 25 F1
Craigcrook Sq EDNW EH4 .... 25 G1
Craigend Pk LIB/NID EH16 .... 45 E5
Craigentinny Av RSTRG EH7 .... 29 G2
Craigentinny Av North LEITH EH6 .... 19 F4
Craigentinny Crs RSTRG EH7 .... 29 G2
Craigentinny Gv RSTRG EH7 .... 29 G2
Craigentinny Pl RSTRG EH7 .... 29 F1
Craigentinny Rd RSTRG EH7 .... 29 F1
Craighall Av LEITH EH6 .... 17 G2
Craighall Crs LEITH EH6 .... 17 G2
Craighall Gdns LEITH EH6 .... 17 G3
Craighall Rd LEITH EH5 .... 17 G2
Craighall Ter LEITH EH6 .... 17 G3
MUS EH21 .... 32 D5
Craighill Gdns MCH/MOR/FMHD EH10 .... 42 D5
Craighouse Av MCH/MOR/FMHD EH10 .... 42 D4
Craighouse Gdns MCH/MOR/FMHD EH10 .... 42 D4
Craighouse Rd MCH/MOR/FMHD EH10 .... 42 D4
Craighouse Ter MCH/MOR/FMHD EH10 .... 42 D4
Craigiebield Crs PNCK EH26 .... 70 C5
Craigievar Sq MRYFD/COR EH12 .... 24 B3
Craigievar Wynd MRYFD/COR EH12 .... 24 A4
Craiglea Dr MCH/MOR/FMHD EH10 .... 42 D5
Craiglea Pl MCH/MOR/FMHD EH10 .... 42 D5
Craigleith Av North EDNW EH4 .... 26 A3
Craigleith Av South EDNW EH4 .... 26 A3
Craigleith Bank EDNW EH4 .... 26 B2
Craigleith Crs EDNW EH4 .... 26 A2
Craigleith Dr EDNW EH4 .... 26 A2
Craigleith Gdns EDNW EH4 .... 26 A2
Craigleith Gv EDNW EH4 .... 26 A2
Craigleith Hill EDNW EH4 .... 26 B1
Craigleith Hill Av EDNW EH4 .... 26 B1
Craigleith Hill Crs EDNW EH4 .... 26 B1
Craigleith Hill Gdns EDNW EH4 .... 26 B1
Craigleith Hill Gv EDNW EH4 .... 26 B1
Craigleith Hill Loan EDNW EH4 .... 26 B1
Craigleith Hill Pk EDNW EH4 .... 26 B1
Craigleith Hill Rd EDNW EH4 .... 26 C2
Craigleith Rd EDNW EH4 .... 26 B2
Craigleith Ter EDNW EH4 .... 26 B2
Craiglockhart Av BAL/CUR EH14 .... 42 A4
Craiglockhart Bank BAL/CUR EH14 .... 42 A5
Craiglockhart Crs BAL/CUR EH14 .... 42 A5
Craiglockhart Dell Rd BAL/CUR EH14 .... 42 A4
Craiglockhart Dr North BAL/CUR EH14 .... 42 A4
Craiglockhart Dr South BAL/CUR EH14 .... 56 D1
Craiglockhart Gdns BAL/CUR EH14 .... 42 A4
Craiglockhart Gv BAL/CUR EH14 .... 57 E1
Craiglockhart Loan BAL/CUR EH14 .... 42 A5
Craiglockhart Pk BAL/CUR EH14 .... 57 E1
Craiglockhart Pl BAL/CUR EH14 .... 42 A5
Craiglockhart Qd BAL/CUR EH14 .... 42 A5
Craiglockhart Rd BAL/CUR EH14 .... 57 E1
Craiglockhart Rd North BAL/CUR EH14 .... 42 A4
Craiglockhart Ter BAL/CUR EH14 .... 42 C4

Craiglockhart Vw BAL/CUR EH14 .... 42 B4
Craigmillar Castle Av LIB/NID EH16 .... 45 F3
Craigmillar Castle Gdns LIB/NID EH16 .... 45 F2
Craigmillar Castle Loan LIB/NID EH16 .... 45 F2
Craigmillar Castle Rd LIB/NID EH16 .... 45 F2
Craigmount Ap MRYFD/COR EH12 .... 24 C4
Craigmount Av EDNW EH4 .... 24 B1
Craigmount Bank EDNW EH4 .... 24 B1
Craigmount Bank West EDNW EH4 .... 24 B1
Craigmount Brae EDNW EH4 .... 24 B2
Craigmount Ct EDNW EH4 .... 24 B2
Craigmount Crs MRYFD/COR EH12 .... 24 B3
Craigmount Dr EDNW EH4 .... 24 B3
Craigmount Gdns MRYFD/COR EH12 .... 24 B4
Craigmount Gv MRYFD/COR EH12 .... 24 B4
Craigmount Gv North MRYFD/COR EH12 .... 24 B4
Craigmount Hi EDNW EH4 .... 24 B2
Craigmount Loan MRYFD/COR EH12 .... 24 B4
Craigmount Pk MRYFD/COR EH12 .... 24 B4
Craigmount Ter MRYFD/COR EH12 .... 24 B3
Craigmount Vw MRYFD/COR EH12 .... 24 B3
Craigmount Wy MRYFD/COR EH12 .... 24 C2
Craigmuir Pl EDNW EH4 .... 16 A3
Craigour Av GIL/MOR EH17 .... 60 C1
Craigour Crs GIL/MOR EH17 .... 60 C1
Craigour Dr GIL/MOR EH17 .... 60 C1
Craigour Gdns GIL/MOR EH17 .... 60 C1
Craigour Gn GIL/MOR EH17 .... 60 C1
Craigour Gv GIL/MOR EH17 .... 60 C1
Craigour Loan GIL/MOR EH17 .... 60 C1
Craigour Pl GIL/MOR EH17 .... 45 F5
Craigpark Av RATHO EH28 .... 37 G4
Craigpark Crs RATHO EH28 .... 37 G4
Craigroyston Gv EDNW EH4 .... 15 G4
Craigroyston Pl EDNW EH4 .... 15 G4
Craigs Av MRYFD/COR EH12 .... 24 B4
Craigs Bank MRYFD/COR EH12 .... 24 B4
Craigs Crs MRYFD/COR EH12 .... 24 B4
Craigs Dr MRYFD/COR EH12 .... 24 B4
Craigs Gdns MRYFD/COR EH12 .... 24 C5
Craigs Loan MRYFD/COR EH12 .... 24 C4
Craigs Pk MRYFD/COR EH12 .... 24 B4
Crame Ter DLKTH EH22 .... 68 A2
Cramond Av EDNW EH4 .... 14 C5
Cramond Bank EDNW EH4 .... 14 B5
Cramond Brige Toll EDNW EH4 .... 13 H4
Cramond Crs EDNW EH4 .... 14 B5
Cramond Gdns EDNW EH4 .... 14 B5
Cramond Glebe Gdns EDNW EH4 .... 14 C2
Cramond Glebe Rd EDNW EH4 .... 14 C2
Cramond Glebe Ter EDNW EH4 .... 14 B2
Cramond Gn EDNW EH4 .... 14 B2
Cramond Pk EDNW EH4 .... 14 B3
Cramond Pl EDNW EH4 .... 14 C5
Cramond Regis EDNW EH4 .... 14 A5
Cramond Rd North EDNW EH4 .... 14 C4
Cramond Rd South EDNW EH4 .... 14 B5
Cramond Ter EDNW EH4 .... 14 B5
Cramond V EDNW EH4 .... 14 B5
Cramond Village EDNW EH4 .... 14 B2
Cranston St EDOT EH1 .... 3 G3
PNCK EH26 .... 70 C5
Crarae Av EDNW EH4 .... 26 B3
Craufurdland EDNW EH4 .... 14 A5
Crawfurd Rd LIB/NID EH16 .... 44 B3
Crawlees Crs DLKTH EH22 .... 77 G1
The Crescent GORBR EH23 .... 76 D4
Crewe Bank GNTN EH5 .... 16 C3
Crewe Crs GNTN EH5 .... 16 C3
Crewe Gv GNTN EH5 .... 16 C3
Crewe Loan GNTN EH5 .... 16 B3
Crewe Pth GNTN EH5 .... 16 B5
Crewe Pl GNTN EH5 .... 16 B5
Crewe Road Gdns GNTN EH5 .... 16 B3
Crewe Rd North GNTN EH5 .... 16 B3
Crewe Rd West GNTN EH5 .... 16 B2
Crewe Ter GNTN EH5 .... 16 B3
Crichton St EDOT EH1 .... 3 F5
Crichton Ter HLYRPK/NF EH8 .... 3 F6
Crockett Gdns PNCK EH26 .... 70 B5
Croft-An-Righ HLYRPK/NF EH8 .... 3 K2
Croft St DLKTH EH22 .... 68 C2
PNCK EH26 .... 70 C5
Cromwell Pl LEITH EH6 .... 18 B2
Crookston Ct MUS EH21 .... 48 A2
Crookston Rd MUS EH21 .... 48 A2
Crosswood Av BAL/CUR EH14 .... 52 D4
Crosswood Crs BAL/CUR EH14 .... 52 D4
Crown Pl LEITH EH6 .... 18 B4
Crown St LEITH EH6 .... 18 B4
Cruickness Rd DFLS KY11 .... 4 A2
Crusader Dr ROSLIN EH25 .... 73 G3
Cuddies La DLKTH EH22 .... 56 C2
Cuddy La MCH/MOR/FMHD EH10 .... 43 E3
Cuguen Pl LSWD EH18 .... 67 F3
Cuiken Av PNCK EH26 .... 70 A4
Cuiken Bank PNCK EH26 .... 70 B3
Cuikenburn PNCK EH26 .... 70 C2
Cuiken Ter PNCK EH26 .... 70 B3

Cumberland St EDNT/CEDW EH3 .... 27 G1
Cumin Pl NWGTN EH9 .... 44 A1
Cumlodden Av MRYFD/COR EH12 .... 26 A3
Cumnor Crs LIB/NID EH16 .... 44 C5
Curriehill Castle Dr BAL/CUR EH14 .... 54 B5
Curriehill Rd BAL/CUR EH14 .... 54 D4
Currievale Dr BAL/CUR EH14 .... 54 C5
Currievale Pk BAL/CUR EH14 .... 54 C5
Currievale Park Gv BAL/CUR EH14 .... 54 C5
Customs Whf LEITH EH6 .... 18 C2
Cutlins Rd DAL/STH/STNH EH11 .... 40 B4

D

Daiches Braes PBLO/DUD EH15 .... 30 D5
Dalgety Av RSTRG EH7 .... 28 D1
Dalgety Rd RSTRG EH7 .... 28 D1
Dalgety St RSTRG EH7 .... 28 D2
Dalhousie Av BNYRG EH19 .... 75 E1
Dalhousie Av West BNYRG EH19 .... 74 D1
Dalhousie Bank DLKTH EH22 .... 68 B2
Dalhousie Crs DLKTH EH22 .... 68 B3
Dalhousie Dr BNYRG EH19 .... 75 E1
Dalhousie Gdns BNYRG EH19 .... 75 E1
Dalhousie Pl DLKTH EH22 .... 68 B3
Dalhousie Rd DLKTH EH22 .... 68 A3
Dalhousie Rd East BNYRG EH19 .... 75 E1
Dalhousie Rd West BNYRG EH19 .... 75 E1
Dalhousie Ter MCH/MOR/FMHD EH10 .... 43 E4
Daikeith Rd HLYRPK/NF EH8 .... 28 A5
NWGTN EH9 .... 44 C2
Dalkeith St PBLO/DUD EH15 .... 30 C5
Dalmahoy Crs BAL/CUR EH14 .... 55 E1
Dalmahoy Rd RATHO EH28 .... 37 H4
Dalmeny Rd LEITH EH6 .... 17 H3
Dalmeny St LEITH EH6 .... 18 B5
Dalrymple Crs MUS EH21 .... 31 G5
NWGTN EH9 .... 44 A2
Dalrymple Loan MUS EH21 .... 32 A5
Dalry Pl DAL/STH/STNH EH11 .... 27 E4
Dalry Rd DAL/STH/STNH EH11 .... 26 D5
Dalton Ct DLKTH EH22 .... 77 G2
Dalum Ct LNHD EH20 .... 65 G4
Dalum Dr LNHD EH20 .... 65 G4
Dalum Gv LNHD EH20 .... 65 G4
Dalum Loan LNHD EH20 .... 65 G4
Damside EDNW EH4 .... 26 D3
Danderhall Crs DLKTH EH22 .... 61 F2
Dania Ct DAL/STH/STNH EH11 .... 41 F2
Danube St EDNW EH4 .... 27 E2
Darnaway St EDNT/CEDW EH3 .... 27 F2
Darnell Rd GNTN EH5 .... 17 E3
David Scott Av DLKTH EH22 .... 77 G1
Davidson Gdns EDNW EH4 .... 15 G5
Davidson Pk EDNW EH4 .... 16 B5
Davidson Rd EDNW EH4 .... 16 B5
Davie St HLYRPK/NF EH8 .... 3 H5
Dean Bank La EDNT/CEDW EH3 .... 27 F1
Deanbank Pl GORBR EH23 .... 79 F5
Deanburn PNCK EH26 .... 70 C4
Deanpark Av BAL/CUR EH14 .... 53 E3
Deanpark Bank BAL/CUR EH14 .... 55 E3
Deanpark Brae BAL/CUR EH14 .... 55 E3
Deanpark Ct BAL/CUR EH14 .... 52 D4
Deanpark Gdns BAL/CUR EH14 .... 53 E3
Deanpark Gv BAL/CUR EH14 .... 53 E3
Dean Park Crs EDNW EH4 .... 27 E2
Dean Park Gdns EDNW EH4 .... 27 E2
Dean Park Ms EDNW EH4 .... 27 E2
Dean Park Pl DLKTH EH22 .... 76 C2
Dean Park St EDNW EH4 .... 27 E2
Dean Pth EDNW EH4 .... 26 D2
Dean St EDNW EH4 .... 27 E2
Dean Ter EDNW EH4 .... 2 A1
Deantown Av MUS EH21 .... 63 G1
Deantown Dr MUS EH21 .... 48 C5
Dechmont Rd MRYFD/COR EH12 .... 24 A4
Dell Rd COLIN EH13 .... 56 D2
Delta Av MUS EH21 .... 49 E1
Delta Dr MUS EH21 .... 49 E1
Delta Gdns MUS EH21 .... 49 E1
Delta Pl MUS EH21 .... 49 E1
Delta Vw MUS EH21 .... 49 E1
Denham Green Av GNTN EH5 .... 17 E3
Denham Green Pl GNTN EH5 .... 17 F3
Denham Green Ter GNTN EH5 .... 17 F3
Denholm Av MUS EH21 .... 47 G2
Denholm Rd MUS EH21 .... 47 G2
Denholm Wy MUS EH21 .... 47 F2
De Quincey Rd LSWD EH18 .... 74 C1
Derby St LEITH EH6 .... 17 H2
Devon Pl MRYFD/COR EH12 .... 26 D4
Dewar Place La EDNT/CEDW EH3 .... 27 E4
Dick Pl NWGTN EH9 .... 43 H2
Dickson St LEITH EH6 .... 18 B5
Dick Ter PNCK EH26 .... 70 D5
Dinmont Dr LIB/NID EH16 .... 44 D5
Dobbie's Rd BNYRG EH19 .... 67 E5
Dochart Dr EDNW EH4 .... 24 C2
Dock Pl LEITH EH6 .... 18 B2
Dock St LEITH EH6 .... 18 B2
Dolphin Av BAL/CUR EH14 .... 54 D5
Dolphin Gdns East BAL/CUR EH14 .... 54 C5
Dolphin Gdns West BAL/CUR EH14 .... 54 C5
Dolphin Rd BAL/CUR EH14 .... 54 C5
Doocot Pl CPS/PPNS EH32 .... 34 B5
Dorset Pl MCH/MOR/FMHD EH10 .... 43 E1
Double Dykes MUS EH21 .... 48 B2
Double Hedges Rd LIB/NID EH16 .... 44 C5

Dougall Ct DLKTH EH22 .... 77 F2
Dougall Pl DLKTH EH22 .... 77 F2
Douglas Crs BNYRG EH19 .... 67 F5
MRYFD/COR EH12 .... 26 D3
Douglas Gardens Ms EDNW EH4 .... 26 D3
Doune Ter EDNT/CEDW EH3 .... 2 A1
Dovecot Brae TRNT EH33 .... 51 E1
Dovecot Gv BAL/CUR EH14 .... 41 G5
Dovecot Pk BAL/CUR EH14 .... 56 C1
Dovecot Rd MRYFD/COR EH12 .... 40 D1
Dowie's Mill La EDNW EH4 .... 13 H4
Downfield Pl DAL/STH/STNH EH11 .... 26 D5
Downie Pl MUS EH21 .... 32 A5
Downing Ct ROSLIN EH25 .... 73 H3
Dreghorn Av COLIN EH13 .... 57 G4
Dreghorn Dr COLIN EH13 .... 57 G4
Dreghorn Gdns COLIN EH13 .... 57 G3
Dreghorn Loan COLIN EH13 .... 57 H4
Dreghorn Jct MCH/MOR/FMHD EH10 .... 57 H5
Dreghorn Link COLIN EH13 .... 57 G4
Dreghorn Loan COLIN EH13 .... 56 D3
Dreghorn Pl COLIN EH13 .... 57 G4
Drum Av GIL/MOR EH17 .... 60 C3
Drum Brae Av MRYFD/COR EH12 .... 24 C3
Drum Brae Crs EDNW EH4 .... 24 C2
Drum Brae Dr EDNW EH4 .... 24 C2
Drum Brae Gdns MRYFD/COR EH12 .... 24 C3
Drum Brae Gv EDNW EH4 .... 24 C2
Drum Brae Neuk MRYFD/COR EH12 .... 24 C3
Drum Brae North EDNW EH4 .... 24 C2
Drum Brae Pk MRYFD/COR EH12 .... 24 C3
Drum Brae Park Ap MRYFD/COR EH12 .... 24 C3
Drum Brae Pl MRYFD/COR EH12 .... 24 C3
Drum Brae South MRYFD/COR EH12 .... 24 C3
Drum Brae Ter EDNW EH4 .... 24 C2
Drum Brae Wk EDNW EH4 .... 24 B2
Drum Crs GIL/MOR EH17 .... 60 D3
Drumdryan St EDNT/CEDW EH3 .... 2 B7
Drummohr Av MUS EH21 .... 49 E1
Drummohr Gdns MUS EH21 .... 49 F1
Drummond Pl EDNT/CEDW EH3 .... 27 G1
Drummond St HLYRPK/NF EH8 .... 3 G5
Drummore Dr CPS/PPNS EH32 .... 34 A5
Drum Pl GIL/MOR EH17 .... 60 D3
Drumsheugh Gdns EDNT/CEDW EH3 .... 27 E3
Drum St GIL/MOR EH17 .... 60 C3
Drum Ter RSTRG EH7 .... 28 C1
Drum View Av DLKTH EH22 .... 61 F2
Drummmohr Ter MUS EH21 .... 49 E2
Dryden Av LNHD EH20 .... 65 G5
Dryden Crs LNHD EH20 .... 65 G5
Dryden Gait RSTRG EH7 .... 18 A5
Dryden Gdns RSTRG EH7 .... 18 A5
Dryden Gln LNHD EH20 .... 65 F5
Dryden Gv LNHD EH20 .... 65 G5
Dryden Loan LNHD EH20 .... 65 F5
Dryden Pl LNHD EH20 .... 65 F5
NWGTN EH9 .... 44 B1
Dryden Rd LNHD EH20 .... 65 G5
Dryden St RSTRG EH7 .... 18 A5
Dryden Ter LNHD EH20 .... 65 G5
RSTRG EH7 .... 18 A5
Dryden V LNHD EH20 .... 65 F5
Drylaw Av EDNW EH4 .... 26 A1
Drylaw Gdns EDNW EH4 .... 15 H5
Drylaw Gv EDNW EH4 .... 15 H5
Drylaw House Gdns EDNW EH4 .... 15 H5
Drylaw House Paddock EDNW EH4 .... 15 H5
Duart Crs MRYFD/COR EH12 .... 24 C2
Dublin Meuse EDNT/CEDW EH3 .... 2 D1
Dublin St EDNT/CEDW EH3 .... 27 H1
Dublin Street La North EDNT/CEDW EH3 .... 27 H1
Dublin Street La South EDOT EH1 .... 2 E1
Duddingston Av PBLO/DUD EH15 .... 29 G5
Duddingston Crs PBLO/DUD EH15 .... 29 G5
Duddingston Gdns North PBLO/DUD EH15 .... 29 H4
Duddingston Gv East PBLO/DUD EH15 .... 29 H4
Duddingston Loan PBLO/DUD EH15 .... 29 G5
Duddingston Mills HLYRPK/NF EH8 .... 29 G4
Duddingston Pk PBLO/DUD EH15 .... 30 A4
Duddingston Rd PBLO/DUD EH15 .... 29 H4
Duddingston Rd West PBLO/DUD EH15 .... 45 H1
Duddingston Rw PBLO/DUD EH15 .... 29 H4
Duddingston Sq East PBLO/DUD EH15 .... 29 H4
Duddingston Sq West PBLO/DUD EH15 .... 29 H4
Duddingston Vw PBLO/DUD EH15 .... 29 H5
Dudgeon Pl KLSTN EH29 .... 21 F1
Dudley Av LEITH EH6 .... 17 H2
Dudley Bank LEITH EH6 .... 17 H2
Dudley Crs LEITH EH6 .... 17 H2
Dudley Gdns LEITH EH6 .... 17 H2
Dudley Gv LEITH EH6 .... 17 H2
Dudley Ter LEITH EH6 .... 17 H2
Duff Rd DAL/STH/STNH EH11 .... 26 D5
Duff St DAL/STH/STNH EH11 .... 26 D5
Duff Street La DAL/STH/STNH EH11 .... 26 C5
Duke Pl LEITH EH6 .... 18 C4
Duke St DLKTH EH22 .... 68 C1
LEITH EH6 .... 18 C4
Duke's Wk HLYRPK/NF EH8 .... 28 D5
Dumbeg Pk BAL/CUR EH14 .... 55 H1

Dumbiedykes Rd HLYRPK/NF EH8 3 J5
Dumbryden Dr BAL/CUR EH14 41 E5
Dumbryden Gdns BAL/CUR EH14 41 E5
Dumbryden Gv BAL/CUR EH14 41 E5
Dumbryden Rd BAL/CUR EH14 41 F5
Dunard Gdn NWGTN EH9 43 H3
Dunbar St EDNT/CEDW EH3 2 B6
Duncan Gdns TRNT EH33 51 E1
Duncan Pl LEITH EH6 18 C4
Duncan St NWGTN EH9 44 A2
Dundas Av QFRY EH30 6 D5
Dundas Crs DLKTH EH22 68 A2
Dundas Gdns GORBR EH23 78 D1
Dundas Gv DLKTH EH22 68 A2
Dundas Pk BNYRG EH19 67 G5
Dundas Pl KLSTN EH29 21 F1
Dundas Rd DLKTH EH22 68 A2
Dundas St BNYRG EH19 67 F5
Dundee St DAL/STH/STNH EH11 27 E5
Dundee Ter DAL/STH/STNH EH11 42 D1
Dundonald St EDNT/CEDW EH3 27 G1
Dundrennan Cottages LIB/NID EH16 45 E4
Dunedin St RSTRG EH7 17 H5
Dunrobin Pl EDNT/CEDW EH3 17 F5
Dunsmuir Ct MRYFD/COR EH12 24 C5
Dunvegan Ct EDNW EH4 14 B4
Durar Dr EDNW EH4 24 C3
Durham Av PBLO/DUD EH15 29 H4
Durham Bank BNYRG EH19 75 G1
Durham Dr PBLO/DUD EH15 29 H5
Durham Gdns North PBLO/DUD EH15 29 H4
Durham Gdns South PBLO/DUD EH15 30 A5
Durham Gv BNYRG EH19 75 G1
PBLO/DUD EH15 30 A4
Durham Pl BNYRG EH19 75 G1
Durham Pl East PBLO/DUD EH15 30 A4
Durham Place La PBLO/DUD EH15 30 A4
Durham Rd PBLO/DUD EH15 30 A4
Durham Rd South PBLO/DUD EH15 30 A5
Durham Sq PBLO/DUD EH15 29 H4
Durham Ter PBLO/DUD EH15 29 G4
Durward Gv LIB/NID EH16 44 D4
Dury Wy MUS EH21 49 E1
Dykes Rd PNCK EH26 70 C2

E

Earl Grey St EDNT/CEDW EH3 2 B6
Earl Haig Gdns GNTN EH5 17 F3
East Adam St HLYRPK/NF EH8 3 G5
East Barnton Av EDNW EH4 15 E4
East Barnton Gdns EDNW EH4 15 E5
East Bay DFLS KY11 4 D5
East Brighton Crs PBLO/DUD EH15 30 A3
East Caiystane Pl MCH/MOR/FMHD EH10 58 A3
East Caiystane Rd MCH/MOR/FMHD EH10 58 A4
East Camus Pl MCH/MOR/FMHD EH10 58 A3
East Camus Rd MCH/MOR/FMHD EH10 58 A3
East Castle Rd DAL/STH/STNH EH11 43 E1
East Champanyie NWGTN EH9 44 A3
East Clapperfield LIB/NID EH16 44 C5
East Claremont St RSTRG EH7 17 H5
East Comiston MCH/MOR/FMHD EH10 58 A3
East Craigs Rigg MRYFD/COR EH12 24 A4
East Craigs Wynd MRYFD/COR EH12 24 A4
East Cft RATHO EH28 38 A4
East Cromwell St LEITH EH6 18 B2
East Crosscauseway HLYRPK/NF EH8 3 H7
Easter Belmont Rd MRYFD/COR EH12 25 H4
Easter Currie Ct BAL/CUR EH14 55 E5
Easter Currie Crs BAL/CUR EH14 55 E4
Easter Currie Pl BAL/CUR EH14 55 E4
Easter Currie Ter BAL/CUR EH14 55 E5
Easter Dalry Dr DAL/STH/STNH EH11 26 D5
Easter Dalry Rd DAL/STH/STNH EH11 26 D4
Easter Dalry Wynd DAL/STH/STNH EH11 26 D4
Easter Drylaw Av EDNW EH4 16 A5
Easter Drylaw Bank EDNW EH4 16 A4
Easter Drylaw Dr EDNW EH4 16 B5
Easter Drylaw Gdns EDNW EH4 16 A5
Easter Drylaw Gv EDNW EH4 16 A5
Easter Drylaw Loan EDNW EH4 16 A5
Easter Drylaw Pl EDNW EH4 16 A5
Easter Drylaw Vw EDNW EH4 16 A4
Easter Haugh COLIN EH13 57 G2
Easter Hermitage LEITH EH6 18 D5
Easter Park Dr EDNW EH4 15 E4
Easter Rd LEITH EH6 18 C5
RSTRG EH7 3 K1
Easter Steil MCH/MOR/FMHD EH10 42 D5
Easter Warriston RSTRG EH7 17 G4
East Farm of Gilmerton GIL/MOR EH17 60 C3
East Fettes Av EDNW EH4 16 D5
Eastfield Av MRYFD/COR EH12 22 D4
Eastfield Dr PNCK EH26 70 D3
Eastfield Farm Rd PNCK EH26 70 D2
Eastfield Gdns PBLO/DUD EH15 31 E4
Eastfield Loan TRNT EH33 51 F1
Eastfield Park Rd PNCK EH26 70 D3
Eastfield Pl PBLO/DUD EH15 31 F4
Eastfield Rd RATHO EH28 22 C4
East Fountainbridge EDNT/CEDW EH3 2 B6
East Hermitage Pl LEITH EH6 18 C4
Easthouses Ct DLKTH EH22 69 E4
Easthouses Rd DLKTH EH22 69 E5
Easthouses Wy DLKTH EH22 69 E3
East Kilngate Pl GIL/MOR EH17 60 B4
East Kilngate Rigg GIL/MOR EH17 60 B4
East Kilngate Wynd GIL/MOR EH17 60 B5
East Lillypot GNTN EH5 17 F3
East Loan CPS/PPNS EH32 34 C4
East London St RSTRG EH7 27 H1
East Lorimer Pl CPS/PPNS EH32 34 D1
East Market St EDOT EH1 3 F3
East Mayfield NWGTN EH9 44 B2
East Montgomery Pl RSTRG EH7 28 B1
East Newington Pl NWGTN EH9 44 A1
East Parkside LIB/NID EH16 28 B5
East Pilton Farm Av GNTN EH5 16 C3
East Pilton Farm Rigg GNTN EH5 16 C3
East Preston St HLYRPK/NF EH8 44 A1
East Preston Street La NWGTN EH9 44 A1
East Queensway PNCK EH26 70 D2
East Restalrig Ter LEITH EH6 18 D4
East Savile Rd LIB/NID EH16 44 B3
East Sciennes St NWGTN EH9 44 A1
East Scotland Street La EDNT/CEDW EH3 27 H1
East Suffolk Rd LIB/NID EH16 44 C3
East Telferton RSTRG EH7 29 H2
East Trinity Rd GNTN EH5 17 F3
East Weberside EDNW EH4 16 C4
Echline QFRY EH30 6 A5
Echline Av QFRY EH30 6 A5
Echline Dr QFRY EH30 6 A4
Echline Gdns QFRY EH30 6 A4
Echline Gn QFRY EH30 6 A4
Echline Gv QFRY EH30 6 B4
Echline Pk QFRY EH30 6 A5
Echline Pl QFRY EH30 6 A5
Echline Rigg QFRY EH30 6 B4
Echline Ter QFRY EH30 6 B5
Echline Vw QFRY EH30 6 A5
Edenhall Bank MUS EH21 48 C1
Edenhall Crs MUS EH21 48 C1
Edenhall Rd MUS EH21 48 C1
Eden La MCH/MOR/FMHD EH10 43 F3
Edgefield Pl LNHD EH20 66 A4
Edgefield Rd LNHD EH20 66 A3
Edina Pl RSTRG EH7 28 B1
Edinburgh Pk MRYFD/COR EH12 39 H1
Edinburgh Rd CPS/PPNS EH32 34 C3
DLKTH EH22 68 C1
MUS EH21 31 F4
PNCK EH26 71 E2
QFRY EH30 6 D4
RATHO EH28 21 E5
TRNT EH33 50 D2
Edmonstone Av DLKTH EH22 61 F1
Edmonstone Dr DLKTH EH22 61 F1
Edmonstone Rd DLKTH EH22 61 G2
Edmonstone Ter DLKTH EH22 61 F1
Eglinton Crs MRYFD/COR EH12 26 D4
Egypt Ms MCH/MOR/FMHD EH10 43 G3
Eighth St DLKTH EH22 76 D2
Eildon St EDNT/CEDW EH3 17 G5
Eildon Ter EDNT/CEDW EH3 17 F5
Elbe St LEITH EH6 18 C3
Elcho Ter PBLO/DUD EH15 30 C3
Elder St EDOT EH1 3 F2
TRNT EH33 51 E2
Elder St East EDOT EH1 3 F1
Eldindean Pl BNYRG EH19 67 F4
Eldindean Rd BNYRG EH19 67 F4
Eldindean Ter BNYRG EH19 67 G4
Electra Pl PBLO/DUD EH15 30 A2
Elgin St RSTRG EH7 28 B1
Elgin Ter RSTRG EH7 28 B1
Elizafield LEITH EH6 18 A4
Ellangowan Ter LIB/NID EH16 44 D5
Ellen's Glen Rd GIL/MOR EH17 60 A2
Ellersly Rd MRYFD/COR EH12 25 H4
Elliot Gdns BAL/CUR EH14 57 E1
Elliot Pk BAL/CUR EH14 57 E1
Elliot Pl BAL/CUR EH14 57 E1
Elliot Rd BAL/CUR EH14 57 E1
Elmfield Pk DLKTH EH22 68 C1
Elmfield Rd DLKTH EH22 68 C1
Elm Pl DLKTH EH22 77 F1
LEITH EH6 18 D4
Elm Rw LSWD EH18 67 E3
Elmwood Ter LEITH EH6 18 D4
Elphinstone Rd TRNT EH33 51 E2
Eltringham Gdns BAL/CUR EH14 42 A2
Eltringham Gv BAL/CUR EH14 42 A2
Eltringham Ter BAL/CUR EH14 42 A2
Emily Pl GORBR EH23 79 E1
Engine Rd GORBR EH23 78 D1
LNHD EH20 66 A4
Eskbank Ct DLKTH EH22 68 A2
Eskbank Rd BNYRG EH19 67 G4
DLKTH EH22 68 B2
Eskbank Ter DLKTH EH22 68 B2
Eskdaill St DLKTH EH22 68 C1
Eskdale Ct BNYRG EH19 67 E5
Eskdale Dr BNYRG EH19 75 E1
Eskdale Ms MUS EH21 32 A5
Eskdale Ter BNYRG EH19 67 E5
Eskfield Gv DLKTH EH22 67 H2
Esk Glades DLKTH EH22 68 D1
Eskhill PNCK EH26 70 D4
Eskmill Rd PNCK EH26 71 E4
Eskside East MUS EH21 32 B5
Eskside West MUS EH21 47 H1
Eskvale Crs PNCK EH26 71 E4
Eskvale Dr PNCK EH26 71 E3
Eskvale Vw PNCK EH26 71 E3
Eskview Av MUS EH21 47 H1
Eskview Crs MUS EH21 47 H1
Eskview Gv DLKTH EH22 68 B1
MUS EH21 47 H1
Eskview Rd DLKTH EH22 77 F1
MUS EH21 47 H1
Eskview Ter MUS EH21 47 H1
Eskview Vls DLKTH EH22 68 A2
Essendean Pl EDNW EH4 24 D2
Essendean Ter EDNW EH4 24 D2
Essex Brae EDNW EH4 14 A4
Essex Pk EDNW EH4 14 A4
Essex Rd EDNW EH4 14 A4
Esslemont Rd LIB/NID EH16 44 B4
Ethel Ter MCH/MOR/FMHD EH10 43 E4
Eton Ter EDNW EH4 27 E2
Ettrick Gv MCH/MOR/FMHD EH10 43 E1
Ettrick Rd MCH/MOR/FMHD EH10 42 D2
Evans Gdns BNYRG EH19 67 H4
Eva Pl NWGTN EH9 44 A4
Ewerland EDNW EH4 14 A4
Ewing St PNCK EH26 70 D2
Eyre Crs EDNT/CEDW EH3 27 G1
Eyre Pl EDNT/CEDW EH3 27 G1
Eyre Place La EDNT/CEDW EH3 27 G1
Eyre Ter EDNT/CEDW EH3 27 G1

F

Fair-a-Far EDNW EH4 14 A3
Fair-a-Far Shot EDNW EH4 14 B3
Fairbrae DAL/STH/STNH EH11 41 F3
Fairford Gdns LIB/NID EH16 44 D5
Fairmile Av MCH/MOR/FMHD EH10 58 B3
Fairview Rd RATHO EH28 22 B4
Falcon Av MCH/MOR/FMHD EH10 43 F3
Falcon Ct MCH/MOR/FMHD EH10 43 F3
Falcon Gdns MCH/MOR/FMHD EH10 43 F2
Falcon Rd MCH/MOR/FMHD EH10 43 F3
Falcon Rd West MCH/MOR/FMHD EH10 43 F3
Falkland Gdns MRYFD/COR EH12 25 E2
Farm Av LSWD EH18 74 D1
Farrer Ter RSTRG EH7 29 G2
Fa'Side Avenue Ct MUS EH21 49 F2
Fa'Side Av North MUS EH21 49 F2
Fa'Side Av South MUS EH21 49 F2
Fa'Side Crs MUS EH21 49 F2
Fa'Side Dr MUS EH21 49 F2
Fa'Side Gdns MUS EH21 49 F2
Fa'Side Rd TRNT EH33 51 F3
Fa'Side Ter MUS EH21 49 F2
Fa'Side Vw TRNT EH33 51 E4
Fauldburn MRYFD/COR EH12 24 B2
Fauldburn Pk MRYFD/COR EH12 24 B2
Featherhall Av MRYFD/COR EH12 24 D5
Featherhall Crs North MRYFD/COR EH12 24 C5
Featherhall Crs South MRYFD/COR EH12 24 C5
Featherhall Gv MRYFD/COR EH12 24 D5
Featherhall Pl MRYFD/COR EH12 24 D5
Featherhall Rd MRYFD/COR EH12 24 D5
Featherhall Ter MRYFD/COR EH12 24 D5
Ferguson Ct MUS EH21 48 A3
Ferguson Gdns MUS EH21 48 A3
Ferguson Gn MUS EH21 47 H3
Ferguson Vw MUS EH21 47 H3
Ferguson Wy DLKTH EH22 76 D3
Ferniehill Av GIL/MOR EH17 60 C3
Ferniehill Dr GIL/MOR EH17 60 D2
Ferniehill Gdns GIL/MOR EH17 60 D2
Ferniehill Pl GIL/MOR EH17 60 C3
Ferniehill Rd GIL/MOR EH17 60 D2
Ferniehill Sq GIL/MOR EH17 60 C3
Ferniehill St GIL/MOR EH17 60 C2
Ferniehill Ter GIL/MOR EH17 60 C3
Ferniehill Wy GIL/MOR EH17 60 C2
Fernielaw Av COLIN EH13 56 B5
Fernieside Av GIL/MOR EH17 60 C2
Fernieside Crs GIL/MOR EH17 60 C2
Fernieside Dr GIL/MOR EH17 60 C2
Fernieside Gdns GIL/MOR EH17 60 C2
Fernieside Gv GIL/MOR EH17 60 D2
Fernieside Pl GIL/MOR EH17 60 C2
Ferrybarns Ct DFLS KY11 4 C4
Ferryburn Gn QFRY EH30 6 D5
Ferryfield GNTN EH5 16 D4
Ferry Gait Dr EDNW EH4 15 G4
Ferry Gait Gdns EDNW EH4 15 G4
Ferry Gait Pl EDNW EH4 15 G4
Ferry Gait Wk EDNW EH4 15 G4
Ferryhill Rd DFLS KY11 4 C2
Ferry La DFLS KY11 4 C4
Ferrymuir Gait QFRY EH30 6 C5
Ferrymuir La QFRY EH30 6 C5
Ferrymuir Rd QFRY EH30 6 C5
Ferry Rd EDNW EH4 15 H5
LEITH EH6 17 H3
Ferry Road Av EDNW EH4 16 A4
Ferry Road Dr EDNW EH4 16 B3
Ferry Road Gdns EDNW EH4 16 A4
Ferry Road Gv EDNW EH4 16 A4
Ferry Road Pl EDNW EH4 16 A4
Ferry Toll Rd DFLS KY11 4 A1
Fettes Av EDNW EH4 16 D4
Fettes Ri EDNW EH4 16 D4
Fettes Rw EDNT/CEDW EH3 27 G1
Fifth St DLKTH EH22 76 C2
Figgate Bank PBLO/DUD EH15 30 B2
Figgate La PBLO/DUD EH15 30 B2
Figgate St PBLO/DUD EH15 30 A2
Fillyside Rd RSTRG EH7 19 G5
Fillyside Ter RSTRG EH7 19 G5
Findhorn Pl NWGTN EH9 44 A1
Findlay Av RSTRG EH7 19 E5
Findlay Cottages RSTRG EH7 19 E5
Findlay Gdns RSTRG EH7 19 E5
Findlay Gv RSTRG EH7 19 E5
Findlay Medway RSTRG EH7 19 E5
Fingal Pl NWGTN EH9 43 H1
Fingzies Pl LEITH EH6 18 D4
Finlay Pl DLKTH EH22 77 H1
Firrhill Crs COLIN EH13 57 G1
Firrhill Dr COLIN EH13 57 G2
Firrhill Loan COLIN EH13 57 G2
First Gait BAL/CUR EH14 54 C1
First St DLKTH EH22 76 D3
Firth Crs PNCK EH26 73 E5
Firth Rd PNCK EH26 73 E5
Fir Vw LNHD EH20 65 F5
Fishergate Rd CPS/PPNS EH32 35 G2
Fishers Rd CPS/PPNS EH32 35 F1
Fishers Wynd MUS EH21 31 H5
Fishmarket Sq LEITH EH6 17 H1
Fishwives' Cswy PBLO/DUD EH15 29 H2
Fleets Gv TRNT EH33 51 F4
Fleets Rd TRNT EH33 51 E3
Fleets Vw TRNT EH33 51 F4
Fletcher Gv PNCK EH26 70 D1
Forbes Rd MCH/MOR/FMHD EH10 43 F2
Forbes St HLYRPK/NF EH8 3 H7
Ford's Rd DAL/STH/STNH EH11 41 H2
Forester's Vw TRNT EH33 51 F2
Forkenford LIB/NID EH16 45 F1
Forres St EDNT/CEDW EH3 2 A2
Forrester Park Av MRYFD/COR EH12 40 D2
Forrester Park Dr MRYFD/COR EH12 40 D2
Forrester Park Gdns MRYFD/COR EH12 40 D2
Forrester Park Gv MRYFD/COR EH12 40 D2
Forrester Park Loan MRYFD/COR EH12 40 D2
Forrester Rd MRYFD/COR EH12 24 D4
Forrest Hl EDOT EH1 2 E6
Forrest Rd EDOT EH1 2 E6
Forth Br DFLS KY11 7 E2
Forth Ct CPS/PPNS EH32 35 G1
Forth Gdns CPS/PPNS EH32 35 G1
Forth Gv CPS/PPNS EH32 35 G1
Forth Pk QFRY EH30 7 E5
Forth Pl QFRY EH30 6 A4
Forth Road Br DFLS KY11 6 C1
Forthside Ter DFLS KY11 4 D5
Forth St EDOT EH1 3 F1
Forthview Ct TRNT EH33 51 F1
Forth View Crs BAL/CUR EH14 54 D5
DLKTH EH22 61 F1
Forth View Rd BAL/CUR EH14 54 D5
Forthview Rd EDNW EH4 25 H1
Forthview Ter EDNW EH4 25 H1
MUS EH21 49 F2
Forthview Wk TRNT EH33 51 F1
Forth Wynd CPS/PPNS EH32 35 G1
Fortland Rw LEITH EH6 18 A2
Foulis Crs BAL/CUR EH14 56 A3
Foundry La LNHD EH20 66 B3
Fountainbridge EDNT/CEDW EH3 2 A7
Fountainhall Rd NWGTN EH9 44 A3
Fountain Pl LNHD EH20 66 A4
Fourth Gait BAL/CUR EH14 54 C2
Fourth St DLKTH EH22 76 C2
Fowler Crs LNHD EH20 66 B4
Fowler St TRNT EH33 51 E1
Fowler Ter DAL/STH/STNH EH11 26 D5
Fox Covert Av MRYFD/COR EH12 25 E2
Fox Spring Crs COLIN EH13 57 H2
Fox Spring Ri MCH/MOR/FMHD EH10 58 A2
Fox St LEITH EH6 18 D3
Fraser Av GNTN EH5 17 E3
Fraser Crs GNTN EH5 17 E3
Fraser La PNCK EH26 72 C4
Frederick St CED/PRST EH2 2 C2
Freelands Rd RATHO EH28 38 A3
Friarton Gdns PNCK EH26 70 A4
Frogston Av MCH/MOR/FMHD EH10 58 B4
Frogston Brae MCH/MOR/FMHD EH10 59 E5
Frogston Gdns MCH/MOR/FMHD EH10 58 B4
Frogston Gv MCH/MOR/FMHD EH10 58 C4
Frogston Rd East GIL/MOR EH17 59 F4
Frogston Rd West MCH/MOR/FMHD EH10 58 C5
Frogston Ter MCH/MOR/FMHD EH10 58 C4
Furcheons Pk HLYRPK/NF EH8 29 G3

G

Galachlawshot MCH/MOR/FMHD EH10 58 C3
Galachlawside MCH/MOR/FMHD EH10 58 C4
Galadale Crs DLKTH EH22 76 C1
Galadale Dr DLKTH EH22 76 C1
The Gallolee COLIN EH13 57 F3
Galloways Entry HLYRPK/NF EH8 3 J3
Galt Av MUS EH21 48 D1
Galt Crs MUS EH21 49 E1
Galt Dr MUS EH21 49 E1
Galt Rd MUS EH21 49 E1
Galt Ter MUS EH21 49 E1
Gamekeeper's Loan EDNW EH4 14 B3
Gamekeeper's Pk EDNW EH4 14 B3
Gamekeeper's Rd EDNW EH4 14 B3
Garden Ter EDNW EH4 14 D4
Gardiner Crs CPS/PPNS EH32 34 D4
Gardiner Gv EDNW EH4 25 H1
Gardiner Pl DLKTH EH22 76 D1
Gardiner Rd CPS/PPNS EH32 34 C4
EDNW EH4 25 H1
Gardner's Crs EDNT/CEDW EH3 2 A6
Garscube Ter MRYFD/COR EH12 26 B3
Gateside Rd KLSTN EH29 20 D2
Gayfield Sq EDOT EH1 28 A1
Gayfield Street La EDOT EH1 27 H1
Gaynor Av LNHD EH20 65 G4
Gelnorchy Ter NWGTN EH9 44 B2
Gentiles Entry HLYRPK/NF EH8 3 J4
George Av LNHD EH20 65 H4
George Crs LNHD EH20 66 A4
George Dr LNHD EH20 65 H4
George IV Br EDOT EH1 2 E5
George Sq HLYRPK/NF EH8 3 F7
George Square La HLYRPK/NF EH8 2 E7
George St CED/PRST EH2 2 B3
George Ter LNHD EH20 65 H4
Gibbs Entry HLYRPK/NF EH8 3 G6
Gibraltar Ct DLKTH EH22 68 D1
Gibraltar Gdns DLKTH EH22 68 C1
Gibraltar Rd DLKTH EH22 68 C1
Gibraltar Ter DLKTH EH22 68 D1
Gibson Dr DLKTH EH22 69 E1
Gibson St LEITH EH6 18 A4
Gibson Ter DAL/STH/STNH EH11 27 E5
Gifford Pk HLYRPK/NF EH8 28 A5
Gilberstoun PBLO/DUD EH15 46 D1
Gilberstoun Brig PBLO/DUD EH15 46 C1
Gilberstoun Loan PBLO/DUD EH15 46 D1
Gilberstoun Pl PBLO/DUD EH15 46 D1
Gilberstoun Wynd PBLO/DUD EH15 46 D1
Giles St LEITH EH6 18 B3
Gillespie Crs MCH/MOR/FMHD EH10 43 F1
Gillespie Rd COLIN EH13 56 C2
Gillespie St EDNT/CEDW EH3 27 F5
Gillsland Rd DAL/STH/STNH EH11 42 D2
Gilmerton Dykes Av GIL/MOR EH17 60 A4
Gilmerton Dykes Crs GIL/MOR EH17 60 A3
Gilmerton Dykes Dr GIL/MOR EH17 60 B4
Gilmerton Dykes Gv GIL/MOR EH17 60 A3
Gilmerton Dykes Loan GIL/MOR EH17 60 A4
Gilmerton Dykes Pl GIL/MOR EH17 60 A3
Gilmerton Dykes Rd GIL/MOR EH17 60 B5
Gilmerton Dykes St GIL/MOR EH17 60 A3
Gilmerton Dykes Ter GIL/MOR EH17 60 B4
Gilmerton Dykes Vw GIL/MOR EH17 60 B4
Gilmerton Jct LSWD EH18 61 E5
Gilmerton Ms GIL/MOR EH17 60 C4
Gilmerton Pl GIL/MOR EH17 60 C4
Gilmerton Rd GIL/MOR EH17 60 A2
LIB/NID EH16 44 D5
Gilmerton Station Rd GIL/MOR EH17 60 D4
Gilmore Pk EDNT/CEDW EH3 27 E5
Gilmore Pl MCH/MOR/FMHD EH10 27 E5
Gilmore Place La EDNT/CEDW EH3 27 F5
Gilmour Rd LIB/NID EH16 44 B3
Gilmour St HLYRPK/NF EH8 3 G6
Gladstone Pl LEITH EH6 18 D4
Gladstone Ter NWGTN EH9 44 A1
Glasgow Rd MRYFD/COR EH12 39 E1
RATHO EH28 21 G5
Glaskhill Ter PNCK EH26 70 C3
Glebe Gv MRYFD/COR EH12 25 E5
Glebe Pk DFLS KY11 4 C1
Glebe Pl LSWD EH18 66 D3
Glebe Rd MRYFD/COR EH12 24 D5
Glebe St DLKTH EH22 68 C1
Glebe Ter MRYFD/COR EH12 24 D5
The Glebe KLSTN EH29 21 E2
Glenallan Dr LIB/NID EH16 44 D4
Glenallan Loan LIB/NID EH16 44 D4
Glenbrook Rd BAL/CUR EH14 52 C3
Glencairn Crs MRYFD/COR EH12 26 D4
Glencorse Pk PNCK EH26 71 G1
Glencross Gdns PNCK EH26 70 A4
Glendevon Av MRYFD/COR EH12 25 H5
Glendevon Gdns MRYFD/COR EH12 25 G5
Glendevon Gv MRYFD/COR EH12 41 H1
Glendevon Pk MRYFD/COR EH12 41 H1
Glendevon Pl MRYFD/COR EH12 25 H5
Glendevon Rd MRYFD/COR EH12 41 H1
Glendevon Ter MRYFD/COR EH12 25 H5
Glendinning Crs LIB/NID EH16 59 G1
Glendinning Dr KLSTN EH29 20 D1
Glendinning Rd KLSTN EH29 20 D1
Glendinning Wy KLSTN EH29 20 D1
Glenesk Crs DLKTH EH22 68 B2
Glenfinlas St EDNT/CEDW EH3 2 A3
Glengyle Ter EDNT/CEDW EH3 27 F5
Glenisla Gardens La NWGTN EH9 43 H3
Glenlee Av HLYRPK/NF EH8 29 E3
Glenlee Gdns HLYRPK/NF EH8 29 E3
Glenlockhart Bank BAL/CUR EH14 42 B5
Glenlockhart Rd BAL/CUR EH14 42 B5
Glenlockhart Va BAL/CUR EH14 42 B4
Glennie Gdns TRNT EH33 51 F2
Glenogle Rd EDNT/CEDW EH3 27 F1
Glen Pl PNCK EH26 70 C3
Glen St EDNT/CEDW EH3 2 C6

Glenure Loan *EDNW* EH4....24 D2
Glenvarloch Crs *LIB/NID* EH16....44 C5
Glenview *PNCK* EH26....70 C3
Glen View Ct *GORBR* EH23....79 E2
Glen View Crs *GORBR* EH23....79 E2
Glen View Pl *GORBR* EH23....79 E3
Glen View Rd *GORBR* EH23....79 E1
Gloucester La *EDNT/CEDW* EH3....2 A1
Gloucester Pl *EDNT/CEDW* EH3....2 A1
Gloucester Sq *EDNT/CEDW* EH3....2 A1
Gloucester St *EDNT/CEDW* EH3....2 A1
Goff Av *RSTRG* EH7....29 H2
Gogar Bridge Rd *MRYFD/COR* EH12....22 C3
Gogarloch Bank *MRYFD/COR* EH12....40 B1
Gogarloch Haugh *MRYFD/COR* EH12....40 B1
Gogarloch Muir *MRYFD/COR* EH12....40 B1
Gogarloch Rd *MRYFD/COR* EH12....40 A1
Gogarloch Syke *MRYFD/COR* EH12....40 A1
Gogar Rbt *MRYFD/COR* EH12....23 C5
Gogar Station Rd *MRYFD/COR* EH12....39 F2
Gogarstone Rd *RATHO* EH28....38 D1
Goldenacre Ter *EDNT/CEDW* EH3....17 F4
Golf Course Rd *BNYRG* EH19....67 F4
Golf Dr *CPS/PPNS* EH32....35 F1
Goodtrees Gdns *GIL/MOR* EH17....60 B1
Goose Green Av *MUS* EH21....32 B4
Goose Green Crs *MUS* EH21....32 B4
Goose Green Rd *MUS* EH21....32 B4
Gordon Av *BNYRG* EH19....67 G5
Gordon Loan *MRYFD/COR* EH12....25 E4
Gordon Rd *MRYFD/COR* EH12....25 E4
Gordon St *DLKTH* EH22....69 E5
  LEITH EH6....18 C4
Gordon Ter *LIB/NID* EH16....44 C4
Gore Av *GORBR* EH23....70 F2
Gorgie Park Cl *DAL/STH/STNH* EH11....42 B1
Gorgie Park Rd *DAL/STH/STNH* EH11....42 B1
Gorgie Rd *DAL/STH/STNH* EH11....41 H5
Gorton Loan *RSWL* EH24....74 B5
Gorton Pl *RSWL* EH24....74 B5
Gorton Rd *RSWL* EH24....74 B5
Gosford Pl *LEITH* EH6....17 H3
Gosford Rd *CPS/PPNS* EH32....35 E1
Gote La *QFRY* EH30....6 C4
Gowanhill Farm Rd *BAL/CUR* EH14....54 A5
Gracefield Ct *MUS* EH21....31 H5
Gracemount Av *LIB/NID* EH16....59 H2
Gracemount Dr *LIB/NID* EH16....59 H4
Gracemount Pl *LIB/NID* EH16....59 H4
Gracemount Rd *LIB/NID* EH16....59 G4
Gracemount Sq *LIB/NID* EH16....59 H2
Graham's Rd *PNCK* EH26....72 C5
Graham Ter *LEITH* EH6....18 A3
Granby Rd *LIB/NID* EH16....44 B5
Grandfield *LEITH* EH6....17 G5
Grandville *LEITH* EH6....17 C3
Grange Crs *BNYRG* EH19....43 H2
Grange Crs East *CPS/PPNS* EH32....34 B4
Grange Crs West *CPS/PPNS* EH32....34 B4
Grange Gv *CPS/PPNS* EH32....34 B4
Grange Loan *NWCTN* EH9....43 G2
Grange Loan Gdns *NWCTN* EH9....43 H2
Grange Rd *CPS/PPNS* EH32....34 B4
  NWCTN EH9....43 H1
Grange Ter *NWCTN* EH9....43 H3
Grannus Ms *MUS* EH21....48 B2
Grant Av *COLIN* EH13....56 C3
Granton Crs *GNTN* EH5....16 D2
Granton Gdns *GNTN* EH5....16 D2
Granton Mains Av *EDNW* EH4....16 A2
Granton Mains Bank *EDNW* EH4....16 A2
Granton Mains East *EDNW* EH4....16 A2
Granton Medway *GNTN* EH5....16 C2
Granton Mill Crs *EDNW* EH4....16 A2
Granton Mill Dr *EDNW* EH4....16 A3
Granton Mill March *EDNW* EH4....16 A2
Granton Mill Pl *EDNW* EH4....16 A3
Granton Mill Rd *EDNW* EH4....15 H3
Granton Mill W *EDNW* EH4....15 H2
Granton Ml West *EDNW* EH4....15 H3
Granton Park Av *GNTN* EH5....16 C1
Granton Pl *GNTN* EH5....16 D2
Granton Rd *GNTN* EH5....16 D2
Granton Ter *GNTN* EH5....16 D2
Granton Vw *GNTN* EH5....16 D2
Grant Rd *CPS/PPNS* EH32....34 C3
Grantully Pl *NWCTN* EH9....44 B2
Granville Ter *MCH/MOR/FMHD* EH10....43 E1
Grassmarket *EDOT* EH1....2 D5
Graysknowe *BAL/CUR* EH14....41 H4
Gray's Loan *DAL/STH/STNH* EH11....42 C2
Great Cannon Bank *PBLO/DUD* EH15....30 A2
Great Carleton Pl *LIB/NID* EH16....46 A3
Great Carleton Sq *LIB/NID* EH16....46 A3
Great Junction St *LEITH* EH6....18 B3
Great King St *EDNT/CEDW* EH3....2 C1
Great Michael Ri *LEITH* EH6....17 H2
Great Michael Sq *LEITH* EH6....17 H1
Great Stuart St *EDNT/CEDW* EH3....2 A2
Greenacre *BAL/CUR* EH14....55 H1
Greenbank Crs *COLIN* EH13....57 H2
  MCH/MOR/FMHD EH10....43 E5
Greenbank Dr *MCH/MOR/FMHD* EH10....57 G1
Greenbank Gdns *MCH/MOR/FMHD* EH10....57 H1
Greenbank Gv *MCH/MOR/FMHD* EH10....57 H1
Greenbank La *MCH/MOR/FMHD* EH10....42 D5
Greenbank Loan *MCH/MOR/FMHD* EH10....42 D5

Greenbank Pk *MCH/MOR/FMHD* EH10....57 H1
Greenbank Ri *MCH/MOR/FMHD* EH10....57 H2
Greenbank Rd *MCH/MOR/FMHD* EH10....57 H1
Greenbank Rw *MCH/MOR/FMHD* EH10....57 H1
Greendale Pk *EDNW* EH4....15 G4
Greendykes Av *LIB/NID* EH16....45 H5
Greendykes Dr *LIB/NID* EH16....45 H5
Greendykes Gdns *LIB/NID* EH16....45 H5
Greendykes Rd *LIB/NID* EH16....45 H5
Greendykes Ter *LIB/NID* EH16....45 H5
Greenend Dr *GIL/MOR* EH17....60 A2
Greenend Gdns *GIL/MOR* EH17....60 A2
Greenend Gv *GIL/MOR* EH17....60 A1
Greenfield Crs *BAL/CUR* EH14....53 E4
Greenfield Pk *MUS* EH21....47 H3
Greenfield Rd *BAL/CUR* EH14....53 E4
Greenhill Ct *MCH/MOR/FMHD* EH10....43 F1
Greenhill Gdns *MCH/MOR/FMHD* EH10....43 F2
Greenhill Pk *MCH/MOR/FMHD* EH10....43 F2
  PNCK EH26....70 B4
Greenhill Pl *MCH/MOR/FMHD* EH10....43 F2
Greenhill Ter *MCH/MOR/FMHD* EH10....43 F2
Green La *LIB/NID* EH18....66 D4
Greenlaw Gv *PNCK* EH26....72 B5
Greenlaw Hedge *COLIN* EH13....57 G1
Greenlaw Rig *COLIN* EH13....57 G1
Greenmantle Loan *LIB/NID* EH16....44 D5
Greenpark *GIL/MOR* EH17....60 A1
Greenside La *EDOT* EH1....3 G1
Greenside Pl *RSWL* EH24....74 B5
Greenside Rw *EDOT* EH1....3 G1
The Green *DAL/CUR* EH14....53 F4
  EDNW EH4....15 F4
  LNHD EH20....66 A3
Greyfriars *EDOT* EH1....2 E6
Grey School Cnr *CPS/PPNS* EH32....34 B4
Grierson Av *GNTN* EH5....17 E2
Grierson Crs *GNTN* EH5....17 E2
Grierson Gdns *GNTN* EH5....17 E2
Grierson Rd *GNTN* EH5....16 D2
Grierson Sq *GNTN* EH5....17 E2
Grierson Vls *GNTN* EH5....17 E3
Grieve Ct *RSTRG* EH7....70 D2
Grigor Av *EDNW* EH4....16 B5
Grigor Dr *EDNW* EH4....16 B5
Grigor Gdns *EDNW* EH4....16 B5
Grigor Ter *EDNW* EH4....16 B5
Grindlay St *EDNT/CEDW* EH3....2 B5
Grindlay Street Ct *EDNT/CEDW* EH3....2 B6
Groathill Av *EDNW* EH4....16 A1
Groathill Loan *EDNW* EH4....16 A1
Groathill Rd North *EDNW* EH4....16 A5
Groathill Rd South *EDNW* EH4....16 A1
Grosvenor Crs *MRYFD/COR* EH12....26 D4
Grosvenor Gdns *MRYFD/COR* EH12....26 D4
Grosvenor St *MRYFD/COR* EH12....26 D4
Grove End *LSWD* EH18....67 F4
Grove St *EDNT/CEDW* EH3....27 E4
  MUS EH21....48 B1
The Grove *MUS* EH21....48 C1
Guardians Wd *MRYFD/COR* EH12....26 A4
Guardwell Crs *GIL/MOR* EH17....60 B2
Gullan's Cl *EDOT* EH1....3 G4
Guthrie St *EDOT* EH1....3 F5
Gyle Av *MRYFD/COR* EH12....39 H1
Gylemuir Rd *MRYFD/COR* EH12....24 C5
Gyle Park Gdns *MRYFD/COR* EH12....24 A5

H

Haddington Rd *MUS* EH21....33 F5
  TRNT EH33....51 G2
Haddon's Ct *HLYRPK/NF* EH8....3 G6
Hailes Ap *COLIN* EH13....56 C2
Hailes Av *COLIN* EH13....56 C1
Hailes Bank *COLIN* EH13....56 C1
Hailes Crs *COLIN* EH13....56 C1
Hailes Gdns *COLIN* EH13....56 B2
Hailes Gv *COLIN* EH13....56 C2
Hailesland Gdns *BAL/CUR* EH14....41 E5
Hailesland Gv *BAL/CUR* EH14....41 E5
Hailesland Pl *BAL/CUR* EH14....41 E5
Hailesland Rd *BAL/CUR* EH14....41 E5
Hailes Pk *COLIN* EH13....56 C1
Hailes St *EDNT/CEDW* EH3....27 F5
Hailes Ter *COLIN* EH13....56 D2
Hainburn Pk *MCH/MOR/FMHD* EH10....57 H4
Hakness Crs *TRNT* EH33....51 F2
Hallcroft Cl *RATHO* EH28....37 G4
Hallcroft Crs *RATHO* EH28....37 G4
Hallcroft Gdns *RATHO* EH28....37 G4
Hallcroft Gn *RATHO* EH28....37 G4
Hallcroft Neuk *RATHO* EH28....37 G4
Hallcroft Pk *RATHO* EH28....37 G4
Hallcroft Ri *RATHO* EH28....37 G4
Hallhead Rd *LIB/NID* EH16....44 B3
Hallyards Rd *KLSTN* EH29....21 F3
Halmyre St *LEITH* EH6....18 B5
Hamilton Crs *DLKTH* EH22....76 D1
Hamilton Dr West *PBLO/DUD* EH15....29 H4
Hamilton Gdns *PBLO/DUD* EH15....29 H4
Hamilton Pk *PBLO/DUD* EH15....29 H4
Hamilton Rd *PBLO/DUD* EH15....29 H4
Hamilton Ter *PBLO/DUD* EH15....30 A3
Hammermen's Entry *HLYRPK/NF* EH8....3 H4

Hanover St *CED/PRST* EH2....2 D3
Harbour Rd *MUS* EH21....31 G5
  PBLO/DUD EH15....30 A2
Hardengreen La *DLKTH* EH22....68 A4
Harden Pl *DAL/STH/STNH* EH11....42 C1
Hardwell Cl *HLYRPK/NF* EH8....3 H7
Harelaw Rd *COLIN* EH13....56 C3
Hares Cl *CPS/PPNS* EH32....35 E1
Harewood Crs *LIB/NID* EH16....45 G2
Harewood Dr *LIB/NID* EH16....45 H2
Harewood Rd *LIB/NID* EH16....45 G2
Harlaw Bank *BAL/CUR* EH14....53 E3
Harlaw Gait *BAL/CUR* EH14....53 F3
Harlaw Gv *PNCK* EH26....70 B4
Harlaw Hl *CPS/PPNS* EH32....34 C4
Harlawhill Gdns *CPS/PPNS* EH32....34 C4
Harlaw March *BAL/CUR* EH14....53 F4
Harlaw Rd *BAL/CUR* EH14....53 E3
Harmony Ct *BNYRG* EH19....67 H5
Harmony Crs *BNYRG* EH19....67 H5
Harmony St *BNYRG* EH19....67 H5
Harmony Wk *BNYRG* EH19....67 H5
Harness Ct *LNHD* EH20....66 A5
Harper's Brae *PNCK* EH26....71 F3
Harrismith Pl *RSTRG* EH7....28 C1
Harrison Gdns *DAL/STH/STNH* EH11....42 C2
Harrison La *DAL/STH/STNH* EH11....42 D1
Harrison Pl *DAL/STH/STNH* EH11....42 D1
Harrison Rd *DAL/STH/STNH* EH11....42 C1
Hartington Gdns *MCH/MOR/FMHD* EH10....43 E1
Hartington Pl *MCH/MOR/FMHD* EH10....43 F1
Hart St *EDOT* EH1....27 H1
Harvest Dr *RATHO* EH28....37 F1
Harvesters Wy *BAL/CUR* EH14....56 A2
Harvest Rd *RATHO* EH28....37 F1
Harvieston Vlas *GORBR* EH23....79 F3
Hatton Pl *NWCTN* EH9....43 H1
Hawes Brae *QFRY* EH30....7 E4
Hawkhead Crs *LIB/NID* EH16....59 G1
Hawkhead Gv *LIB/NID* EH16....59 G1
Hawkhill *LEITH* EH6....18 D5
Hawkhill Av *RSTRG* EH7....18 D5
Hawkill Cl *RSTRG* EH7....18 D5
Hawkins Ter *PNCK* EH26....72 C5
Hawthorn Bank *QFRY* EH30....6 C4
Hawthornbank La *EDNW* EH4....27 E5
Hawthornbank Pl *LEITH* EH6....18 A2
Hawthornden Av *BNYRG* EH19....75 E1
Hawthornden Gdns *BNYRG* EH19....75 E1
Hawthornden Pl *RSTRG* EH7....18 A5
Hawthorn Gdns *LNHD* EH20....65 H5
Hawthorn Rd *CPS/PPNS* EH32....34 D4
Hawthorn Ter *CPS/PPNS* EH32....34 D2
Hawthornvale *LEITH* EH6....17 H2
Hay Av *LIB/NID* EH16....45 H2
Hay Dr *LIB/NID* EH16....46 A2
Hayfield *MRYFD/COR* EH12....24 A3
Hay Gdns *LIB/NID* EH16....45 H2
Haymarket *MRYFD/COR* EH12....26 D4
Haymarket Ter *MRYFD/COR* EH12....26 D4
Haymarket Yards *MRYFD/COR* EH12....26 D4
Hay Pl *LIB/NID* EH16....45 H2
Hay Ter *LIB/NID* EH16....45 H2
Hazelbank Ter *DAL/STH/STNH* EH11....42 C2
Hazeldean Ter *LIB/NID* EH16....44 D5
Hazel Dr *BNYRG* EH19....75 E1
Hazel La *LNHD* EH20....65 E5
Hazelwood Gv *LIB/NID* EH16....45 E4
Headrigg Rw *LIB/NID* EH16....44 D5
Helen La *DFLS* KY11....4 D5
Henderland Rd *MRYFD/COR* EH12....26 B4
Henderson Gdns *LEITH* EH6....18 B3
  TRNT EH33....51 F2
Henderson Pl *EDNT/CEDW* EH3....27 G1
Henderson Place La *EDNT/CEDW* EH3....27 F1
Henderson Rw *EDNT/CEDW* EH3....27 F1
Henderson St *LEITH* EH6....18 B3
Henderson Ter *DAL/STH/STNH* EH11....42 D1
Henry Ross Pl *QFRY* EH30....6 C4
Hepburn Dr *DLKTH* EH22....69 E2
Hercus Loan *MUS* EH21....31 H5
Herd Ter *LNHD* EH20....65 G5
Heriot Br *EDOT* EH1....2 D5
Heriot Hill Ter *RSTRG* EH7....17 H5
Heriot Pl *EDNT/CEDW* EH3....2 D6
Heriot Rw *EDNT/CEDW* EH3....2 B2
Hermand Crs *DAL/STH/STNH* EH11....42 C2
Hermand St *DAL/STH/STNH* EH11....42 B2
Hermand Ter *DAL/STH/STNH* EH11....42 B2
Hermiston House Rd *MRYFD/COR* EH12....39 C2
Hermitage Dr *MCH/MOR/FMHD* EH10....43 F5
Hermitage Gdns *MCH/MOR/FMHD* EH10....43 F5
Hermitage Park *LEITH* EH6....18 D5
Hermitage Park Gv *LEITH* EH6....18 D5
Hermitage Park South *LEITH* EH6....18 D5
Hermitage Ter *MCH/MOR/FMHD* EH10....43 F4
Hermits Cft *HLYRPK/NF* EH8....3 J7
The Heugh *TRNT* EH33....51 E1
Higginson Loan *DLKTH* EH22....77 G2
High Buckstone *MCH/MOR/FMHD* EH10....58 C3
Highlea Cir *BAL/CUR* EH14....52 D5
Highlea Gv *BAL/CUR* EH14....52 D4
High Park Dr *PNCK* EH26....70 D5
High Park Ri *PNCK* EH26....70 D5
High Riggs *EDNT/CEDW* EH3....2 B5
High School Yards *EDOT* EH1....3 G5
High St *BNYRG* EH19....67 H4
  CPS/PPNS EH32....34 B3
  EDOT EH1....3 F4
  KLSTN EH29....21 F2
  LNHD EH20....66 A5
  LSWD EH18....67 E3
  MUS EH21....32 B5
  PNCK EH26....70 D5
  QFRY EH30....6 C4
  RSTRG EH7....51 F2
Hillcoat Loan *PBLO/DUD* EH15....30 B4
Hillcoat Pl *PBLO/DUD* EH15....30 B4
Hillhead *BNYRG* EH19....67 H4
Hillhouse Rd *EDNW* EH4....25 H1
Hillpark Av *EDNW* EH4....15 E5
Hillpark Brae *EDNW* EH4....25 F2
Hillpark Crs *EDNW* EH4....25 F1
Hillpark Dr *EDNW* EH4....15 F5
Hillpark Gdns *EDNW* EH4....25 F1
Hillpark Gn *EDNW* EH4....25 F1
Hillpark Gv *EDNW* EH4....25 F1
Hillpark Loan *EDNW* EH4....25 G1
Hillpark Rd *EDNW* EH4....25 F1
Hillpark Ter *EDNW* EH4....25 F1
Hillpark Wy *EDNW* EH4....25 F1
Hill Pl *HLYRPK/NF* EH8....3 G6
Hillside Crs *RSTRG* EH7....28 A1
Hillside Crs North *GORBR* EH23....79 F2
Hillside Crs South *GORBR* EH23....79 F2
Hillside Rd *QFRY* EH30....13 F4
Hillside St *RSTRG* EH7....28 B1
Hill Sq *HLYRPK/NF* EH8....3 G6
Hill St *CED/PRST* EH2....2 B3
Hill Street North La *CED/PRST* EH2....2 B2
Hill Street South La *CED/PRST* EH2....2 B3
Hill Vw *PNCK* EH26....71 E4
Hillview Cottages *MRYFD/COR* EH12....37 H4
Hillview Crs *MRYFD/COR* EH12....24 D4
Hillview Dr *MRYFD/COR* EH12....24 D4
Hillview Rd *MRYFD/COR* EH12....24 D4
Hillview Ter *MRYFD/COR* EH12....24 D4
Hillwood Crs *RATHO* EH28....37 G1
Hillwood Gdns *RATHO* EH28....21 G5
Hillwood Ri *RATHO* EH28....37 G1
Hillwood Rd *RATHO* EH28....37 G1
Hillwood Ter *RATHO* EH28....37 G1
Hogarth Av *GORBR* EH23....76 D5
Holly Bank *DLKTH* EH22....69 G5
Hollybank Ter *DAL/STH/STNH* EH11....42 C2
Holly Ter *BNYRG* EH19....75 E1
Holly Wk *LNHD* EH20....65 E5
Holyrood Park Rd *LIB/NID* EH16....28 B5
Holyrood Rd *HLYRPK/NF* EH8....3 H4
Home St *EDNT/CEDW* EH3....2 B7
Hopefield Pk *BNYRG* EH19....75 E1
Hopefield Pl *BNYRG* EH19....75 E1
Hopefield Ter *BNYRG* EH19....75 E1
  LEITH EH6....18 A2
Hope La *PBLO/DUD* EH15....30 B4
Hope La North *PBLO/DUD* EH15....30 B4
Hope Park Ter *HLYRPK/NF* EH8....28 A5
Hope Pl *MUS* EH21....32 D4
Hope St *CED/PRST* EH2....2 A4
  DFLS KY11....4 C1
Hope Street La *CED/PRST* EH2....2 A4
Hope Ter *NWCTN* EH9....43 G2
Hopetoun Rd *QFRY* EH30....6 C5
Hopetoun St *RSTRG* EH7....28 A1
Horne Ter *DAL/STH/STNH* EH11....27 E5
Horsburgh Bank *BAL/CUR* EH14....53 E1
Horsburgh Gdns *BAL/CUR* EH14....53 E1
Horse Wynd *HLYRPK/NF* EH8....3 K3
Hoseason Gdns *EDNW* EH4....24 D2
Hosie Rigg *PBLO/DUD* EH15....46 B1
House O'Hill Av *EDNW* EH4....15 G5
House O'Hill Brae *EDNW* EH4....15 G5
House O'Hill Crs *EDNW* EH4....15 G5
House O'Hill Gdns *EDNW* EH4....15 G5
House O'Hill Gn *EDNW* EH4....15 G5
House O'Hill Gv *EDNW* EH4....15 G5
House O'Hill Pl *EDNW* EH4....15 G5
House O'Hill Rd *EDNW* EH4....15 G5
House O'Hill Row *EDNW* EH4....15 H5
Howden Hall Crs *LIB/NID* EH16....59 F4
Howden Hall Dr *LIB/NID* EH16....59 F4
Howden Hall Gdns *LIB/NID* EH16....59 F4
Howden Hall Loan *LIB/NID* EH16....59 F4
Howden Hall Pk *LIB/NID* EH16....59 E4
Howden Hall Rd *LIB/NID* EH16....59 F4
Howden Hall Wy *LIB/NID* EH16....59 F4
Howe Pk *MCH/MOR/FMHD* EH10....57 H4
Howe St *EDNT/CEDW* EH3....2 C1
Hughes Crs *DLKTH* EH22....77 H1
Hugh Miller Pl *EDNT/CEDW* EH3....27 E1
Hugh Russell Pl *QFRY* EH30....6 C5
Huly Hill Rd *RATHO* EH28....37 E1
Humbie Rd *KLSTN* EH29....20 A5
Hungerage Sq *TRNT* EH33....51 F3
Hunter Av *LNHD* EH20....66 B4
Hunter Ct *LNHD* EH20....66 B4
Hunterfield Ct *GORBR* EH23....79 E2
Hunterfield Pk *GORBR* EH23....79 E1
Hunterfield Rd *GORBR* EH23....78 E5
Hunter's Cl *EDOT* EH1....3 F6
Hunter Sq *EDOT* EH1....3 F4
  GORBR EH23....79 F2
Hunter Ter *BNYRG* EH19....75 E1
  LNHD EH20....66 B4
Huntingdon Pl *RSTRG* EH7....28 A1
Hursted Av *DLKTH* EH22....69 F5
Hutchison Gv *BAL/CUR* EH14....42 B3
Hutchison Av *BAL/CUR* EH14....42 A3
Hutchison Crossway *BAL/CUR* EH14....42 A2
Hutchison Gdns *BAL/CUR* EH14....42 A3
Hutchison Loan *BAL/CUR* EH14....42 A3

Hutchison Medway *BAL/CUR* EH14....42 A3
Hutchison Pk *BAL/CUR* EH14....42 A2
Hutchison Pl *BAL/CUR* EH14....42 A3
Hutchison Rd *BAL/CUR* EH14....42 A3
Hutchison Ter *BAL/CUR* EH14....42 A3
Hutchison Vw *BAL/CUR* EH14....42 A3
Hutton Rd *HLYRPK/NF* EH8....3 J4
Hyvot Av *GIL/MOR* EH17....60 B3
Hyvot Bank Av *GIL/MOR* EH17....60 B4
Hyvot Gdns *GIL/MOR* EH17....60 B3
Hyvot Gn *GIL/MOR* EH17....60 B3
Hyvot Gv *GIL/MOR* EH17....60 B3
Hyvot Loan *GIL/MOR* EH17....60 B3
Hyvot Pk *GIL/MOR* EH17....60 B3
Hyvot Ter *GIL/MOR* EH17....60 B3
Hyvot Vw *GIL/MOR* EH17....60 B3

I

Imrie Pl *PNCK* EH26....70 D4
Inchcolm Dr *DFLS* KY11....4 A4
Inchcolm Ter *QFRY* EH30....6 C5
Inchkeith Av *QFRY* EH30....6 D5
Inchkeith Gv *TRNT* EH33....51 F1
Inchview *MUS* EH21....49 G1
Inchview North *CPS/PPNS* EH32....33 H2
Inchview Ter *MUS* EH21....49 F1
India Pl *EDNT/CEDW* EH3....2 A1
India St *EDNT/CEDW* EH3....2 B1
Industrial Rd *LEITH* EH6....18 C4
Industry La *LEITH* EH6....18 A3
Infirmary St *EDOT* EH1....3 G5
Inglewood Pl *LIB/NID* EH16....59 H1
Inglis Av *CPS/PPNS* EH32....35 E1
Inglis Farm *CPS/PPNS* EH32....35 E2
Inglis Green Gait *BAL/CUR* EH14....41 H4
Inglis Green Rd *BAL/CUR* EH14....41 H4
Ingliston Rd *RATHO* EH28....22 B5
Inkerman Ct *PNCK* EH26....72 B5
Inveralmond Dr *EDNW* EH4....14 A3
Inveralmond Gdns *EDNW* EH4....14 A3
Inveralmond Gv *EDNW* EH4....14 A3
Inveravon Rd *LNHD* EH20....65 H5
Inveravon Ter *MUS* EH21....48 A5
Inveresk Brae *MUS* EH21....48 B1
Inveresk Rd *MUS* EH21....48 B1
The Inveresk Est *MUS* EH21....48 B1
Inveresk Village Rd *MUS* EH21....48 B1
Inverleith Av *EDNT/CEDW* EH3....17 F4
Inverleith Av South *EDNT/CEDW* EH3....17 F4
Inverleith Gdns *EDNT/CEDW* EH3....16 D5
Inverleith Pl *EDNT/CEDW* EH3....16 D5
Inverleith Place La *EDNT/CEDW* EH3....17 F4
Inverleith Rw *EDNT/CEDW* EH3....17 F5
Inverleith Terrace La *EDNT/CEDW* EH3....17 F5
Iona St *LEITH* EH6....18 B5
Ironmills Rd *DLKTH* EH22....68 B1
Ivanhoe Crs *LIB/NID* EH16....44 D3

J

Jackson's Entry *HLYRPK/NF* EH8....3 J4
Jackson St *PNCK* EH26....70 C4
Jacobite Wy *CPS/PPNS* EH32....33 H2
Jacobs Wy *GORBR* EH23....79 E2
Jamaica St North *EDNT/CEDW* EH3....2 C1
Jamaica St South *EDNT/CEDW* EH3....2 B1
Jamaica St West *EDNT/CEDW* EH3....2 B1
James Lean Av *DLKTH* EH22....68 D1
James Leary Wy *BNYRG* EH19....67 G4
Jameson Pl *LEITH* EH6....18 B5
James St *MUS* EH21....32 B5
  PBLO/DUD EH15....30 A3
James Street La *PBLO/DUD* EH15....30 C3
Janefield *GIL/MOR* EH17....59 G5
Jane St *LEITH* EH6....18 B4
Jean Armour Dr *DLKTH* EH22....69 F2
Jeanette Stewart Dr *DLKTH* EH22....76 B3
Jeffrey Av *EDNW* EH4....25 H2
Jeffrey St *EDOT* EH1....3 F3
Jenks Loan *DLKTH* EH22....76 C2
Jessfield Ter *LEITH* EH6....17 H2
The Jewel *PBLO/DUD* EH15....46 B1
John Bernard Wy *GORBR* EH23....79 E3
John Cotton Dr *RSTRG* EH7....51 E2
John Humble St *DLKTH* EH22....77 G2
Johnnie Cope's Rd *CPS/PPNS* EH32....34 C2
Johnsburn Haugh *BAL/CUR* EH14....52 D3
Johnsburn Rd *BAL/CUR* EH14....52 D3
Johns La *LEITH* EH6....18 C3
John's Pl *LEITH* EH6....18 C5
Johnston Pl *PNCK* EH26....70 D1
Johnston Ter *CPS/PPNS* EH32....35 F1
  EDOT EH1....2 C5
John St *PBLO/DUD* EH15....30 C4
  PNCK EH26....70 C4
John Street La *PBLO/DUD* EH15....30 C4
John Street La East *PBLO/DUD* EH15....30 C3
John Street La West *PBLO/DUD* EH15....30 C3
Joppa Gdns *PBLO/DUD* EH15....30 C4
Joppa Gv *PBLO/DUD* EH15....30 C4
Joppa Pk *PBLO/DUD* EH15....30 C4
Joppa Rd *PBLO/DUD* EH15....30 C4

Joppa Station Pl PBLO/DUD EH15 .... 30 C4
Joppa Ter PBLO/DUD EH15 .... 30 C4
Jordan La MCH/MOR/FMHD EH10 .... 43 F3
Jubilee Crs GORBR EH23 .... 79 E1
Jubilee Rd MRYFD/COR EH12 .... 22 D4
Junction Pl LEITH EH6 .... 18 B4
Juner Pl GORBR EH23 .... 79 E1
Juniper Av BAL/CUR EH14 .... 55 G3
Juniper Gdns BAL/CUR EH14 .... 55 G3
Juniper Gv BAL/CUR EH14 .... 55 G3
Juniperlee BAL/CUR EH14 .... 55 H3
Juniper Park Rd BAL/CUR EH14 .... 55 G3
Juniper Pl BAL/CUR EH14 .... 55 G3

K

Kaimes Rd MRYFD/COR EH12 .... 25 E4
Kaimes Vw DLKTH EH22 .... 61 G1
Katesmill Rd BAL/CUR EH14 .... 56 D1
Kay Gdns CPS/PPNS EH32 .... 35 E1
Kedslie Pl LIB/NID EH16 .... 59 F2
Kedslie Rd LIB/NID EH16 .... 59 F2
Keir Hardie Dr DLKTH EH22 .... 77 F3
Keir St EDNT/CEDW EH3 .... 2 D6
Keith Ter EDNW EH4 .... 25 H2
Kekewich Av RSTRG EH7 .... 29 H1
Kemp Pl EDNT/CEDW EH3 .... 17 F5
Kemp's End TRNT EH33 .... 51 E4
Kenilworth Dr LIB/NID EH16 .... 59 G1
Kenmure Av HLYRPK/NF EH8 .... 29 F2
Kennedy Crs TRNT EH33 .... 51 F1
Kennington Av LNHD EH20 .... 65 H5
Kennington Ter LNHD EH20 .... 65 H4
Keppock Crs CPS/PPNS EH32 .... 34 D5
Kerr Av DLKTH EH22 .... 68 A2
Kerr Rd TRNT EH33 .... 51 E2
Kerr's Wynd MUS EH21 .... 32 B5
Kevock Rd LSWD EH18 .... 66 D4
Kilgraston Rd NWGTN EH9 .... 43 G2
Kilmaurs Rd LIB/NID EH16 .... 44 C2
Kilmaurs Ter LIB/NID EH16 .... 44 C2
Kilncroft Side BAL/CUR EH14 .... 41 H4
Kilngate Brae GIL/MOR EH17 .... 60 B4
Kilwinning Pl MUS EH21 .... 32 A5
Kilwinning St MUS EH21 .... 32 B5
Kilwinning Ter MUS EH21 .... 32 B5
Kinellan Rd MRYFD/COR EH12 .... 26 A4
King Edwards Wy KLSTN EH29 .... 20 D2
Kinghorn Pl LEITH EH6 .... 17 H3
King Malcolm Cl MCH/MOR/FMHD EH10 .... 58 D4
Kingsburgh Rd MRYFD/COR EH12 .... 26 B4
King's Cramond EDNW EH4 .... 14 B3
Kings Haugh LIB/NID EH16 .... 45 E2
Kingsknowe Av BAL/CUR EH14 .... 56 C1
Kingsknowe Ct BAL/CUR EH14 .... 41 F5
Kingsknowe Dr BAL/CUR EH14 .... 41 G5
Kingsknowe Gdns BAL/CUR EH14 .... 56 C1
Kingsknowe Gv BAL/CUR EH14 .... 56 C1
Kingsknowe Pk BAL/CUR EH14 .... 56 C1
Kingsknowe Pl BAL/CUR EH14 .... 41 F5
Kingsknowe Rd North BAL/CUR EH14 .... 41 G5
Kingsknowe Rd South BAL/CUR EH14 .... 41 G5
Kingslaw Ct TRNT EH33 .... 51 F3
King's Meadow LIB/NID EH16 .... 44 D2
King's Rd PBLO/DUD EH15 .... 30 A2
  TRNT EH33 .... 51 E3
King's Stables La EDOT EH1 .... 2 C5
King's Stables Rd EDOT EH1 .... 2 B4
Kingston Av LIB/NID EH16 .... 29 H2
King St LEITH EH6 .... 18 B3
  MUS EH21 .... 32 B5
Kinnear Rd EDNT/CEDW EH3 .... 16 D4
Kippielaw Dr DLKTH EH22 .... 69 E3
Kippielaw Medway DLKTH EH22 .... 69 E3
Kippielaw Pk DLKTH EH22 .... 69 F4
Kippielaw Rd DLKTH EH22 .... 69 E3
Kippielaw Wk DLKTH EH22 .... 69 E3
Kirk Brae LIB/NID EH16 .... 59 F4
Kirk Cramond EDNW EH4 .... 14 C2
Kirkgate LIB/NID EH16 .... 59 G2
Kirkhill Ct GORBR EH23 .... 79 E3
Kirkhill Dr LIB/NID EH16 .... 44 C2
Kirkhill Gdns LIB/NID EH16 .... 44 C1
  PNCK EH26 .... 70 D4
Kirkhill Rd LIB/NID EH16 .... 44 C1
  PNCK EH26 .... 70 D4
Kirkhill Ter LIB/NID EH16 .... 44 C1
Kirkhill Wy PNCK EH26 .... 70 D4
Kirklands MRYFD/COR EH12 .... 40 D2
Kirklands Park Ct KLSTN EH29 .... 20 D1
Kirklands Park Gv KLSTN EH29 .... 20 D1
Kirklands Park Rigg KLSTN EH29 .... 20 D1
Kirklands Park St KLSTN EH29 .... 20 D1
Kirkliston Rd QFRY EH30 .... 6 C4
Kirk Loan MRYFD/COR EH12 .... 25 E5
Kirk Pk LIB/NID EH16 .... 59 G1
Kirk St CPS/PPNS EH32 .... 34 B4
  LEITH EH6 .... 18 B4
Kirkstyle Gdns KLSTN EH29 .... 21 F2
Kittle Yards NWGTN EH9 .... 44 A1
Klondyke St MUS EH21 .... 47 E2
Knowetop Pl ROSLIN EH25 .... 73 G3
Komarom Pl DLKTH EH22 .... 69 F1
Kyle Pl RSTRG EH7 .... 3 K1

L

Laburnum Arch Ct CPS/PPNS EH32 .... 34 B4
Laburnum Av CPS/PPNS EH32 .... 35 F2
Laburnum Pl DLKTH EH22 .... 69 G5
The Lade BAL/CUR EH14 .... 53 F4
Lady Brae GORBR EH23 .... 79 F3

Lady Brae Pl GORBR EH23 .... 79 G2
Ladycroft BAL/CUR EH14 .... 53 E3
Lady Emily Wy GORBR EH23 .... 79 E2
Lady Lawson St EDNT/CEDW EH3 .... 2 C6
Lady Nairne Crs HLYRPK/NF EH8 .... 29 F4
Lady Nairne Gv HLYRPK/NF EH8 .... 29 F4
Lady Nairne Loan HLYRPK/NF EH8 .... 29 F4
Lady Nairne Pl HLYRPK/NF EH8 .... 29 F4
Lady Rd LIB/NID EH16 .... 44 C3
Lady Road Pl DLKTH EH22 .... 76 D1
Ladysmith Rd NWGTN EH9 .... 43 H4
Ladywell MUS EH21 .... 32 A5
Ladywell Av MRYFD/COR EH12 .... 24 D5
Ladywell Wy MUS EH21 .... 32 A5
Ladywell Gdns MRYFD/COR EH12 .... 24 D5
Ladywell Rd MRYFD/COR EH12 .... 24 D5
Laichfield BAL/CUR EH14 .... 41 H3
Laichpark Pl BAL/CUR EH14 .... 41 H3
Laichpark Rd BAL/CUR EH14 .... 41 H3
Laidlaw Gdns TRNT EH33 .... 51 E3
Laing Ter PBLO/DUD EH15 .... 30 C5
  PNCK EH26 .... 70 D2
Laird Ter BNYRG EH19 .... 75 G1
Lamb's Cl EDNT/CEDW EH8 .... 3 H7
Lammermoor Gdns TRNT EH33 .... 50 D2
Lammermoor Ter LIB/NID EH16 .... 45 G5
Lampacre Rd MRYFD/COR EH12 .... 25 E5
Lanark Rd BAL/CUR EH14 .... 55 H4
  COLIN EH13 .... 56 B2
Lanark Rd West BAL/CUR EH14 .... 52 D2
The Lane MUS EH21 .... 48 C3
Langlaw Rd DLKTH EH22 .... 69 F4
Lang Loan GIL/MOR EH17 .... 65 H2
Langton Rd NWGTN EH9 .... 44 A2
Lansbury Ct DLKTH EH22 .... 68 C1
Lansdowne Crs MRYFD/COR EH12 .... 27 E4
Lapicide Pl LEITH EH6 .... 18 A3
Larbourfield DAL/STH/STNH EH11 .... 40 D5
Larch Crs DLKTH EH22 .... 77 H1
Larchfield BAL/CUR EH14 .... 53 E2
Largo Pl LEITH EH6 .... 18 A3
Larkfield Dr DLKTH EH22 .... 67 H3
Larkfield Rd DLKTH EH22 .... 68 A2
Lasswade Bank GIL/MOR EH17 .... 60 A4
Lasswade Gv GIL/MOR EH17 .... 60 A4
Lasswade Jct GIL/MOR EH17 .... 66 C1
Lasswade Rd LIB/NID EH16 .... 59 H2
  LIB/NID EH16 .... 59 H2
  PNCK EH26 .... 66 B4
Latch Hk COLIN EH13 .... 57 E2
Lauder Loan NWGTN EH9 .... 43 G1
Lauderdale St NWGTN EH9 .... 43 G1
Lauder Loan NWGTN EH9 .... 43 H2
Lauder Rd NWGTN EH9 .... 43 G2
  NWGTN EH9 .... 43 G1
Laurel Bank DLKTH EH22 .... 69 E2
Laurel Bank Rd DLKTH EH22 .... 77 G1
Laurie St LEITH EH6 .... 18 C4
Lauriston Farm Rd EDNW EH4 .... 15 E4
Lauriston Gdns EDNT/CEDW EH3 .... 2 C6
Lauriston Pk EDNT/CEDW EH3 .... 2 D6
Lauriston Pl EDNT/CEDW EH3 .... 2 C6
Lauriston St EDNT/CEDW EH3 .... 2 C6
Laverockbank Gv GNTN EH5 .... 17 G2
Laverockbank Rd GNTN EH5 .... 17 G2
Laverockbank Ter GNTN EH5 .... 17 G2
Laverockdale Crs COLIN EH13 .... 56 D4
Laverockdale Loan COLIN EH13 .... 56 D4
Laverockdale Pk COLIN EH13 .... 56 D4
Laverock Dr PNCK EH26 .... 70 B3
Lawfield Rd DLKTH EH22 .... 69 F5
Lawhead Pl PNCK EH26 .... 70 A4
Lawnmarket EDOT EH1 .... 2 E4
Lawrie Dr PNCK EH26 .... 70 C2
Lawson Crs QFRY EH30 .... 6 D5
Lawson Wy TRNT EH33 .... 51 E3
Leadervale Rd LIB/NID EH16 .... 59 F1
Leadervale Ter LIB/NID EH16 .... 59 F1
Leamington La MCH/MOR/FMHD EH10 * 43 F1
Leamington Rd MCH/MOR/FMHD EH10 .... 43 F1
Leamington Ter MCH/MOR/FMHD EH10 .... 43 F1
Learmonth Ct EDNW EH4 .... 26 D1
Learmonth Crs EDNW EH4 .... 26 D2
Learmonth Gdns EDNW EH4 .... 26 D2
Learmonth Gardens Ms EDNW EH4 .... 27 E2
Learmonth Gv EDNW EH4 .... 26 D1
Learmonth Pk EDNW EH4 .... 26 D1
Learmonth Pl EDNW EH4 .... 26 D1
Learmonth Ter EDNW EH4 .... 26 D2
Lee Crs PBLO/DUD EH15 .... 30 A3
Leighton Crs DLKTH EH22 .... 69 E5
Leith St EDOT EH1 .... 3 F2
Leith Wk EDOT EH1 .... 3 G1
  RSTRG EH7 .... 28 A1
Lennel Av MRYFD/COR EH12 .... 26 A3
Lenniemuir MRYFD/COR EH12 .... 22 D2
Lennox Rw GNTN EH5 .... 17 F2
Lennox Street La EDNW EH4 .... 27 E2
Leslie Pl EDNW EH4 .... 27 E1
Leven St EDNT/CEDW EH3 .... 27 G5
Leven Ter EDNT/CEDW EH3 .... 27 G5
Lewisvale Av MUS EH21 .... 48 C1
Lewisvale Ct MUS EH21 .... 48 C1
Leyden Pk BNYRG EH19 .... 67 F4
Leyden Ter BNYRG EH19 .... 75 F1
Liberton Brae LIB/NID EH16 .... 59 G1
Liberton Dr LIB/NID EH16 .... 58 C3
Liberton Gdns LIB/NID EH16 .... 59 G3
Liberton Pl LIB/NID EH16 .... 59 G2
Liberton Rd LIB/NID EH16 .... 44 C5
Liberton Tower La LIB/NID EH16 .... 59 F1
Liddesdale Pl EDNT/CEDW EH3 .... 27 F1

Lidgate Shot RATHO EH28 .... 37 H4
Lilac Av DLKTH EH22 .... 77 H1
Lilyhill Ter HLYRPK/NF EH8 .... 29 E2
Limefield GIL/MOR EH17 .... 60 C4
Lime Pl BNYRG EH19 .... 75 F1
Lindean Pl LEITH EH6 .... 18 D4
Linden Pl LNHD EH20 .... 66 B4
Lindores Dr TRNT EH33 .... 51 F1
Lindores Wood Dr TRNT EH33 .... 51 F2
Lindsay Rd LEITH EH6 .... 17 H2
Lindsay St LEITH EH6 .... 18 A2
Lingerwood Rd DLKTH EH22 .... 76 D3
Lingerwood Wk DLKTH EH22 .... 76 D3
Linkfield Rd MUS EH21 .... 32 D5
Links Av MUS EH21 .... 31 H4
Links Ct CPS/PPNS EH32 .... 35 F1
Links Gdns LEITH EH6 .... 18 D3
Links Gardens La LEITH EH6 .... 18 D3
Links Pl CPS/PPNS EH32 .... 35 G1
  LEITH EH6 .... 18 C3
Links St MUS EH21 .... 32 A5
Links Vw CPS/PPNS EH32 .... 35 G1
  MUS EH21 .... 31 H4
Lismore Av HLYRPK/NF EH8 .... 29 E2
Lismore Crs HLYRPK/NF EH8 .... 29 E2
Liston Dr KLSTN EH29 .... 21 E1
Liston Pl KLSTN EH29 .... 21 E1
Liston Rd KLSTN EH29 .... 21 E2
Little Acre DLKTH EH22 .... 69 F4
Little France Crs LIB/NID EH16 .... 45 F5
Little France Dr LIB/NID EH16 .... 45 G5
Little France Mills GIL/MOR EH17 .... 45 F5
Littlejohn Av MCH/MOR/FMHD EH10 .... 57 H1
Little John Rd MCH/MOR/FMHD EH10 .... 57 H1
Little King St EDOT EH1 .... 3 F2
Little Rd LIB/NID EH16 .... 59 H2
Livesey Ter PNCK EH26 .... 71 E1
Livingstone Pl NWGTN EH9 .... 43 H1
Lixmount Av GNTN EH5 .... 17 G2
Lixmount Gdns GNTN EH5 .... 17 G2
Loanburn PNCK EH26 .... 70 C4
Loanburn Av PNCK EH26 .... 70 D4
Loanhead Rd LNHD EH20 .... 65 H3
Loaning Crs RSTRG EH7 .... 29 E1
Loaning Rd RSTRG EH7 .... 29 E1
The Loan LNHD EH20 .... 65 H5
  QFRY EH30 .... 6 C4
Lochend Av RSTRG EH7 .... 28 D1
Lochend Cl HLYRPK/NF EH8 .... 3 J3
Lochend Crs RSTRG EH7 .... 29 E1
Lochend Dr RSTRG EH7 .... 28 D1
Lochend Gdns RSTRG EH7 .... 28 D1
Lochend Pk RSTRG EH7 .... 28 D1
Lochend Qd RSTRG EH7 .... 29 E1
Lochend Rd LEITH EH6 .... 18 D5
  RATHO EH28 .... 21 E4
Lochend Rd North MUS EH21 .... 31 H5
Lochend Rd South MUS EH21 .... 31 H5
  RSTRG EH7 .... 28 D1
Loch Pl QFRY EH30 .... 6 C4
Lochrin Pl EDNT/CEDW EH3 .... 2 B7
Loch Rd EDNW EH4 .... 25 G1
  QFRY EH30 .... 12 A1
  RATHO EH28 .... 37 H4
  ROSLIN EH25 .... 73 G2
Lochside Av MRYFD/COR EH12 .... 39 H2
Lochside Ct MRYFD/COR EH12 .... 40 A2
Lochside Pl MRYFD/COR EH12 .... 39 H1
Lochside Vw MRYFD/COR EH12 .... 39 H2
Lochside Wy MRYFD/COR EH12 .... 40 A2
Loch Sq TRNT EH33 .... 51 F1
Lockerby Cottages LIB/NID EH16 .... 60 A3
Lockerby Crs LIB/NID EH16 .... 60 A3
Lockerby Gv LIB/NID EH16 .... 60 A3
Lockharton Av BAL/CUR EH14 .... 42 B4
Lockharton Crs BAL/CUR EH14 .... 42 C4
Lockharton Gdns BAL/CUR EH14 .... 42 C3
Lockhart Ter ROSLIN EH25 .... 73 G5
Loganlea Av RSTRG EH7 .... 29 E2
Loganlea Dr RSTRG EH7 .... 29 E2
Loganlea Gdns RSTRG EH7 .... 29 E1
Loganlea Pl RSTRG EH7 .... 29 F2
Loganlea Rd RSTRG EH7 .... 29 E2
Loganlea Ter RSTRG EH7 .... 29 F1
Logan St EDNT/CEDW EH3 .... 27 G1
Logie Green Gdns RSTRG EH7 .... 17 G5
Logie Green La RSTRG EH7 .... 17 G5
Logie Green Rd RSTRG EH7 .... 17 G5
Logie Mill RSTRG EH7 .... 17 H5
Lomond Rd GNTN EH5 .... 17 E3
Lomond Wk LNHD EH20 .... 66 B5
London Rd RSTRG EH7 .... 28 C1
London Rd DLKTH EH22 .... 68 C1
  RSTRG EH7 .... 3 H1
Long Craig Rigg GNTN EH5 .... 16 A1
Long Craigs CPS/PPNS EH32 .... 35 G2
Long Crook QFRY EH30 .... 6 B5
Long Dalmahoy Rd BAL/CUR EH14 .... 54 B4
Longdykes Rd CPS/PPNS EH32 .... 34 D3
Longformacus Rd LIB/NID EH16 .... 59 G2
Longstone Av BAL/CUR EH14 .... 41 G4
Longstone Crs BAL/CUR EH14 .... 41 G4
Longstone Gdns BAL/CUR EH14 .... 41 F3
Longstone Gv BAL/CUR EH14 .... 41 G4
Longstone Pk BAL/CUR EH14 .... 41 G4
Longstone Pl BAL/CUR EH14 .... 41 G4
Longstone Rd BAL/CUR EH14 .... 41 G4
Longstone St BAL/CUR EH14 .... 41 G4
Longstone Ter BAL/CUR EH14 .... 41 F3
Lonsdale Ter EDNT/CEDW EH3 .... 2 C7
Loretto Ct MUS EH21 .... 47 H2
Lorimer Vw BAL/CUR EH14 .... 56 A3
Lorne Gv LNHD EH20 .... 65 H5
Lorne St LEITH EH6 .... 18 B5
Lothianburn Jct MCH/MOR/FMHD EH10 .... 58 B5
Lothian Dr DLKTH EH22 .... 69 E4
Lothian Rd DLKTH EH22 .... 68 C1
  EDOT EH1 .... 2 A4

Lothian St BNYRG EH19 .... 67 G5
  EDOT EH1 .... 3 F6
  RSWL EH24 .... 74 B5
Lothian Ter DLKTH EH22 .... 76 D3
Louisa Sq RSWL EH24 .... 74 B5
Lovedale Av BAL/CUR EH14 .... 52 D3
Lovedale Crs BAL/CUR EH14 .... 52 D3
Lovedale Gdns BAL/CUR EH14 .... 53 E3
Lovedale Gv BAL/CUR EH14 .... 52 D3
Lovedale Rd BAL/CUR EH14 .... 53 E3
Lovers La QFRY EH30 .... 6 D3
Lower Broomieknowe LSWD EH18 .... 67 E5
Lower Gilmore Pl EDNT/CEDW EH3 .... 27 E5
Lower Granton Rd GNTN EH5 .... 16 D1
Lower Joppa PBLO/DUD EH15 .... 30 C3
Lower London Rd RSTRG EH7 .... 28 C2
Lower Valleyfield Vw PNCK EH26 .... 70 D5
Lowrie Av PNCK EH26 .... 70 A4
Lugton Brae DLKTH EH22 .... 62 B5
Lumsdaine Dr DFLS KY11 .... 5 H1
Lussielaw Rd NWGTN EH9 .... 44 B4
Lutton Pl HLYRPK/NF EH8 .... 28 A5
Lygon Rd LIB/NID EH16 .... 44 B2
Lyndene Sq LNHD EH20 .... 65 F3
Lynedoch Place La EDNT/CEDW EH3 .... 27 E3

M

Macbeth Moir Rd MUS EH21 .... 33 E5
Mac Cormick Ter PNCK EH26 .... 70 D4
Maccormick Ter PNCK EH26 .... 70 D1
Macdowall Rd NWGTN EH9 .... 44 A3
Mackenzie Pl EDNT/CEDW EH3 .... 27 E3
Mactaggart Loan DLKTH EH22 .... 76 D4
Madeira Pl LEITH EH6 .... 18 A3
Madeira St LEITH EH6 .... 18 A2
Magdala Crs MRYFD/COR EH12 .... 26 D3
Magdala Ms MRYFD/COR EH12 .... 26 D3
Magdalene Av PBLO/DUD EH15 .... 30 B5
Magdalene Ct PBLO/DUD EH15 .... 30 A5
Magdalene Gdns PBLO/DUD EH15 .... 30 C5
Magdalene Loan PBLO/DUD EH15 .... 30 B5
Magdalene Medway PBLO/DUD EH15 .... 30 B5
Magdalene Pl PBLO/DUD EH15 .... 30 B5
Maidencraig Crs EDNW EH4 .... 26 A1
Maine Gdns TRNT EH33 .... 50 D2
Main St BAL/CUR EH14 .... 53 E2
  DFLS KY11 .... 5 J3
  DLKTH EH22 .... 76 C2
  EDNW EH4 .... 15 F5
  GORBR EH23 .... 79 F3
  KLSTN EH29 .... 21 F1
  LEITH EH6 .... 18 B3
  LNHD EH20 .... 65 H5
  QFRY EH30 .... 12 A1
  RATHO EH28 .... 37 H4
  ROSLIN EH25 .... 73 G2
Maitland Av MUS EH21 .... 31 G5
Maitland Hog La KLSTN EH29 .... 21 E2
Maitland Park Rd MUS EH21 .... 31 G5
Maitland St MUS EH21 .... 21 E1
Malbet Pk LIB/NID EH16 .... 59 H2
Malbet Wynd LIB/NID EH16 .... 59 H2
Mall Av MUS EH21 .... 32 A5
Malleny Av BAL/CUR EH14 .... 53 E3
Malleny Millgate BAL/CUR EH14 .... 53 F5
Malta Gn EDNW EH4 .... 27 F1
Malta Ter EDNW EH4 .... 27 F1
Manderston St LEITH EH6 .... 18 B4
Mannering Pl LIB/NID EH16 .... 59 H1
Manor Pl EDNT/CEDW EH3 .... 26 D3
Manse La CPS/PPNS EH32 .... 35 E1
  MUS EH21 .... 32 A5
Manse Rd KLSTN EH29 .... 21 E2
  MRYFD/COR EH12 .... 24 C5
  ROSLIN EH25 .... 73 H3
Manse St MRYFD/COR EH12 .... 24 C5
Mansfield Av DLKTH EH22 .... 76 D3
  MUS EH21 .... 32 A5
Mansfield Ct MUS EH21 .... 48 B1
Mansfield Pl DLKTH EH22 .... 48 A1
  MUS EH21 .... 48 A1
Mansfield Rd BAL/CUR EH14 .... 53 E2
  DLKTH EH22 .... 76 D1
  MUS EH21 .... 48 A1
Mansionhouse Rd NWGTN EH9 .... 43 H1
Marchbank Dr BAL/CUR EH14 .... 53 E4
Marchbank Gdns BAL/CUR EH14 .... 53 E4
Marchbank Gv BAL/CUR EH14 .... 53 E4
Marchbank Pl BAL/CUR EH14 .... 53 E4
Marchbank Wy BAL/CUR EH14 .... 53 E3
Marchburn Dr PNCK EH26 .... 70 B4
Marchfield Gv EDNW EH4 .... 15 E4
Marchfield Pk EDNW EH4 .... 15 E4
Marchfield Park La EDNW EH4 .... 15 F5
Marchfield Ter EDNW EH4 .... 25 E1
March Gait EDNW EH4 .... 15 E5
Marchhall Crs LIB/NID EH16 .... 44 C1
Marchhall Pl LIB/NID EH16 .... 44 C1
Marchhall Rd LIB/NID EH16 .... 44 C1
Marchmont Crs NWGTN EH9 .... 43 G1
Marchmont Rd NWGTN EH9 .... 43 G1
Marchmont St NWGTN EH9 .... 43 G1
March Pines EDNW EH4 .... 25 F1
March Rd EDNW EH4 .... 25 F1
Mardale Crs MCH/MOR/FMHD EH10 .... 43 E2
Margaret Rose Av MCH/MOR/FMHD EH10 .... 58 C4
Margaret Rose Crs MCH/MOR/FMHD EH10 .... 58 C4
Margaret Rose Dr MCH/MOR/FMHD EH10 .... 58 C4
Margaret Rose Loan MCH/MOR/FMHD EH10 .... 58 C4

Margaret Rose Wk MCH/MOR/FMHD EH10 .... 58 C4
Margaret Rose Wy MCH/MOR/FMHD EH10 .... 58 C4
Marine Dr EDNW EH4 .... 15 F2
Marine Esp LEITH EH6 .... 19 E3
Marionville Av RSTRG EH7 .... 28 D1
Marionville Crs RSTRG EH7 .... 29 E1
Marionville Dr RSTRG EH7 .... 29 E1
Marionville Gv RSTRG EH7 .... 29 E1
Marionville Rd RSTRG EH7 .... 28 D2
Maritime St LEITH EH6 .... 18 C3
Market La TRNT EH33 .... 51 E1
Market St EDOT EH1 .... 2 E4
  MUS EH21 .... 31 H5
Market Vw TRNT EH33 .... 51 E2
Market Wy TRNT EH33 .... 51 E1
Marlborough St PBLO/DUD EH15 .... 30 B3
Marmion Av ROSLIN EH25 .... 73 G2
Marmion Crs LIB/NID EH16 .... 44 D5
Marshall Rd KLSTN EH29 .... 21 E2
Marshall St EDOT EH1 .... 3 G1
Marshall St CPS/PPNS EH32 .... 34 D1
  HLYRPK/NF EH8 .... 3 F6
Martin Gv BNYRG EH19 .... 67 H4
Martin Pl DLKTH EH22 .... 68 A2
Maryburn Rd DLKTH EH22 .... 69 E4
Maryfield PBLO/DUD EH15 .... 30 B2
  RSTRG EH7 .... 3 K1
Maryfield Pl BNYRG EH19 .... 67 G5
  RSTRG EH7 .... 28 C2
Masefield Wy MRYFD/COR EH12 .... 22 D2
Mason Pl LSWD EH18 .... 74 D1
Matthews Dr DLKTH EH22 .... 78 B3
Maulsford Av DLKTH EH22 .... 61 F2
Maurice Pl NWGTN EH9 .... 43 H4
Mauricewood Av PNCK EH26 .... 70 D2
Mauricewood Bank PNCK EH26 .... 70 D2
Mauricewood Gv PNCK EH26 .... 70 D2
Mauricewood Pk PNCK EH26 .... 70 D2
Mauricewood Ri PNCK EH26 .... 70 D2
Mavisbank LNHD EH20 .... 66 A5
Mavisbank Pl LSWD EH18 .... 74 C1
Maxton Ct DLKTH EH22 .... 68 C1
Maxwell St MCH/MOR/FMHD EH10 .... 43 E3
Maybank Vls MRYFD/COR EH12 .... 24 D4
Mayburn Av LNHD EH20 .... 65 H5
Mayburn Bank LNHD EH20 .... 65 H4
Mayburn Ct LNHD EH20 .... 65 H4
Mayburn Crs LNHD EH20 .... 65 H4
Mayburn Dr LNHD EH20 .... 65 H4
Mayburn Gv LNHD EH20 .... 65 H5
Mayburn Hl LNHD EH20 .... 65 H5
Mayburn Loan LNHD EH20 .... 65 H3
Mayburn Ter LNHD EH20 .... 65 H4
Mayburn V LNHD EH20 .... 65 H5
Mayburn Wk LNHD EH20 .... 65 G4
Maybury Dr MRYFD/COR EH12 .... 24 A4
Maybury Rd MRYFD/COR EH12 .... 24 A4
Mayfield Av MUS EH21 .... 47 G5
Mayfield Crs LNHD EH20 .... 66 A4
  MUS EH21 .... 47 G2
Mayfield Gdns NWGTN EH9 .... 44 B2
Mayfield Gardens La NWGTN EH9 .... 44 B2
Mayfield Pl DLKTH EH22 .... 77 F1
  MUS EH21 .... 47 G2
Mayfield Rd NWGTN EH9 .... 44 B4
Mayshade Rd LNHD EH20 .... 65 H3
Mayville Bank MUS EH21 .... 33 E5
Mayville Gdns East GNTN EH5 .... 17 G2
McCathie Dr DLKTH EH22 .... 76 D1
McDiarmid Gv DLKTH EH22 .... 76 D4
McDonald Pl RSTRG EH7 .... 17 H5
McDonald Rd RSTRG EH7 .... 17 H5
McDonald St RSTRG EH7 .... 18 A5
McGahey Ct DLKTH EH22 .... 76 D3
McGregor Pend CPS/PPNS EH32 .... 34 D3
McKinlay Ter LNHD EH20 .... 65 G5
McKinnon Dr DLKTH EH22 .... 77 G3
McLaren Rd NWGTN EH9 .... 44 C2
McLean Pl GORBR EH23 .... 79 F1
Mc Lean Pl LSWD EH18 .... 74 D1
McLean Wk DLKTH EH22 .... 76 D3
McLeod Crs CPS/PPNS EH32 .... 34 B4
McLeod St DAL/STH/STNH EH11 .... 26 D5
McNeill Av LNHD EH20 .... 65 H4
McNeill Pl LNHD EH20 .... 65 H4
McNeill St DAL/STH/STNH EH11 .... 26 D5
McNeill Ter LNHD EH20 .... 65 G5
McPhail Sq TRNT EH33 .... 51 F2
McQuade St BNYRG EH19 .... 67 H4
Meadowbank HLYRPK/NF EH8 .... 28 D2
Meadowbank Crs HLYRPK/NF EH8 .... 28 D2
Meadowfield Av HLYRPK/NF EH8 .... 29 G4
Meadowfield Ct HLYRPK/NF EH8 .... 29 F4
Meadowfield Dr HLYRPK/NF EH8 .... 29 F4
Meadowfield Gdns HLYRPK/NF EH8 .... 29 F5
Meadowfield Rd MRYFD/COR EH12 .... 23 G4
Meadowfield Ter HLYRPK/NF EH8 .... 29 F5
Meadowhouse Rd MRYFD/COR EH12 .... 25 F5
Meadow La HLYRPK/NF EH8 .... 3 F7
Meadowmill Loan TRNT EH33 .... 51 F1
Meadow Pl NWGTN EH9 .... 43 G1
Meadow Place Rd MRYFD/COR EH12 .... 24 D5
Meadow Rd BAL/CUR EH14 .... 54 D2
Meadowside TRNT EH33 .... 51 G3
Meadowspot MCH/MOR/FMHD EH10 .... 42 C4
Mearenside MRYFD/COR EH12 .... 23 G4
Meeting House La TRNT EH33 .... 51 E2
Meggetgate BAL/CUR EH14 .... 42 B3
Meggetland Ter BAL/CUR EH14 .... 42 C4

Melville Dr EDNT/CEDW EH3 .... 27 G5
Melville Dykes Rd LSWD EH18 .... 67 F3
Melville Gate Rd LSWD EH18 .... 67 H1
Melville Rd DLKTH EH22 .... 68 A2
Melville St EDNT/CEDW EH3 .... 27 E3
Melville Street La
    EDNT/CEDW EH3 .... 27 E3
Melville Ter DLKTH EH22 .... 68 A3
    NWGTN EH6 .... 44 A1
Mentone Av PBLO/DUD EH15 .... 30 B5
Mentone Gdns NWGTN EH9 .... 44 B2
Mentone Ter NWGTN EH9 .... 44 B3
Merchant St EDOT EH1 .... 2 E5
Merchiston Av
    MCH/MOR/FMHD EH10 .... 43 E1
Merchiston Bank Av
    MCH/MOR/FMHD EH10 .... 43 E2
Merchiston Bank Gdns
    MCH/MOR/FMHD EH10 .... 43 E2
Merchiston Crs
    MCH/MOR/FMHD EH10 .... 43 E2
Merchiston Gdns
    MCH/MOR/FMHD EH10 .... 42 D3
Merchiston Gv
    DAL/STH/STNH EH11 .... 42 C2
Merchiston Ms
    MCH/MOR/FMHD EH10 .... 43 E1
Merchiston Pk
    MCH/MOR/FMHD EH10 .... 43 E1
Merchiston Pl
    MCH/MOR/FMHD EH10 .... 43 E2
Mertyon Wy PNCK EH26 .... 70 B3
Mertoun Pl
    DAL/STH/STNH EH11 .... 42 D1
Methven Ter LSWD EH18 .... 74 D1
Meuse La EDT/PRST EH2 .... 2 E3
Middleby St NWGTN EH9 .... 44 B2
Middlefield RSTRG EH7 .... 18 A5
Middleknowe BAL/CUR EH14 .... 55 G1
Middlepark BAL/CUR EH14 .... 55 G1
Middle Pier GNTN EH5 .... 16 D1
Middleshot Sq CPS/PPNS EH32 .... 34 D3
Mid Gilliland Rd
    MCH/MOR/FMHD EH10 .... 42 D2
Mid Liberton LIB/NID EH16 .... 44 C4
Midmar Av
    MCH/MOR/FMHD EH10 .... 43 G4
Midmar Dr
    MCH/MOR/FMHD EH10 .... 43 G4
Midmar Gdns
    MCH/MOR/FMHD EH10 .... 43 F4
Mid New Cultins
    DAL/STH/STNH EH11 .... 40 A4
Mid Steil
    MCH/MOR/FMHD EH10 .... 42 C5
Millar Crs
    MCH/MOR/FMHD EH10 .... 43 E3
Millar Pl
    MCH/MOR/FMHD EH10 .... 43 E3
Millar Place La
    MCH/MOR/FMHD EH10 .... 43 E3
Millar Rd TRNT EH33 .... 51 E5
Millbank BAL/CUR EH14 .... 53 E3
Millbank Gv GORBR EH23 .... 79 E3
Millbrae Wynd BAL/CUR EH14 ...... 41 H4
Millerfield Pl NWGTN EH9 .... 43 H1
Millerhill Rd DLKTH EH22 .... 46 D4
Miller Rw EDNW EH4 .... 27 E5
Millers Ct TRNT EH33 .... 50 D3
Millhill MUS EH21 .... 32 B5
Millhill La LEITH EH6 .... 18 B3
Mill Wynd CPS/PPNS EH32 .... 34 B3
Milton Crs PBLO/DUD EH15 .... 30 A5
Milton Dr PBLO/DUD EH15 .... 30 D4
Milton Gdns North
    PBLO/DUD EH15 .... 30 A5
Milton Gdns South
    PBLO/DUD EH15 .... 30 A5
Milton Gln PBLO/DUD EH15 .... 31 E4
Milton Gv PBLO/DUD EH15 .... 31 E4
Milton Link PBLO/DUD EH15 .... 30 C5
Milton Rd PBLO/DUD EH15 .... 30 D5
Milton Rd East PBLO/DUD EH15 ... 30 D5
Milton Rd West
    PBLO/DUD EH15 .... 29 H5
Milton St HLYRPK/NF EH8 .... 28 C2
Milton Ter PBLO/DUD EH15 .... 30 D4
Miner's Ter MUS EH21 .... 49 F1
Minstrel Ct ROSLIN EH25 .... 75 H3
Minto St NWGTN EH9 .... 44 B1
Mitchell St DLKTH EH22 .... 68 B1
    LEITH EH6 .... 18 C5
Mitchell Wy TRNT EH33 .... 51 F1
Moat Dr BAL/CUR EH14 .... 42 B2
Moat St BAL/CUR EH14 .... 42 B2
Moat Ter BAL/CUR EH14 .... 42 B2
Moat Vw ROSLIN EH25 .... 75 G3
Moffat Av BNYRG EH19 .... 75 F1
Moffat Wk TRNT EH33 .... 51 E4
Moira Pl RSTRG EH7 .... 29 G2
Moira Terrace La RSTRG EH7 .... 29 G2
Moir Av MUS EH21 .... 33 E5
Moir Crs MUS EH21 .... 33 E5
Moir Dr MUS EH21 .... 33 F5
Moir Pl MUS EH21 .... 33 E5
Moir Ter MUS EH21 .... 33 E5
Moncrieff Ter NWGTN EH9 .... 44 A1
Monkbarns Gdns LIB/NID EH16 .... 59 H1
Monksrig Rd PNCK EH26 .... 70 B3
Monkswood Rd DLKTH EH22 .... 76 D3
Monktonhall Pl MUS EH21 .... 47 H3
Monktonhall Ter MUS EH21 .... 47 H2
Monkwood Ct NWGTN EH9 .... 43 H2
Monmouth Ter
    EDNT/CEDW EH3 .... 17 F4
Montague St HLYRPK/NF EH8 ...... 28 A5
Montgomery St RSTRG EH7 .... 28 A1
Montgomery Street La
    RSTRG EH7 .... 28 A1
Montpelier
    MCH/MOR/FMHD EH10 .... 43 E1
Montpelier Pk
    MCH/MOR/FMHD EH10 .... 43 E1
Montrose Ter RSTRG EH7 .... 3 K1
Moorfoot Pl BNYRG EH19 .... 75 F1
    PNCK EH26 .... 70 C3
Moorfoot Vw BNYRG EH19 .... 75 F1

Moorfoot View GORBR EH23 .... 79 E3
Moray Park Ter RSTRG EH7 .... 28 C2
Moray Pl EDT/PRST EH2 .... 2 A2
Moredun Dell GIL/MOR EH17 .... 60 C2
Moredun Dykes Rd
    GIL/MOR EH17 .... 60 B3
Moredun Park Ct
    GIL/MOR EH17 .... 60 B2
Moredun Park Dr
    GIL/MOR EH17 .... 60 B2
Moredun Park Gdns
    GIL/MOR EH17 .... 60 C2
Moredun Park Gn
    GIL/MOR EH17 .... 60 C2
Moredun Park Gv
    GIL/MOR EH17 .... 60 C3
Moredun Park Loan
    GIL/MOR EH17 .... 60 B2
Moredun Park Rd
    GIL/MOR EH17 .... 60 B2
Moredun Park St
    GIL/MOR EH17 .... 60 B2
Moredun Park Vw
    GIL/MOR EH17 .... 60 C3
Moredun Park Wy
    GIL/MOR EH17 .... 60 B2
Moredunvale GIL/MOR EH17 .... 60 B1
Moredunvale Bank
    GIL/MOR EH17 .... 60 B1
Moredunvale Gn
    GIL/MOR EH17 .... 60 B1
Moredunvale Gv
    GIL/MOR EH17 .... 60 B1
Moredunvale Loan
    GIL/MOR EH17 .... 60 B1
Moredunvale Rd
    GIL/MOR EH17 .... 60 B1
Moredunvale Vw
    GIL/MOR EH17 .... 60 B1
Moredunvale Wy
    GIL/MOR EH17 .... 60 B1
Morham Gait
    MCH/MOR/FMHD EH10 .... 57 G1
Morham Lea
    MCH/MOR/FMHD EH10 .... 57 G1
Morham Pk
    MCH/MOR/FMHD EH10 .... 57 G1
Morison Gdns QFRY EH30 .... 6 C4
Morningside Dr
    MCH/MOR/FMHD EH10 .... 42 D4
Morningside Gdns
    MCH/MOR/FMHD EH10 .... 42 D4
Morningside Gv
    MCH/MOR/FMHD EH10 .... 42 D4
Morningside Pk
    MCH/MOR/FMHD EH10 .... 43 E3
Morningside Pl
    MCH/MOR/FMHD EH10 .... 43 E3
Morningside Rd
    MCH/MOR/FMHD EH10 .... 43 E2
Morningside Ter
    MCH/MOR/FMHD EH10 .... 43 E3
Morrison Av TRNT EH33 .... 51 G2
Morrison Crs EDNT/CEDW EH3 ..... 27 E4
Morrison Link EDNT/CEDW EH3 .... 27 E4
Morrison St EDNT/CEDW EH3 .... 2 A6
    MRYFD/COR EH12 .... 27 E4
Morris Rd DLKTH EH22 .... 77 F3
Mortonhall Ga DLKTH EH22 .... 58 D4
Mortonhall Park Av
    GIL/MOR EH17 .... 59 F4
Mortonhall Park Bank
    GIL/MOR EH17 .... 59 G4
Mortonhall Park Crs
    GIL/MOR EH17 .... 59 G4
Mortonhall Park Dr
    GIL/MOR EH17 .... 59 G4
Mortonhall Park Gdns
    GIL/MOR EH17 .... 59 F4
Mortonhall Park Gv
    GIL/MOR EH17 .... 59 F4
Mortonhall Park Loan
    GIL/MOR EH17 .... 59 F4
Mortonhall Park Pl
    GIL/MOR EH17 .... 59 G4
Mortonhall Park Ter
    GIL/MOR EH17 .... 59 G4
Mortonhall Park Vw
    GIL/MOR EH17 .... 59 F4
Mortonhall Park Wy
    LIB/NID EH16 .... 59 F4
Mortonhall Rd NWGTN EH9 .... 43 H3
Morton St PBLO/DUD EH15 .... 30 C4
Morvenside BAL/CUR EH14 .... 55 G1
Morven St EDNW EH4 .... 24 C2
Moston Ter NWGTN EH9 .... 44 B2
Moubray Gr QFRY EH30 .... 6 D5
Mound Pl EDOT EH1 .... 2 D4
The Mound EDT/PRST EH2 .... 2 D3
Mountcastle Bank
    HLYRPK/NF EH8 .... 29 H3
Mountcastle Crs
    HLYRPK/NF EH8 .... 29 H3
Mountcastle Dr North
    HLYRPK/NF EH8 .... 29 G3
Mountcastle Dr South
    PBLO/DUD EH15 .... 29 H4
Mountcastle Gdns
    HLYRPK/NF EH8 .... 29 H3
Mountcastle Gn
    HLYRPK/NF EH8 .... 29 H3
Mountcastle Gv
    HLYRPK/NF EH8 .... 29 G3
Mountcastle Loan
    HLYRPK/NF EH8 .... 29 H3
Mountcastle Pk
    HLYRPK/NF EH8 .... 29 G3
Mountcastle Pl
    HLYRPK/NF EH8 .... 29 G2
Mountcastle Ter
    HLYRPK/NF EH8 .... 29 G3
Mount Gra NWGTN EH9 .... 43 G2
Mount Hooly Crs DFLS KY11 .... 4 D4
Mounthooly Loan
    MCH/MOR/FMHD EH10 .... 58 C4
Mountjoy Ter MUS EH21 .... 32 A5
Mount Lodge Pl
    PBLO/DUD EH15 .... 30 B5

Mount Vernon Rd
    LIB/NID EH16 .... 59 H1
Mucklets Av MUS EH21 .... 47 G2
Mucklets Ct MUS EH21 .... 47 G2
Mucklets Crs MUS EH21 .... 47 G2
Mucklets Dr MUS EH21 .... 47 G2
Mucklets Pl MUS EH21 .... 47 G2
Muirend Av BAL/CUR EH14 .... 41 H2
Muirfield Gdns LHND EH20 .... 66 A5
Muirhead Pl PNCK EH26 .... 70 D1
Muirhouse Av
    EDNW EH4 .... 15 H3
Muirhouse Av North
    EDNW EH4 .... 15 H3
Muirhouse Bank EDNW EH4 .... 15 H4
Muirhouse Ct EDNW EH4 .... 15 G4
Muirhouse Crs EDNW EH4 .... 15 G3
Muirhouse Dr EDNW EH4 .... 15 G3
Muirhouse Gn EDNW EH4 .... 15 H4
Muirhouse Gv EDNW EH4 .... 15 G3
Muirhouse Medway EDNW EH4 .... 15 G4
Muirhouse Pk EDNW EH4 .... 15 G4
Muirhouse Pkwy EDNW EH4 .... 15 H4
Muirhouse Pl East EDNW EH4 .... 15 H4
Muirhouse Pl West EDNW EH4 ...... 15 H4
Muirhouse Ter EDNW EH4 .... 15 H4
Muirhouse Wy EDNW EH4 .... 15 H4
Muirpark DLKTH EH22 .... 68 A3
Muirpark Ct TRNT EH33 .... 51 G3
Muirpark Gdns TRNT EH33 .... 51 G3
Muirpark Gv TRNT EH33 .... 51 G3
Muirpark Rd TRNT EH33 .... 51 G3
Muirpark Ter TRNT EH33 .... 51 G3
Muirpark Wynd TRNT EH33 .... 51 G3
Muirside Dr TRNT EH33 .... 51 E3
Muir Wood Crs BAL/CUR EH14 ..... 55 F4
Muir Wood Dr BAL/CUR EH14 ...... 55 F4
Muir Wood Gv BAL/CUR EH14 ...... 55 F4
Muir Wood Pl BAL/CUR EH14 .... 55 F4
Muir Wood Rd BAL/CUR EH14 ...... 55 F4
Munro Dr COLIN EH13 .... 56 C4
Murderdean Rd DLKTH EH22 .... 76 C2
Murdoch Ter
    DAL/STH/STNH EH11 .... 27 E5
Murham Gdn
    MCH/MOR/FMHD EH10 .... 57 G1
Murieston Crs
    DAL/STH/STNH EH11 .... 26 C5
Murieston Crescent La
    DAL/STH/STNH EH11 .... 26 C5
Murieston La
    DAL/STH/STNH EH11 .... 42 C1
Murieston Pl
    DAL/STH/STNH EH11 .... 26 C5
Murieston Rd
    DAL/STH/STNH EH11 .... 26 C5
Murieston Ter
    DAL/STH/STNH EH11 .... 26 C5
Murrayburn Ap
    DAL/STH/STNH EH11 .... 40 D5
Murrayburn Dr
    DAL/STH/STNH EH11 .... 40 C5
Murrayburn Gdns
    BAL/CUR EH14 .... 41 E5
Murrayburn Ga BAL/CUR EH14 .... 55 H1
Murrayburn Gn BAL/CUR EH14 .... 41 E5
Murrayburn Pl BAL/CUR EH14 ..... 40 D5
Murrayburn Rd BAL/CUR EH14 .... 41 E4
Murray Cottages
    MRYFD/COR EH12 .... 24 C5
Murrayfield Av
    MRYFD/COR EH12 .... 26 B4
Murrayfield Dr
    MRYFD/COR EH12 .... 26 A4
Murrayfield Gdns
    MRYFD/COR EH12 .... 26 B3
Murrayfield Rd
    MRYFD/COR EH12 .... 26 A3
The Murrays Brae
    GIL/MOR EH17 .... 60 A5
The Murrays GIL/MOR EH17 .... 60 A5
Musselburgh Rd DLKTH EH22 .... 31 F4
    PBLO/DUD EH15 .... 31 F4
Myre Di BNYRG EH19 .... 75 G1
Myreside Ct
    MCH/MOR/FMHD EH10 .... 42 C4
Myreside Rd
    MCH/MOR/FMHD EH10 .... 42 D3
Myreside Vw BAL/CUR EH14 .... 42 C3
Myrtle Gv PNCK EH26 .... 69 F5

N

Namur Rd PNCK EH26 .... 70 B1
Nantwich Dr RSTRG EH7 .... 29 H1
Napier Rd
    MCH/MOR/FMHD EH10 .... 42 D2
Neidfield LIB/NID EH16 .... 59 H1
Nelson Pl EDNT/CEDW EH3 .... 2 D1
Nelson St EDNT/CEDW EH3 .... 2 D1
Ness St TRNT EH33 .... 51 E4
Netherbank LIB/NID EH16 .... 59 F4
Netherbank Vw LIB/NID EH16 .... 59 F5
Netherby Rd GNTN EH5 .... 17 F5
Nether Craigour GIL/MOR EH17 ... 45 F5
Nether Craigwell
    HLYRPK/NF EH8 .... 3 J5
Nether Currie Crs
    BAL/CUR EH14 .... 55 F4
Nether Currie Pl BAL/CUR EH14 ... 55 F4
Nether Currie Rd
    BAL/CUR EH14 .... 55 F4
Nethershot Rd CPS/PPNS EH32 ... 34 C3
New Arthur Pl HLYRPK/NF EH8 .... 3 H5
New Arthur St HLYRPK/NF EH8 .... 3 H5
Newbattle Abbey Crs
    DLKTH 68 B5
Newbattle Gdns DLKTH EH22 .... 68 B5
Newbattle Rd DLKTH EH22 .... 68 B2
Newbattle Ter
    MCH/MOR/FMHD EH10 .... 43 F2
Newbigging MUS EH21 .... 48 B1

Newbridge Rd RATHO EH28 .... 21 E5
New Broompark GNTN EH5 .... 16 C1
New Broughton
    EDNT/CEDW EH3 .... 27 H1
Newbyres Av GORBR EH23 .... 79 F2
Newbyres Crs GORBR EH23 .... 79 F2
Newbyres Gdns GORBR EH23 ...... 79 E2
Newcraighall Rd MUS EH21 .... 46 D2
Newcraighall Rd MUS EH21 .... 47 E2
New Cut Rigg LEITH EH6 .... 17 H3
Newhailes Av MUS EH21 .... 31 G5
Newhailes Crs MUS EH21 .... 47 F5
Newhailes Rd MUS EH21 .... 47 F1
Newhaven Rd (Edinburgh Rd)
    QFRY EH30 .... 11 G1
Newhaven Pl LEITH EH6 .... 17 H1
Newhaven Rd LEITH EH6 .... 17 H2
Newington Rd NWGTN EH9 .... 44 A1
New John's Pl HLYRPK/NF EH8 .... 3 H7
New Lairdship Yards
    DAL/STH/STNH EH11 .... 40 D3
Newlands Pk NWGTN EH9 .... 44 B2
New La LEITH EH6 .... 17 H2
New Liston Rd KLSTN EH29 .... 21 E5
Newmains Rd KLSTN EH29 .... 21 E1
New Market Rd BAL/CUR EH14 .... 42 A3
New Mart Rd BAL/CUR EH14 .... 41 H3
New Matt Pl BAL/CUR EH14 .... 41 H3
New Matt Sq BAL/CUR EH14 .... 41 H3
Newmills Av BAL/CUR EH14 .... 54 B5
Newmills Crs BAL/CUR EH14 .... 53 F1
Newmills Gv BAL/CUR EH14 .... 53 F1
Newmills Rd BAL/CUR EH14 .... 53 F1
    DLKTH EH22 .... 68 C1
New Skinner's Cl EDOT EH1 .... 3 G4
New Orchardfield LEITH EH6 .... 18 B4
New Rw TRNT EH33 .... 51 E2
New Skinner's Cl EDOT EH1 .... 3 G4
New Star Bank DLKTH EH22 .... 76 D4
New St CPS/PPNS EH32 .... 34 B4
    HLYRPK/NF EH8 .... 3 G5
    MUS EH21 .... 48 B1
    TRNT EH33 .... 51 E1
New Swanston
    MCH/MOR/FMHD EH10 .... 57 H4
Newtoft St GIL/MOR EH17 .... 60 C4
Newton Church Rd
    DLKTH EH22 .... 61 F2
Newton Loan Ct GORBR EH23 ...... 76 D5
Newton St
    DAL/STH/STNH EH11 .... 27 E5
    DLKTH EH22 .... 69 E4
New Tower Pl PBLO/DUD EH15 .... 30 B2
Nicholfield LEITH EH6 .... 17 H2
Nicolson Sq HLYRPK/NF EH8 .... 3 G6
Nicolson St HLYRPK/NF EH8 .... 3 G6
Niddrie Farm Gv LIB/NID EH16 .... 45 H3
Niddrie House Av LIB/NID EH16 ... 45 H3
Niddrie House Dr LIB/NID EH16 ... 46 A3
Niddrie House Gdns
    LIB/NID EH16 .... 45 H3
Niddrie House Gn
    LIB/NID EH16 .... 45 H3
Niddrie House Pk LIB/NID EH16 ... 45 H3
Niddrie House Sq LIB/NID EH16 ... 45 H3
Niddrie Mains Dr LIB/NID EH16 ... 45 H3
Niddrie Mains Rd LIB/NID EH16 ... 45 G2
Niddrie Mains Ter LIB/NID EH16 .. 45 G2
Niddrie Marischal Crs
    LIB/NID EH16 .... 45 H2
Niddrie Marischal Dr
    LIB/NID EH16 .... 45 H3
Niddrie Marischal Gdns
    LIB/NID EH16 .... 45 H3
Niddrie Marischal Gn
    LIB/NID EH16 .... 45 H3
Niddrie Marischal Gv
    LIB/NID EH16 .... 46 A2
Niddrie Marischal Pl
    LIB/NID EH16 .... 45 H3
Niddrie Marischal Rd
    LIB/NID EH16 .... 46 A2
Niddrie Mill Av PBLO/DUD EH15 .. 46 A2
Niddrie Mill Ter
    PBLO/DUD EH15 .... 36 F4
Niddry Mill Cr PBLO/DUD EH15 ... 46 A1
Niddrie Mill Dr PBLO/DUD EH15 .. 46 A2
Niddrie Mill Gv PBLO/DUD EH15 .. 46 A2
Niddrie Mill Pl PBLO/DUD EH15 ... 46 A2
Niddry St EDOT EH1 .... 3 F4
Niddry St South EDOT EH1 .... 3 G5
Nigel Loan LIB/NID EH16 .... 59 H1
Nile Gv MCH/MOR/FMHD EH10 ... 43 E3
Nimmo Av CPS/PPNS EH32 .... 34 C4
Ninth St DLKTH EH22 .... 76 D2
Niven's Knowe Rd LHND EH20 ..... 65 F5
Nobel Pl ROSLIN EH25 .... 73 G3
Noble Pl LEITH EH6 .... 18 B2
North Bank CPS/PPNS EH32 .... 34 A5
North Bank St EDOT EH1 .... 2 E4
North Br EDOT EH1 .... 3 F4
North Bughtlin Bank
    MRYFD/COR EH12 .... 24 B2
North Bughtlin Brae
    MRYFD/COR EH12 .... 24 B2
North Bughtlinfield
    MRYFD/COR EH12 .... 24 A2
North Bughtlin Ga
    MRYFD/COR EH12 .... 24 A2
North Bughtlin Neuk
    MRYFD/COR EH12 * 24 A2
North Bughtlin Pl
    MRYFD/COR EH12 .... 24 B3
North Bughtlinrig
    MRYFD/COR EH12 .... 24 A2
North Bughtlin Rd
    MRYFD/COR EH12 .... 24 B2
North Bughtlinside
    MRYFD/COR EH12 .... 24 A2
North Charlotte St
    EDNT/CEDW EH3 .... 2 A2
North Clyde Street La
    EDT/PRST EH2 .... 2 E2
Northcote St
    DAL/STH/STNH EH11 .... 26 D5
North Crs CPS/PPNS EH32 .... 34 C4
North East Circus Pl
    EDNT/CEDW EH3 .... 2 B1

North East Cumberland
    Street La EDNT/CEDW EH3 ..... 27 G1
Northfield TRNT EH33 .... 51 G2
Northfield Av HLYRPK/NF EH8 ..... 29 F3
Northfield Broadway
    HLYRPK/NF EH8 .... 29 F2
Northfield Circ HLYRPK/NF EH8 .. 29 F2
Northfield Ct CPS/PPNS EH32 ...... 34 B5
Northfield Crs HLYRPK/NF EH8 ... 29 F3
Northfield Dr HLYRPK/NF EH8 ..... 29 F3
Northfield East TRNT EH33 .... 51 G2
Northfield Farm Av
    HLYRPK/NF EH8 .... 29 G4
Northfield Farm Rd
    HLYRPK/NF EH8 .... 29 G4
Northfield Gdns
    HLYRPK/NF EH8 .... 29 G4
Northfield Pk HLYRPK/NF EH8 .... 29 G3
Northfield Park Gv
    HLYRPK/NF EH8 .... 29 F3
Northfield Rd HLYRPK/NF EH8 .... 29 F3
Northfield Sq HLYRPK/NF EH8 .... 29 G3
North Fort St LEITH EH6 .... 18 A2
North Grange Av
    CPS/PPNS EH32 .... 34 A5
North Grange Gv CPS/PPNS EH32 34 A4
North Grange Rd
    CPS/PPNS EH32 .... 34 B4
North Greens PBLO/DUD EH15 .... 46 A1
North Gyle Av
    MRYFD/COR EH12 .... 24 B5
North Gyle Dr
    MRYFD/COR EH12 .... 24 B4
North Gyle Farm Ct
    MRYFD/COR EH12 .... 24 A5
North Gyle Farm La
    MRYFD/COR EH12 .... 24 A5
North Gyle Gv
    MRYFD/COR EH12 .... 24 A5
North Gyle Loan
    MRYFD/COR EH12 .... 24 A4
North Gyle Pk
    MRYFD/COR EH12 .... 24 A5
North Gyle Rd
    MRYFD/COR EH12 .... 24 B4
North Gyle Ter
    MRYFD/COR EH12 .... 24 A5
North High St MUS EH21 .... 31 G5
North Hillhousefield LEITH EH6 ... 18 A2
North Junction St LEITH EH6 .... 18 A2
Northlawn Ter EDNW EH4 .... 15 E4
North Leith Mill LEITH EH6 .... 18 A2
North Leith Sands LEITH EH6 .... 18 A2
North Meggetland
    BAL/CUR EH14 .... 42 B3
North Park Ter EDNW EH4 .... 27 E1
North Peffer Pl LIB/NID EH16 .... 45 H2
North Richmond St
    HLYRPK/NF EH8 .... 3 G5
North St Andrew La
    CED/PRST EH1 .... 2 E2
North St Andrew St EDOT EH1 ...... 2 E1
North St David St CED/PRST EH2 .. 2 D2
North Seton Pk
    CPS/PPNS EH32 .... 35 F1
North St RATHO EH28 .... 37 H4
North West Cumberland
    EDNT/CEDW EH3 .... 2 D1
Northumberland St
    EDNT/CEDW EH3 .... 2 D1
Northumberland Street North
    East La EDNT/CEDW EH3 .... 2 D1
Northumberland Street
    North West La
    EDNT/CEDW EH3 .... 2 C1
North Weber Pl EDNW EH4 .... 16 C5
North Werber Pk EDNW EH4 .... 16 C5
North West Circus Pl
    EDNT/CEDW EH3 .... 2 A1
North West Cumberland
    Street La EDNT/CEDW EH3 ..... 27 G1
North Wynd DLKTH EH22 .... 68 C1
Norton Pk RSTRG EH7 .... 28 C1
Nottingham Pl EDOT EH1 .... 3 G2

O

Oak Crs DLKTH EH22 .... 77 G5
Oakfield Pl HLYRPK/NF EH8 .... 3 H5
Oak La MRYFD/COR EH12 .... 25 F2
Oak Pl DLKTH EH22 .... 77 H1
Oak St TRNT EH33 .... 18 D4
Oak Wy PNCK EH26 .... 72 B5
Observatory Gn NWGTN EH9 .... 44 A4
Observatory Rd NWGTN EH9 .... 43 I4
Ocean Dr LEITH EH6 .... 18 B2
Ocean Wy LEITH EH6 .... 18 C2
Ochil Ct QFRY EH30 .... 6 D5
Ochiltree Gdns LIB/NID EH16 .... 45 E5
Ogilvie Ter DAL/STH/STNH EH11 . 42 C2
Old Burdiehouse Rd
    .... 65 G1
Old Church La PBLO/DUD EH15 ... 29 G5
Old Course Ga MUS EH21 .... 32 B4
Old Craighall Jct MUS EH21 .... 47 H4
Old Craighall Rd DLKTH EH22 ...... 47 F4
Old Dalkeith Rd DLKTH EH22 .... 61 F3
    GIL/MOR EH17 .... 60 D1
    LIB/NID EH16 .... 45 E1
Old Edinburgh Rd DLKTH EH22 ... 68 B1
Old Farm Av COLIN EH13 .... 56 D2
Old Farm Pl COLIN EH13 .... 56 C2
Old Fishmarket Cl EDOT EH1 .... 3 F4
Old Kirk Rd DFLS KY11 .... 4 D4
    MRYFD/COR EH12 .... 25 F3
Old Liston Rd RATHO EH28 .... 21 E5
Old Mill La LIB/NID EH16 .... 44 C4
Old Newmills Rd BAL/CUR EH14 .. 53 F4
Old Star Rd DLKTH EH22 .... 76 C2
Old Tolbooth Wynd
    HLYRPK/NF EH8 .... 3 H3
Oliphant Gdns MUS EH21 .... 49 F1
Olive Bank Rd MUS EH21 .... 47 H1
Orchard Bank EDNW EH4 .... 26 C2
Orchard Brae EDNW EH4 .... 26 D2

Orchard Brae Av EDNW EH4 .... 26 C2
Orchard Brae Gdns EDNW EH4 ...... 26 C2
Orchard Crs CPS/PPNS EH32 .... 34 B4
Orchard Dr EDNW EH4 .... 26 B2
Orchard Dr EDNW EH4 .... 26 B2
Orchardfield Av
  MRYFD/COR EH12 .... 24 D5
Orchardhead Loan
  LIB/NID EH16 .... 59 G1
Orchardhead Rd LIB/NID EH16 ...... 59 G1
Orchard Pl EDNW EH4 .... 26 C1
Orchard Rd EDNW EH4 .... 26 C1
Orchard Rd South EDNW EH4 .... 26 B2
The Orchard MUS EH21 .... 47 H1
  TRNT EH33 .... 51 E1
Orchard Toll EDNW EH4 .... 26 C2
Orchard Vw DLKTH EH22 .... 67 H2
Ormidale Ter MRYFD/COR EH12 .... 67 H2
Ormiston Av TRNT EH33 .... 51 G2
Ormiston Crs East TRNT EH33 ...... 51 G2
Ormiston Crs West TRNT EH33 ..... 51 G2
Ormiston Pl CPS/PPNS EH32 .... 34 A4
Ormiston Rd TRNT EH33 .... 51 G2
Orrok Pk LIB/NID EH16 .... 44 C4
Orwell Pl DAL/STH/STNH EH11 ..... 26 D5
Orwell Ter DAL/STH/STNH EH11 .... 26 D5
Osborne Ct CPS/PPNS EH32 .... 35 E1
Osborne Ter CPS/PPNS EH32 .... 35 E1
Oswald Ct NWGTN EH9 .... 43 H5
Oswald Rd NWGTN EH9 .... 43 H5
Oswald Ter MRYFD/COR EH12 ...... 24 D5
Otterburn Pk BAL/CUR EH14 .... 41 H5
Oxcraig St GNTN EH5 .... 16 D1
Oxenfoord Ct HLYRPK/NF EH8 ...... 29 E6
Oxford Ter EDNW EH4 .... 27 E1
Oxgangs Av COLIN EH13 .... 57 F2
Oxgangs Bank COLIN EH13 .... 57 H3
Oxgangs Brae COLIN EH13 .... 57 H3
Oxgangs Crs COLIN EH13 .... 57 H3
Oxgangs Dr COLIN EH13 .... 57 H2
Oxgangs Farm Av COLIN EH13 ..... 57 G3
Oxgangs Farm Dr COLIN EH13 ..... 57 G3
Oxgangs Farm Gdns
  COLIN EH13 .... 57 G3
Oxgangs Farm Gv COLIN EH13 ..... 57 G3
Oxgangs Farm Loan
  COLIN EH13 .... 57 G3
Oxgangs Farm Ter COLIN EH13 .... 57 G3
Oxgangs Gdns COLIN EH13 .... 57 G2
Oxgangs Gn COLIN EH13 .... 57 G2
Oxgangs Gv COLIN EH13 .... 57 H2
Oxgangs Hl COLIN EH13 .... 57 H2
Oxgangs Loan COLIN EH13 .... 57 H2
Oxgangs Medway COLIN EH13 ..... 57 H3
Oxgangs Pk COLIN EH13 .... 57 H3
Oxgangs Ph COLIN EH13 .... 57 H2
Oxgangs Pl COLIN EH13 .... 57 G2
Oxgangs Ri COLIN EH13 .... 57 H2
Oxgangs Rd
  MCH/MOR/FMHD EH10 .... 58 A4
Oxgangs Rd North COLIN EH13 .... 57 G2
Oxgangs Rw COLIN EH13 .... 57 H3
Oxgangs Ter COLIN EH13 .... 57 H3
Oxgangs Vw COLIN EH13 .... 57 H3

P

The Paddockholm
  MRYFD/COR EH12 .... 25 E5
Paisley Av HLYRPK/NF EH8 .... 29 F3
Paisley Crs HLYRPK/NF EH8 .... 29 F3
Paisley Dr HLYRPK/NF EH8 .... 29 F4
Paisley Gdns HLYRPK/NF EH8 ...... 29 E3
Palmer Pl BAL/CUR EH14 .... 54 D4
Palmerston Pl
  MRYFD/COR EH12 .... 27 E3
Palmerston Place La
  MRYFD/COR EH12 .... 27 E4
Pankhurst Loan DLKTH EH22 .... 69 F1
Panmure Pl EDNT/CEDW EH3 ...... 2 C7
Papermill Wynd RSTRC EH7 .... 18 A5
Paradykes Av LNHD EH20 .... 65 G5
Park Av GORBR EH23 .... 79 E1
  LNHD EH20 .... 65 G5
  MUS EH21 .... 48 C1
  PBLO/DUD EH15 .... 30 A4
Park Dr MUS EH21 .... 48 C1
Park Crs BNYRC EH19 .... 67 F5
  DLKTH EH22 .... 59 H1
  LIB/NID EH16 .... 59 H1
  LNHD EH20 .... 65 H5
Parker Rd RSTRC EH7 .... 29 E2
Park Gdns LIB/NID EH16 .... 59 H1
Park Gv LIB/NID EH16 .... 59 H2
Parkgrove Av EDNW EH4 .... 24 C1
Parkgrove Bank EDNW EH4 .... 24 C1
Parkgrove Crs EDNW EH4 .... 24 C1
Parkgrove Dr EDNW EH4 .... 24 C1
Parkgrove Gdns EDNW EH4 .... 24 C1
Parkgrove Gn EDNW EH4 .... 24 C1
Parkgrove Loan EDNW EH4 .... 24 C1
Parkgrove Neuk EDNW EH4 .... 24 D1
Parkgrove Pth EDNW EH4 .... 24 D1
Parkgrove Pl EDNW EH4 .... 24 C1
Parkgrove Rw EDNW EH4 .... 24 C1
Parkgrove Ter EDNW EH4 .... 24 C1
Park Grove Ter MUS EH21 .... 48 C1
Parkgrove Vw EDNW EH4 .... 24 C1
Parkhead Av
  DAL/STH/STNH EH11 .... 41 E4
Parkhead Crs
  DAL/STH/STNH EH11 .... 41 E4
Parkhead Dr
  DAL/STH/STNH EH11 .... 41 F4
Parkhead Gdns
  DAL/STH/STNH EH11 .... 41 E4
Parkhead Loan
  DAL/STH/STNH EH11 .... 41 F4

Parkhead Pk DLKTH EH22 .... 69 E4
Parkhead Pl
  DAL/STH/STNH EH11 .... 41 E4
  DLKTH EH22 .... 69 E4
Parkhead St
  DAL/STH/STNH EH11 .... 41 E4
Parkhead Ter
  DAL/STH/STNH EH11 .... 41 F3
Parkhead Vw
  DAL/STH/STNH EH11 .... 41 E4
Park Hl GORBR EH23 .... 78 D1
Park La MUS EH21 .... 48 C1
Park Pl EDNW EH4 .... 30 A4
Park Rd BNYRC EH19 .... 67 F5
  CPS/PPNS EH32 .... 35 F1
  DLKTH EH22 .... 76 D1
  GORBR EH23 .... 79 E1
  LEITH EH6 .... 17 G2
Parkside Ct DLKTH EH22 .... 68 B1
Parkside Pl DLKTH EH22 .... 68 B1
Parkside St HLYRPK/NF EH8 .... 28 B5
Parkside Ter LIB/NID EH16 .... 28 B5
Parkvale Pl LEITH EH6 .... 18 D4
Park Vw CPS/PPNS EH32 .... 34 C4
  LNHD EH20 .... 65 H5
  MUS EH21 .... 46 D2
  MUS EH21 .... 48 C1
Park Vw East CPS/PPNS EH32 ..... 35 F1
Park Vw West CPS/PPNS EH32 .... 35 F1
Parliament Sq EDOT EH1 .... 2 E4
Parliament St LEITH EH6 .... 18 B3
Parrot La GORBR EH23 .... 79 E2
The Parsonage MUS EH21 .... 32 B5
Parsons Green Ter
  HLYRPK/NF EH8 .... 29 E2
Parsonspool BNYRC EH19 .... 75 G2
Path Brae KLSTN EH29 .... 21 E2
Patie's Rd BAL/CUR EH14 .... 57 F2
Pattison St LEITH EH6 .... 18 C3
Peacock Av BNYRC EH19 .... 76 A1
Peacock Ct LEITH EH6 .... 17 H2
Peacock Pkwy BNYRC EH19 .... 76 A1
Peacocktail Cl PBLO/DUD EH15 ... 46 B2
Pearce Av MRYFD/COR EH12 ...... 24 C4
Pearce Gv MRYFD/COR EH12 ...... 24 C4
Pearce Rd MRYFD/COR EH12 ...... 24 C4
Peatville Gdns BAL/CUR EH14 ..... 41 G5
Peatville Ter BAL/CUR EH14 .... 41 G5
Peel Ter NWGTN EH9 .... 44 B2
Peffer Bank LIB/NID EH16 .... 45 F2
Peffermill Rd LIB/NID EH16 .... 44 D3
Peffer Pl LIB/NID EH16 .... 45 F2
Peffer St LIB/NID EH16 .... 45 F2
Peggy's Mill Rd EDNW EH4 .... 14 A4
Pembroke Pl MRYFD/COR EH12 ... 26 C4
Pendreich Av BNYRC EH19 .... 67 G4
Pendreich Dr BNYRC EH19 .... 67 G4
Pendreich Gv BNYRC EH19 .... 67 G4
Pendreich Ter BNYRC EH19 .... 67 G4
Pendreich Vw BNYRC EH19 .... 67 G4
Penicuik Rd ROSLIN EH25 .... 73 F3
Pennywell Ct EDNW EH4 .... 15 G5
Pennywell Gv EDNW EH4 .... 15 G5
Pennywell Medway EDNW EH4 .... 15 H3
Pennywell Pl EDNW EH4 .... 15 H3
Pentland Av BAL/CUR EH14 .... 54 D5
  COLIN EH13 .... 56 C3
  GORBR EH23 .... 76 D4
  PNCK EH26 .... 70 C3
Pentland Crs
  MCH/MOR/FMHD EH10 .... 58 A2
  RSWL EH24 .... 74 B5
Pentland Dr
  MCH/MOR/FMHD EH10 .... 57 H3
Pentland Gait
  DAL/STH/STNH EH11 .... 40 B5
Pentland Gv
  MCH/MOR/FMHD EH10 .... 58 A2
Pentland Pl BAL/CUR EH14 .... 54 D5
Pentland Rd BNYRC EH19 .... 74 D1
  COLIN EH13 .... 56 C2
  MCH/MOR/FMHD EH10 .... 64 D3
Pentlands Gdns
  MCH/MOR/FMHD EH10 .... 57 H2
Pentland Vw BNYRC EH19 .... 70 C3
Pentland Vw BAL/CUR EH14 .... 54 D5
  DLKTH EH22 .... 69 E2
  MCH/MOR/FMHD EH10 .... 58 A3
Pentland View Crs
  ROSLIN EH25 .... 73 G3
Pentland View Pl ROSLIN EH25 ... 73 G3
Pentland View Rd KLSTN EH29 .... 21 E2
  ROSLIN EH25 .... 73 G3
Pentland View Ter
  ROSLIN EH25 .... 73 G3
Perdrixknowe BAL/CUR EH14 ...... 42 A5
Perth's Gv CPS/PPNS EH32 .... 34 C3
Perth St EDNT/CEDW EH3 .... 27 F1
Pettigrew's Cl DLKTH EH22 .... 68 C1
Peveril Ter LIB/NID EH16 .... 59 G1
Picardy Pl EDOT EH1 .... 3 F1
Pier Pl LEITH EH6 .... 17 G1
Piersfield Gv HLYRPK/NF EH8 ..... 29 F2
Piersfield Pl HLYRPK/NF EH8 ...... 29 F2
Piershill La HLYRPK/NF EH8 .... 29 F2
Piershill Ter HLYRPK/NF EH8 ...... 29 F2
Pilrig Gdns LEITH EH6 .... 18 A4
Pilrig Glebe LEITH EH6 .... 18 A5
Pilrig Hts LEITH EH6 .... 18 A4
Pilrig House Cl LEITH EH6 .... 18 A4
Pilrig St LEITH EH6 .... 18 A5
Pilton Av GNTN EH5 .... 16 C5
Pilton Crs GNTN EH5 .... 16 D5
Pilton Dr GNTN EH5 .... 16 C5
Pilton Dr North GNTN EH5 .... 16 C5
Pilton Gdns GNTN EH5 .... 16 C5
Pilton Loan GNTN EH5 .... 16 C5
Pilton Pk GNTN EH5 .... 16 C5
Pilton Pl GNTN EH5 .... 16 C5
Pine Ct PNCK EH26 .... 72 B5
Pinewood Gdns EDNW EH4 .... 15 F2
Pinewood Pl DLKTH EH22 .... 77 G1
Pinewood Rd DLKTH EH22 .... 77 G1
Pinewood Vw DLKTH EH22 .... 77 G1
Pinkhill MRYFD/COR EH12 .... 25 F5

Pinkie Av MUS EH21 .... 48 C1
Pinkie Dr MUS EH21 .... 48 C1
Pinkie Hill Crs MUS EH21 .... 48 D1
Pinkie Pl MUS EH21 .... 48 C1
Pinkie Rd MUS EH21 .... 48 C1
Pinkie Ter MUS EH21 .... 48 C1
Pipe La PBLO/DUD EH15 .... 30 A2
Pipe St PBLO/DUD EH15 .... 30 A2
Pirniefield Bank LEITH EH6 .... 19 E4
Pirniefield Gdns LEITH EH6 .... 19 E4
Pirniefield Pl LEITH EH6 .... 19 E4
Pirniefield Ter LEITH EH6 .... 19 E4
Pirrie St LEITH EH6 .... 18 B4
Pitsligo Rd
  MCH/MOR/FMHD EH10 .... 43 F2
Pitt St LEITH EH6 .... 18 A3
Pittville St PBLO/DUD EH15 .... 30 B3
Pittville Street La
  PBLO/DUD EH15 .... 30 B3
Pleasance HLYRPK/NF EH8 .... 3 H5
Plewlandcroft QFRY EH30 .... 6 C4
Plewlands Av
  MCH/MOR/FMHD EH10 .... 42 D4
Plewlands Gdns
  MCH/MOR/FMHD EH10 .... 42 D4
Plewlands Pl QFRY EH30 .... 6 C5
Plewlands Ter
  MCH/MOR/FMHD EH10 .... 42 D4
Pleydell Pl LIB/NID EH16 .... 59 H1
Polson Gdns TRNT EH33 .... 50 D2
Polton Avenue Rd BNYRC EH19 ... 74 D1
Polton Bank LSWD EH18 .... 74 C1
Polton Bank Ter LSWD EH18 .... 74 C1
Polton Cottages LSWD EH18 .... 74 B1
Polton Ct BNYRC EH19 .... 75 F4
Polton Gdns LSWD EH18 .... 74 D1
Polton Rd LNHD EH20 .... 66 A5
  LSWD EH18 .... 74 D1
Polton Rd West BNYRC EH19 ...... 74 C1
Polton St BNYRC EH19 .... 75 F4
Polton V LNHD EH20 .... 66 A5
Polwarth Crs CPS/PPNS EH32 ..... 34 C4
  DAL/STH/STNH EH11 .... 43 E1
Polwarth Gdns
  DAL/STH/STNH EH11 .... 42 D1
Polwarth Gv
  DAL/STH/STNH EH11 .... 42 D2
Polwarth Pk
  DAL/STH/STNH EH11 .... 42 D1
Polwarth Pl
  DAL/STH/STNH EH11 .... 42 D1
Polwarth Ter CPS/PPNS EH32 ..... 34 C4
  DAL/STH/STNH EH11 .... 42 C3
Pomathorn Bank PNCK EH26 ...... 70 D5
Ponton St EDNT/CEDW EH3 .... 2 A7
Poplar La LEITH EH6 .... 18 C5
Poplar Pk CPS/PPNS EH32 .... 35 F2
Poplar St DLKTH EH22 .... 77 C1
Poplar Ter BNYRC EH19 .... 75 F1
Porterfield Rd EDNW EH4 .... 16 C5
Portgower Pl EDNW EH4 .... 27 E2
Port Hamilton EDNT/CEDW EH3 ... 2 A7
Port Long Wynd DFLS KY11 .... 4 D3
Portland Gdns LEITH EH6 .... 18 A2
Portland St LEITH EH6 .... 18 A2
Portobello High St
  PBLO/DUD EH15 .... 30 A2
Portobello Rd RSTRC EH7 .... 29 C2
Post Office La DFLS KY11 .... 4 B4
Potterrow HLYRPK/NF EH8 .... 3 F6
The Pottery CPS/PPNS EH32 .... 34 A4
Povert Rd GORBR EH23 .... 76 B5
Powderhall Brae RSTRC EH7 .... 17 H4
Powderhall Rigg RSTRC EH7 .... 17 H4
Powderhall Rd RSTRC EH7 .... 17 H5
Powdermill Brae GORBR EH23 .... 79 E4
Preston Av CPS/PPNS EH32 .... 34 D5
Preston Ct CPS/PPNS EH32 .... 34 B5
Preston Crs CPS/PPNS EH32 ...... 34 C5
Preston Rd CPS/PPNS EH32 .... 34 D5
Prestonfield Av LIB/NID EH16 ...... 44 C2
Prestonfield Bank
  LIB/NID EH16 .... 44 C2
Prestonfield Crs LIB/NID EH16 .... 44 C3
Prestonfield Gdns
  LIB/NID EH16 .... 44 C2
Prestonfield Rd LIB/NID EH16 ..... 44 C2
Prestonfield Ter LIB/NID EH16 ..... 44 C2
Prestongrange Rd
  CPS/PPNS EH32 .... 33 H2
Prestongrange Ter
  CPS/PPNS EH32 .... 34 A5
Prestonhall Crs RSWL EH24 .... 74 B5
Prestonhall Rd RSWL EH24 .... 74 B5
Preston Rd CPS/PPNS EH32 .... 34 B5
Preston St RSWL EH24 .... 74 B5
Preston Ter CPS/PPNS EH32 ...... 34 D4
  DFLS KY11 .... 5 E1
Priestfield Av LIB/NID EH16 .... 44 D2
Priestfield Crs LIB/NID EH16 .... 44 D2
Priestfield Gdns LIB/NID EH16 .... 44 D2
Priestfield Gv LIB/NID EH16 .... 44 C1
Priestfield Rd LIB/NID EH16 .... 44 C1
Priestfield Rd North
  LIB/NID EH16 .... 44 C1
Priesthill Pl LIB/NID EH16 .... 59 H5
Priesthill St LIB/NID EH16 .... 59 H5
Primrose Bank Rd GNTN EH5 ...... 17 F2
Primrose Crs DLKTH EH22 .... 69 E2
Primrose Dr QFRY EH30 .... 13 F5
Primrose Gdns QFRY EH30 .... 6 B5
Primrose St LEITH EH6 .... 18 C4
Primrose Ter DLKTH EH22 .... 69 E2
Prince Regent St LEITH EH6 .... 18 A2
Princes St EDOT EH1 .... 2 A4
Priory Gv QFRY EH30 .... 6 C5
Promenade MUS EH21 .... 31 H4
  PBLO/DUD EH15 .... 19 H5
  PBLO/DUD EH15 .... 30 A1
Prospect Bank Crs LEITH EH6 ..... 18 D4
Prospect Bank Gdns LEITH EH6 .. 18 D5
Prospect Bank Gv LEITH EH6 ...... 19 E4
Prospect Bank Pl LEITH EH6 .... 19 E5
Prospect Bank Rd LEITH EH6 ...... 18 D4
Prospect Bank Ter LEITH EH6 ..... 19 E4
Provost Haugh BAL/CUR EH14 .... 55 F4
Provost Milne Gv QFRY EH30 ...... 6 D5
Pryde Av BNYRC EH19 .... 67 E5
Pryde Ter BNYRC EH19 .... 67 E5
Pypers Wynd CPS/PPNS EH32 .... 34 C3

Q

The Quadrant PNCK EH26 .... 70 D3
Quality St EDNW EH4 .... 15 F5
Quality Street La EDNW EH4 .... 15 F5
Quarry Bank BAL/CUR EH14 .... 55 G1
Quarrybank Cl BAL/CUR EH14 ..... 40 C5
Quarrybank Ct BAL/CUR EH14 .... 40 C5
Quarrybank End
  BAL/CUR EH14 .... 55 G1
Quarry Cl HLYRPK/NF EH8 .... 3 G7
Quarryfoot Gdns BNYRC EH19 .... 67 G5
Quarryfoot Gn BNYRC EH19 .... 67 G5
Quarryfoot Pl BNYRC EH19 .... 67 F5
Quayside St LEITH EH6 .... 18 B3
Queen Anne Dr RATHO EH28 ...... 37 F1
Queen Charlotte St LEITH EH6 .... 18 C3
Queen Margaret Cl
  MCH/MOR/FMHD EH10 .... 58 D5
Queen Margaret Dr QFRY EH30 ... 6 D5
Queen Margaret's Pl DFLS KY11 .. 4 D4
Queen Margaret University Wy
  MUS EH21 .... 49 E4
Queen's Av EDNW EH4 .... 25 H1
Queen's Av South EDNW EH4 ...... 26 A1
Queen's Bay Crs
  PBLO/DUD EH15 .... 30 D4
Queen's Crs NWGTN EH9 .... 44 B2
Queen's Dr HLYRPK/NF EH8 .... 3 J7
Queensferry Rd EDNW EH4 .... 24 B1
  KLSTN EH29 .... 11 E5
Queensferry St
  EDNT/CEDW EH3 .... 27 E3
Queensferry Ter EDNW EH4 .... 26 C2
Queen's Gdns EDNW EH4 .... 26 A1
Queen's Park Av
  HLYRPK/NF EH8 .... 28 D2
Queen's Rd EDNW EH4 .... 26 A1
Queen Street Gdns East
  EDNT/CEDW EH3 .... 2 D1
Queen Street Gdns West
  EDNT/CEDW EH3 .... 2 D1
Queensway PNCK EH26 .... 70 D4
The Quilts LEITH EH6 .... 18 A3

R

Raeburn Ms EDNW EH4 .... 27 E1
Raeburn Pl EDNW EH4 .... 27 E1
Raeburn St EDNW EH4 .... 27 E1
Raes Gdns BNYRC EH19 .... 67 G4
Ramillies Ct PNCK EH26 .... 71 E1
Ramsay Gdn EDOT EH1 .... 2 D4
Ramsay La EDOT EH1 .... 2 D4
Ramsay Pl PBLO/DUD EH15 .... 30 A3
Ramsay Ter LSWD EH18 .... 74 D1
Ramsey Pl PNCK EH26 .... 70 A3
Randolph Crs EDNT/CEDW EH3 ... 27 E3
Randolph La EDNT/CEDW EH3 .... 2 A5
Randolph Pl EDNT/CEDW EH3 .... 2 A5
Rankeillor St HLYRPK/NF EH8 ..... 3 H7
Rankin Av NWGTN EH9 .... 44 A4
Rankin Dr NWGTN EH9 .... 44 A4
Rankin Rd NWGTN EH9 .... 44 A4
Rannoch Gv EDNW EH4 .... 24 D2
Rannoch Pl EDNW EH4 .... 24 D2
Rannoch Rd EDNW EH4 .... 24 D2
Rannoch Ter EDNW EH4 .... 24 D2
Ransome Gdns EDNW EH4 .... 24 D2
Ratcliffe Ter NWGTN EH9 .... 44 A1
Rathbone Pl PBLO/DUD EH15 ..... 30 B2
Ratho Park Rd RATHO EH28 .... 38 A4
Rattray Dr
  MCH/MOR/FMHD EH10 .... 57 G1
Rattray Gv
  MCH/MOR/FMHD EH10 .... 57 G1
Rattray Loan
  MCH/MOR/FMHD EH10 .... 57 G1
Rattray Wy
  MCH/MOR/FMHD EH10 .... 57 H1
Ravelrig Dr BAL/CUR EH14 .... 52 D2
Ravelrig Gait BAL/CUR EH14 ...... 52 D2
Ravelrig Pk BAL/CUR EH14 .... 52 D1
Ravelrig Rd BAL/CUR EH14 .... 52 D1
Ravelrig Wynd BAL/CUR EH14 ..... 52 D2
Ravelston Dykes EDNW EH4 .... 26 B3
Ravelston Dykes La EDNW EH4 ... 25 G3
Ravelston Gdns EDNW EH4 .... 26 A3
Ravelston House Loan
  EDNW EH4 .... 25 H2
Ravelston House Pk EDNW EH4 ... 26 A3
Ravelston House Rd
  EDNW EH4 .... 26 A3
Ravelston Pk EDNW EH4 .... 26 C3
Ravelston Pl EDNW EH4 .... 26 D2
Ravelsykes Rd PNCK EH26 .... 70 A4
Ravendean Gdns PNCK EH26 ..... 70 A4
Ravenscroft Gdns
  GIL/MOR EH17 .... 60 C4
Ravenscroft Pl GIL/MOR EH17 .... 60 C4
Ravenscroft St GIL/MOR EH17 .... 60 C4
Ravenshaugh Rd MUS EH21 .... 33 E5
Ravenswood Av LIB/NID EH16 ..... 45 E5
Redbraes Gv RSTRC EH7 .... 17 H4
Redbraes Pl RSTRC EH7 .... 17 H4
Redburn Rd CPS/PPNS EH32 ...... 34 A4
Redburn Rd North
  CPS/PPNS EH32 .... 34 A4
Redcroft St EDNT/CEDW EH3 ..... 56 D5
Redford Av COLIN EH13 .... 56 D3
Redford Bank COLIN EH13 .... 57 E3
Redford Crs COLIN EH13 .... 57 E3
Redford Dr COLIN EH13 .... 56 D3
Redford Gdns COLIN EH13 .... 57 E3
Redford Gv COLIN EH13 .... 57 F3
Redford Loan COLIN EH13 .... 57 E3
Redford Neuk COLIN EH13 .... 57 E3
Redford Pl COLIN EH13 .... 57 F2
Redford Rd COLIN EH13 .... 57 F2

Redford Rd COLIN EH13 .... 57 E3
Redford Ter COLIN EH13 .... 57 E3
Redford Wk COLIN EH13 .... 57 E3
Red Fox Crs PNCK EH26 .... 70 C5
Redgauntlet Ter LIB/NID EH16 ..... 44 D5
Redhall Av BAL/CUR EH14 .... 41 H5
Redhall Bank Rd BAL/CUR EH14 .. 41 H5
Redhall Crs BAL/CUR EH14 .... 41 G4
Redhall Dr BAL/CUR EH14 .... 41 G4
Redhall Gdns BAL/CUR EH14 ...... 41 G4
Redhall Gv BAL/CUR EH14 .... 41 G4
Redhall House Dr
  BAL/CUR EH14 .... 42 A5
Redhall Pl BAL/CUR EH14 .... 41 G4
Redhall Rd BAL/CUR EH14 .... 41 G4
Redhall Vw BAL/CUR EH14 .... 41 H5
Redheughs Av
  MRYFD/COR EH12 .... 40 A2
Redheughs Rigg
  MRYFD/COR EH12 .... 40 A1
Redwood Gv DLKTH EH22 .... 76 B1
Redwood Wk DLKTH EH22 .... 76 C2
Reed Dr DLKTH EH22 .... 68 D5
Regent Pl RSTRC EH7 .... 18 B3
Regent St PBLO/DUD EH15 .... 30 B3
Regent Street La
  PBLO/DUD EH15 .... 30 B3
Regent Ter RSTRC EH7 .... 3 J2
Regent Terrace Ms RSTRC EH7 ... 3 J2
Regis Ct EDNW EH4 .... 14 B4
Register Pl CED/PRST EH2 .... 2 D2
Reid St HLYRPK/NF EH8 .... 3 J5
Reid Ter EDNT/CEDW EH3 .... 27 E1
Relugas Gdns NWGTN EH9 .... 44 A3
Relugas Pl NWGTN EH9 .... 44 A3
Relugas Rd NWGTN EH9 .... 44 A3
Rennie's Isle LEITH EH6 .... 18 B2
Research Avenue 1
  BAL/CUR EH14 .... 54 D1
Research Avenue 2
  BAL/CUR EH14 .... 54 D1
Research Av North
  BAL/CUR EH14 .... 54 C1
Research Av South
  BAL/CUR EH14 .... 54 C1
Restalrig Av RSTRC EH7 .... 29 E2
Restalrig Circ RSTRC EH7 .... 18 D5
Restalrig Gdns RSTRC EH7 .... 29 E1
Restalrig Pk RSTRC EH7 .... 29 E1
Restalrig Rd LEITH EH6 .... 18 C4
Restalrig Rd South RSTRC EH7 ... 29 E2
Restalrig Sq RSTRC EH7 .... 19 E5
Restalrig Ter LEITH EH6 .... 18 C4
Riccarton Av BAL/CUR EH14 .... 54 D4
Riccarton Crs BAL/CUR EH14 ..... 55 E5
Riccarton Gv BAL/CUR EH14 ...... 54 D4
Riccarton St BAL/CUR EH14 .... 55 E4
Riccarton Mains Rd
  BAL/CUR EH14 .... 54 D1
Richmond La HLYRPK/NF EH8 ..... 3 G6
Richmond Pl HLYRPK/NF EH8 ..... 3 G5
Riding Pk EDNW EH4 .... 14 B4
Riego St EDNT/CEDW EH3 .... 2 B6
Riggonhead Ct TRNT EH33 .... 51 F1
Riggonhead Gdns TRNT EH33 .... 51 F1
Rigley Ter CPS/PPNS EH32 .... 34 A5
Rillbank Crs NWGTN EH9 .... 43 H1
Rillbank Ter NWGTN EH9 .... 43 H1
Ringwood Pl LIB/NID EH16 .... 59 H1
Rintoul Pl EDNT/CEDW EH3 .... 27 F1
Riselaw Crs
  MCH/MOR/FMHD EH10 .... 58 A2
Riselaw Pl
  MCH/MOR/FMHD EH10 .... 58 A1
Riselaw Rd
  MCH/MOR/FMHD EH10 .... 58 A1
Riselaw Ter
  MCH/MOR/FMHD EH10 .... 58 A1
Ritchie Pl DAL/STH/STNH EH11 ... 42 D1
River Gore Gv GORBR EH23 .... 79 E2
River Gore Rd GORBR EH23 .... 79 E2
River Gore Vw GORBR EH23 .... 79 E2
Riversdale Crs
  MRYFD/COR EH12 .... 26 A4
Riversdale Gv
  MRYFD/COR EH12 .... 26 A4
Riversdale Rd
  MRYFD/COR EH12 .... 25 H4
Riverside RATHO EH28 .... 20 D5
Riverside Gdns MUS EH21 .... 47 H1
Riverside Rd QFRY EH30 .... 13 G4
Roanshead Rd DLKTH EH22 .... 69 E4
Robb's Loan BAL/CUR EH14 .... 42 A2
Robb's Loan Gv BAL/CUR EH14 .. 42 A2
Robert Burns Dr LIB/NID EH16 .... 44 C5
Robert Burns Ms DLKTH EH22 .... 68 F4
Robert Smillie Av DLKTH EH22 .... 77 G2
Robertson Av CPS/PPNS EH32 .... 34 B1
  DAL/STH/STNH EH11 .... 42 B1
  TRNT EH33 .... 51 F2
Robertson Dr TRNT EH33 .... 51 F1
Robertsons Bank GORBR EH23 ... 79 E1
Robertson's Cl DLKTH EH22 .... 68 C1
  EDOT EH1 .... 3 G5
Robertson's Ct HLYRPK/NF EH8 .. 3 J3
Rocheid Pk EDNW EH4 .... 16 C4
Rochester Ter
  MCH/MOR/FMHD EH10 .... 43 E2
Rockville Ter LSWD EH18 .... 67 F4
Roddinglaw Rd
  MRYFD/COR EH12 .... 39 E3
Rodney St EDNT/CEDW EH3 .... 27 G1
Roman Dr DLKTH EH22 .... 69 F2
Roman St DLKTH EH22 .... 69 F2
Roman Vw DLKTH EH22 .... 69 F2
Romero Pl LIB/NID EH16 .... 44 B1
Ronaldson's Wharf LEITH EH6 ..... 18 B3
Rosabelle Rd ROSLIN EH25 .... 73 F3
Rose Av BNYRC EH19 .... 75 H1
Rosebank Gv GNTN EH5 .... 17 E3
Rosebank Rd GNTN EH5 .... 17 E3
Rosebery Av QFRY EH30 .... 13 G4
Rosebery Crs GORBR EH23 .... 79 E4
  MRYFD/COR EH12 .... 26 D4
Rosebery Crescent La
  MRYFD/COR EH12 .... 26 D4

Roseburn Av
MRYFD/COR EH12 ....26 B4
Roseburn Crs
MRYFD/COR EH12 ....26 B4
Roseburn Dr MRYFD/COR EH12 ..26 B4
Roseburn Gdns
MRYFD/COR EH12 ....26 B4
Roseburn Maltings
MRYFD/COR EH12 ....26 C4
Roseburn Pl MRYFD/COR EH12 ..26 B5
Roseburn Ter
MRYFD/COR EH12 ....26 B4
Rose Cottages BNYRG EH19 ....75 H1
Rosefield Av PBLO/DUD EH15 ..30 A3
Rosefield Avenue La
PBLO/DUD EH15 ....30 A3
Rosefield La PBLO/DUD EH15 ..30 A3
Rosefield Pl PBLO/DUD EH15 ..30 A3
Rosefield St PBLO/DUD EH15 ..30 A3
Rose Gdns BNYRG EH19 ....75 H1
Rose Gv BNYRG EH19 ....75 H1
Rose La QFRY EH30 ....6 C4
Roseneath Pl NWGTN EH9 ......43 H1
Roseneath Ter NWGTN EH9 ......43 H1
Rose Neuk BNYRG EH19 ....75 H1
Rose Pk BNYRG EH19 ....75 H1
CNTN EH5 ....17 F3
Rose Pth BNYRG EH19 ....75 H1
Rose Pl BNYRG EH19 ....75 H1
Rose St CED/PRST EH2 ....2 D3
Rose Street North La
CED/PRST EH2 ....2 B3
Rose Street South La
CED/PRST EH2 ....2 B3
Rose Ter BNYRG EH19 ....75 H1
Rosevale Pl LEITH EH6 ....18 D4
Rosevale Ter LEITH EH6 ......18 C4
Roseville Gdns CNTN EH5 ......17 G2
Rose Wy BNYRG EH19 ....75 H1
Rosewell Rd RSWL EH24 ....74 D3
Ross Crs TRNT EH33 ....51 F3
Ross Gdns NWGTN EH9 ....44 B3
Rossie Pl RSTRC EH7 ....18 A5
Rosslyn Crs LEITH EH6 ....18 A5
Ross Pl DLKTH EH22 ....76 D1
NWGTN EH9 ....44 B3
Ross Rd NWGTN EH9 ....44 B4
Rothesay Ms EDNT/CEDW EH3 ..26 D5
Rothesay Pl EDNT/CEDW EH3 ..26 D5
MUS EH21 ....48 B1
Rothesay Ter EDNT/CEDW EH3 ..26 D3
Roull Rd MRYFD/COR EH12 ....40 D1
Rowan Gdns BNYRG EH19 ......75 F1
Rowanhill Cl CPS/PPNS EH32 ..35 F2
Rowanhill Dr CPS/PPNS EH32 ..35 F2
Rowanhill Pk CPS/PPNS EH32 ..35 F2
Rowanhill Wy CPS/PPNS EH32 ..35 F2
Rowan Tree Av BAL/CUR EH14 ..54 C5
Rowan Tree Rd DLKTH EH22 ....69 C5
Roxburgh Pl HLYRPK/NF EH8 ..3 G5
Roxburgh St HLYRPK/NF EH8 ..3 G5
Royal Circ EDNT/CEDW EH3 ..2 B1
Royal Ct PNCK EH26 ....70 B2
Royal Crs EDNT/CEDW EH3 ..2 B1
Royal Park Ter HLYRPK/NF EH8 ..28 D2
Royal Ter EDNT/CEDW EH7 ....3 J1
Royston Mains Av CNTN EH5 ..16 C2
Royston Mains Crescent
CNTN EH5 ....16 B2
Royston Mains Gdn CNTN EH5 ..16 B2
Royston Mains Gn CNTN EH5 ..16 B2
Royston Mains Pl CNTN EH5 ..16 B2
Royston Mains Rd CNTN EH5 ..16 B2
Royston Mains St CNTN EH5 ..16 B2
Royston Ter EDNT/CEDW EH3 ..17 F4
Rullion Green Av PNCK EH26 ..70 B2
Rullion Green Crs PNCK EH26 ..70 B2
Rullion Green Gv PNCK EH26 ..70 B2
Rullion Rd PNCK EH26 ....70 B3
Russell Gdns MRYFD/COR EH12 ..26 B5
Russell Pl CNTN EH5 ....17 F2
Russell Rd LEITH EH11 ....26 C5
Rutherford Dr LIB/NID EH16 ..44 D5
Ruthven Pl LIB/NID EH16 ......44 D5
Rutland Court La
EDNT/CEDW EH3 ....2 A5
Rutland Sq EDOT EH1 ....2 A4
Rutland St EDOT EH1 ....2 A4
Ryehill Av LEITH EH6 ....18 D4
Ryehill Gdns LEITH EH6 ......18 D4
Ryehill Gv LEITH EH6 ....18 D5
Ryehill Pl LEITH EH6 ....18 D4
Ryehill Ter LEITH EH6 ......18 D4

S

Saddletree Loan LIB/NID EH16 ..45 E4
St Alban's Rd NWGTN EH9 ......44 A3
St Andrew Pl LEITH EH6 ....18 C4
St Andrew Sq CED/PRST EH2 ..2 E2
St Andrew St DLKTH EH22 ......68 C1
St Ann's Av LSWD EH18 ....74 C1
St Anthony La LEITH EH6 ......18 B3
St Bernard's Crs EDNW EH4 ..27 E2
St Bernard's Rw EDNW EH4 ....27 F1
St Catherine's Mnr
MUS EH21 ....25 C5
St Catherine's Pl NWGTN EH9 ..44 A1
St Clair Av LEITH EH6 ....18 B5
St Clair Crs ROSLIN EH25 ....73 H3
St Clair Pl LEITH EH6 ....18 C5
St Clair Rd LEITH EH6 ....18 C5
St Clair St LEITH EH6 ....18 C5
St Clair Ter
MCH/MOR/FMHD EH10 ....42 D4
St Clements Gdns North
MUS EH21 ....49 F2
St Clements Gdns
MUS EH21 ....49 F2
St Clements Ter MUS EH21 ....49 F2
St Colme St EDNT/CEDW EH3 ..2 A3
St David's Pl EDNT/CEDW EH3 ..27 E4
St David's Ter EDNT/CEDW EH3 ..27 E4

St Fillan's Ter
MCH/MOR/FMHD EH10 ....42 D4
St Germains Cnr TRNT EH33 ..51 F1
St Giles' St EDOT EH1 ....2 E4
St James' Pl EDOT EH1 ....3 F1
St James' Gdns PNCK EH26 ....70 C5
St James Sq EDOT EH1 ....3 F1
St James's Vw PNCK EH26 ....70 C5
St John's Av MRYFD/COR EH12 ..25 E5
St John's Crs MRYFD/COR EH12 ..25 F5
St John's Hl HLYRPK/NF EH8 ..3 H5
St John's Rd MRYFD/COR EH12 ..24 D5
St John's Ter MRYFD/COR EH12 ..25 E5
St John St HLYRPK/NF EH8 ....3 H4
St Katharine's Brae
LIB/NID EH16 ....59 G3
St Katharine's Crs LIB/NID EH16 ..59 G3
St Katharine's Loan
LIB/NID EH16 ....59 H4
St Katherine's Brae
LIB/NID EH16 ....59 G3
St Kentigern Rd PNCK EH26 ..70 A3
St Leonard's Bank
HLYRPK/NF EH8 ....3 J7
St Leonard's Hl HLYRPK/NF EH8 ..3 H7
St Leonard's La HLYRPK/NF EH8 ..3 H7
St Leonard's St HLYRPK/NF EH8 ..3 H7
St Margaret's Pl NWGTN EH9 ..43 G2
St Margaret's Rd
MCH/MOR/FMHD EH10 ....43 F2
St Mark's La PBLO/DUD EH15 ..30 B3
St Mark's Pl PBLO/DUD EH15 ..30 B3
St Mary's Pl PBLO/DUD EH15 ..30 C4
St Mary's Place La
PBLO/DUD EH15 ....30 C3
St Mary's St EDOT EH1 ....3 G4
St Michael's Av MUS EH21 ....48 A1
St Mungo's Vw PNCK EH26 ....70 D4
St Ninian's Dr
MRYFD/COR EH12 ....24 D4
St Ninian's Rd
MRYFD/COR EH12 ....24 D4
St Ninian's Rw EDOT EH1 ....3 F2
St Ninian's Ter
MCH/MOR/FMHD EH10 ....42 D4
St Ninians Wy MUS EH21 ......33 E5
St Patrick Sq HLYRPK/NF EH8 ..3 G7
St Ronan's Ter
MCH/MOR/FMHD EH10 ....43 E4
St Stephen Pl EDNT/CEDW EH3 ..27 F1
St Stephen St EDNT/CEDW EH3 ..27 F1
St Teresa Pl
MCH/MOR/FMHD EH10 ....42 D2
St Thomas Rd NWGTN EH9 ....43 H2
St Triduana's Rest RSTRC EH7 ..29 E1
St Vincent St EDNT/CEDW EH3 ..2 B1
Salamanca Crs PNCK EH26 ....71 E1
Salamander Pl LEITH EH6 ....18 D3
Salamander St LEITH EH6 ....18 D3
Salamander Yards LEITH EH6 ..19 E4
Salisbury Pl NWGTN EH9 ......44 A1
Salisbury Rd LIB/NID EH16 ..44 B1
Salisbury Vw DLKTH EH22 ......77 F1
Salters' Gv DLKTH EH22 ......63 E5
Salters Rd DLKTH EH22 ......69 E1
Saltire St LEITH EH6 ....16 B1
Salt Preston Pl
CPS/PPNS EH32 ....34 B3
Salvesen Crs EDNW EH4 ......15 G3
Salvesen Gdns EDNW EH4 ....15 H3
Samoa Ter PNCK EH26 ....71 E1
Sanderson's Gv TRNT EH33 ..51 F1
Sanderson's Wynd TRNT EH33 ..51 F1
Sandford Gdns
PBLO/DUD EH15 ....30 A3
Sand Port LEITH EH6 ....18 C2
Sandport Pl LEITH EH6 ......18 B2
Sandport St LEITH EH6 ......18 B2
Sandport Wy LEITH EH6 ......18 B2
Sauchiebank
DAL/STH/STNH EH11 ....26 C5
The Saughs DLKTH EH22 ......76 C3
Saughton Av
DAL/STH/STNH EH11 ....42 A2
Saughton Crs
MRYFD/COR EH12 ....25 H5
Saughton Gdns
MRYFD/COR EH12 ....25 H5
Saughton Gv
MRYFD/COR EH12 ....25 H5
Saughtonhall Av
MRYFD/COR EH12 ....25 H5
Saughtonhall Av West
MRYFD/COR EH12 ....25 H5
Saughtonhall Circ
MRYFD/COR EH12 ....26 A5
Saughtonhall Crs
MRYFD/COR EH12 ....25 H5
Saughtonhall Dr
MRYFD/COR EH12 ....25 H5
Saughtonhall Gdns
MRYFD/COR EH12 ....26 A5
Saughtonhall Gv
MRYFD/COR EH12 ....26 A5
Saughtonhall Pl
MRYFD/COR EH12 ....25 H5
Saughtonhall Ter
MRYFD/COR EH12 ....26 A5
Saughton Loan
MRYFD/COR EH12 ....25 H5
Saughton Mains Av
DAL/STH/STNH EH11 ....41 F2
Saughton Mains Bank
DAL/STH/STNH EH11 ....41 G2
Saughton Mains Dr
DAL/STH/STNH EH11 ....41 F3
Saughton Mains Gdns
DAL/STH/STNH EH11 ....41 F3
Saughton Mains Gv
DAL/STH/STNH EH11 ....41 G3
Saughton Mains Loan
DAL/STH/STNH EH11 ....41 F3
Saughton Mains Pk
DAL/STH/STNH EH11 ....41 F2
Saughton Mains Pl
DAL/STH/STNH EH11 ....41 F2
Saughton Mains St
DAL/STH/STNH EH11 ....41 F2

Saughton Mains Ter
DAL/STH/STNH EH11 ....41 F2
Saughton Pk MRYFD/COR EH12 ..25 H5
Saughton Rd
DAL/STH/STNH EH11 ....41 F2
Saughton Rd North
MRYFD/COR EH12 ....41 E2
Saunders St EDNT/CEDW EH3 ..2 A1
Savile Pl NWGTN EH9 ....44 B3
Savile Ter NWGTN EH9 ....44 B3
Saxe Coburg St
EDNT/CEDW EH3 ....27 F1
Scarlett Pk MUS EH21 ....49 E1
Schaw Rd CPS/PPNS EH32 ....34 D4
School Brae EDNW EH4 ....14 B3
School La
LSWD EH18 ....67 E3
School Gn LSWD EH18 ....67 E3
School La CPS/PPNS EH32 ....35 E1
QFRY EH30 ....6 C4
Schoolyard Ct ROSLIN EH25 ..73 H3
Sciennes NWGTN EH9 ....44 A1
Sciennes Gdns NWGTN EH9 ..44 A1
Sciennes House Pl NWGTN EH9 ..44 A1
Sciennes Pl NWGTN EH9 ......44 A1
Sciennes Rd NWGTN EH9 ......43 H1
Scollon Av BNYRG EH19 ......67 G4
Scone Gdns HLYRPK/NF EH8 ..29 E2
Scotland St EDNT/CEDW EH3 ..27 G1
Scotstoun Av QFRY EH30 ....11 G1
Scotstoun Gn QFRY EH30 ......6 C5
Scotstoun Interchange
QFRY EH30 ....11 H2
Scotstoun Pk QFRY EH30 ......11 G1
Scott Rd PNCK EH26 ....70 C2
Seafield Av LEITH EH6 ....19 E4
Seafield Moor Rd
MCH/MOR/FMHD EH10 ....64 C3
Seafield Pl LEITH EH6 ....19 E4
Seafield Rd LEITH EH6 ....19 E4
Seafield Rd East
PBLO/DUD EH15 ....19 H5
Seafield St LEITH EH6 ......19 E4
Seaforth Dr EDNW EH4 ....26 A1
Seaforth Ter BNYRG EH19 ....75 H4
Seaport St LEITH EH6 ....18 C3
Seaview Crs PBLO/DUD EH15 ..30 C4
Second Gait BAL/CUR EH14 ..54 C1
Second St DLKTH EH22 ......76 D3
Semple St EDNT/CEDW EH3 ..2 A6
Seton Ct CPS/PPNS EH32 ....35 G2
Seton Pl NWGTN EH9 ....44 A1
Seton Vw CPS/PPNS EH32 ....35 G2
Seton Wynd CPS/PPNS EH32 ..35 G1
Seventh St DLKTH EH22 ......76 D2
Shadepark Crs DLKTH EH22 ..62 D5
Shadepark Dr DLKTH EH22 ..62 D5
Shadepark Gdns DLKTH EH22 ..62 D5
Shaftesbury Pk
DAL/STH/STNH EH11 ....42 C2
Shandon Crs
DAL/STH/STNH EH11 ....42 C2
Shandon Pl
DAL/STH/STNH EH11 ....42 C2
Shandon Rd
DAL/STH/STNH EH11 ....42 C2
Shandon St
DAL/STH/STNH EH11 ....42 C2
Shandon Ter
DAL/STH/STNH EH11 ....42 C2
Shandwick Pl EDNT/CEDW EH3 ..27 E4
Shank Br CORBR EH23 ....78 D3
Shaw Pl DLKTH EH22 ....69 F4
Shaws Ct PNCK EH26 ....72 B5
Shaws Pl PNCK EH26 ....72 B5
Sheriff Brae LEITH EH6 ......18 B3
Sheriffhall Rdt DLKTH EH22 ..77 H4
Sheriff Pk LEITH EH6 ....18 B3
Sherwood Ct BNYRG EH19 ....75 C1
Sherwood Crs BNYRG EH19 ..75 C1
Sherwood Dr BNYRG EH19 ....75 C1
Sherwood Gv BNYRG EH19 ....75 C1
Sherwood Loan BNYRG EH19 ..75 C1
Sherwood Pk BNYRG EH19 ....75 C1
Sherwood Pl BNYRG EH19 ....75 C1
Sherwood Ter BNYRG EH19 ..75 C1
Sherwood Vw BNYRG EH19 ..75 C1
Shore LEITH EH6 ....18 C2
Shore Pl LEITH EH6 ....18 C3
Shore Rd QFRY EH30 ....6 C5
Shorthope St MUS EH21 ......32 A5
Shrub Mt PBLO/DUD EH15 ....30 A2
Shrub Place La RSTRC EH7 ..28 A1
Sienna Gdns NWGTN EH9 ....44 A1
Sighthill Av
DAL/STH/STNH EH11 ....41 E4
Sighthill Bank
DAL/STH/STNH EH11 ....40 D4
Sighthill Ct
DAL/STH/STNH EH11 ....40 D4
Sighthill Crs
DAL/STH/STNH EH11 ....40 D5
Sighthill Dr
DAL/STH/STNH EH11 ....40 D5
Sighthill Gdns
DAL/STH/STNH EH11 ....40 D4
Sighthill Gn
DAL/STH/STNH EH11 ....40 D4
Sighthill Loan
DAL/STH/STNH EH11 ....40 C4
Sighthill Neuk
DAL/STH/STNH EH11 ....40 D4
Sighthill Pk
DAL/STH/STNH EH11 ....40 D4
Sighthill Pl
DAL/STH/STNH EH11 ....40 D4
Sighthill Rd
DAL/STH/STNH EH11 ....40 D5
Sighthill St
DAL/STH/STNH EH11 ....40 D5
Sighthill Ter
DAL/STH/STNH EH11 ....40 D4
Sighthill Vw
DAL/STH/STNH EH11 ....40 D4
Sighthill Wynd
DAL/STH/STNH EH11 ....40 D4
Silverburn Dr PNCK EH26 ....70 A3
Silverknowes Av EDNW EH4 ..15 E4

Silverknowes Bank EDNW EH4 ..15 F4
Silverknowes Brae EDNW EH4 ..15 F4
Silverknowes Ct EDNW EH4 ..15 F4
Silverknowes Crs EDNW EH4 ..15 F4
Silverknowes Dell EDNW EH4 ..15 F4
Silverknowes Dr EDNW EH4 ..15 F4
Silverknowes Eastway
EDNW EH4 ....15 G3
Silverknowes Gdns EDNW EH4 ..15 G4
Silverknowes Gn EDNW EH4 ..15 G4
Silverknowes Gv EDNW EH4 ..15 G4
Silverknowes Hl EDNW EH4 ..15 G4
Silverknowes Loan EDNW EH4 ..15 F4
Silverknowes Midway
EDNW EH4 ....15 G4
Silverknowes Neuk EDNW EH4 ..15 G4
Silverknowes Pkwy
EDNW EH4 ....15 F3
Silverknowes Pl EDNW EH4 ..15 F3
Silverknowes Rd EDNW EH4 ..15 F3
Silverknowes Rd East
EDNW EH4 ....15 G4
Silverknowes Rd South
EDNW EH4 ....15 F5
Silverknowes Southway
EDNW EH4 ....15 G4
Silverknowes Ter EDNW EH4 ..15 G4
Silverknowes Vw EDNW EH4 ..15 G4
Silvermills EDNT/CEDW EH3 ..27 F1
Simon Sq HLYRPK/NF EH8 ....3 G6
Sinclair Cl DAL/STH/STNH EH11 ..42 C2
Sinclair Gdns
DAL/STH/STNH EH11 ....42 B1
Sinclair Pl DAL/STH/STNH EH11 ..42 B1
Sir Harry Lauder Rd
PBLO/DUD EH15 ....29 H2
Sixth St DLKTH EH22 ....76 D2
Skeltiemuir Av BNYRG EH19 ..75 E1
Skeltiemuir Ct BNYRG EH19 ..75 F2
Skeltiemuir Gv BNYRG EH19 ..75 F2
Slaeside BAL/CUR EH14 ......53 E5
Slateford Gn BAL/CUR EH14 ..42 B1
Slateford Rd BAL/CUR EH14 ..42 B3
Sleigh Dr RSTRC EH7 ....28 D1
Sleigh Gdns RSTRC EH7 ......29 E1
Sloan St LEITH EH6 ....18 A5
Smithfield St
DAL/STH/STNH EH11 ....42 B1
Smith's Pl LEITH EH6 ....18 B4
Smithy Green Av DLKTH EH22 ..61 E2
Society Rd QFRY EH30 ....5 G2
Somerset Pl LEITH EH6 ......18 C4
Sommerville Gdns QFRY EH30 ..11 H1
South Barnton Av EDNW EH4 ..15 E4
South Beechwood
MRYFD/COR EH12 ....25 C5
South Br EDOT EH1 ....3 F5
South Charlotte St
CED/PRST EH2 ....2 B4
South Clerk St HLYRPK/NF EH8 ..28 A5
South College St
HLYRPK/NF EH8 ....3 F5
South Crs CPS/PPNS EH32 ..34 C4
South Doors CPS/PPNS EH32 ..35 E1
South East Circus Pl
EDNT/CEDW EH3 ....2 B1
South East Cumberland
Street La EDNT/CEDW EH3 ..27 G1
South Elixa Pl HLYRPK/NF EH8 ..29 F3
South Ettrick Rd
MCH/MOR/FMHD EH10 ....42 D2
Southfield Farm Gv
PBLO/DUD EH15 ....29 G4
Southfield Gdns East
PBLO/DUD EH15 ....29 H4
Southfield Gdns West
PBLO/DUD EH15 ....29 H4
Southfield Loan
PBLO/DUD EH15 ....29 H4
Southfield Pl PBLO/DUD EH15 ..30 A4
Southfield Rd East
PBLO/DUD EH15 ....29 H5
Southfield Rd West
PBLO/DUD EH15 ....29 G5
Southfield Ter PBLO/DUD EH15 ..29 H5
South Fort St LEITH EH6 ....18 A3
South Gillsland Rd
MCH/MOR/FMHD EH10 ....42 D2
South Grange Av
CPS/PPNS EH32 ....34 A5
South Gray's Cl EDOT EH1 ..3 G4
South Gray St NWGTN EH9 ..44 B2
South Groathill Av EDNW EH4 ..26 A3
South Gyle Access
MRYFD/COR EH12 ....40 C2
South Gyle Broadway
MRYFD/COR EH12 ....39 H1
South Gyle Crs
MRYFD/COR EH12 ....40 D2
South Gyle Crescent La
MRYFD/COR EH12 ....40 B2
South Gyle Gdns
MRYFD/COR EH12 ....40 C1
South Gyle Loan
MRYFD/COR EH12 ....40 B1
South Gyle Mains
MRYFD/COR EH12 ....40 C1
South Gyle Pk
MRYFD/COR EH12 ....40 B2
South Gyle Rd
MRYFD/COR EH12 ....40 C1
South Gyle Wynd
MRYFD/COR EH12 ....40 C2
Southhouse Av
GIL/MOR EH17 ....59 H4
Southhouse Broadway
GIL/MOR EH17 ....59 H5
Southhouse Crs GIL/MOR EH17 ..59 H5
Southhouse Dr GIL/MOR EH17 ..59 H4
Southhouse Gdns
GIL/MOR EH17 ....59 H5
Southhouse Gv GIL/MOR EH17 ..59 H5
Southhouse Loan
GIL/MOR EH17 ....59 H4
Southhouse Rd GIL/MOR EH17 ..59 H5
Southhouse Sq GIL/MOR EH17 ..59 H5
Southhouse Ter GIL/MOR EH17 ..60 A4
Southhouse Wk
GIL/MOR EH17 ....59 H4

South Lauder Rd NWGTN EH9 ..44 A2
South Laverockbank Av
CNTN EH5 ....17 G2
South Learmonth Av
EDNW EH4 ....26 D2
South Learmonth Gdns
EDNW EH4 ....26 D2
South Lorimer Pl
CPS/PPNS EH32 ....35 E2
South Maybury
MRYFD/COR EH12 ....24 A5
South Mellis Pk
HLYRPK/NF EH8 ....29 G3
South Morton St
PBLO/DUD EH15 ....30 C4
South Oswald Rd NWGTN EH9 ..43 H3
Southouse Cl GIL/MOR EH17 ..59 H5
Southouse Crossway
GIL/MOR EH17 ....59 H4
Southouse Pl GIL/MOR EH17 ..59 H4
South Oxford St
HLYRPK/NF EH8 ....44 B1
South Pk LEITH EH6 ....17 G2
South Parrotshot
PBLO/DUD EH15 ....46 A1
South St Andrew St
CED/PRST EH2 ....2 E3
South St David St
CED/PRST EH2 ....2 E3
South Scotstoun QFRY EH30 ..11 G1
South Seton Pk
CPS/PPNS EH32 ....35 F2
South Sloan St LEITH EH6 ..18 B5
South St Clair St LEITH EH6 ..68 C1
MUS EH21 ....31 H5
South Trinity Rd CNTN EH5 ..17 F3
South West Cumberland
Street La EDNT/CEDW EH3 ..27 G1
Spalding Crs DLKTH EH22 ....68 D1
Spa Pl PBLO/DUD EH15 ......30 A2
Speedwell Av DLKTH EH22 ....61 E1
Spencer Pl CNTN EH5 ....17 F2
Spence St NWGTN EH9 ......44 B1
Spey St RSTRC EH7 ....18 B5
Spey Street La RSTRC EH7 ..18 A5
Spey Ter RSTRC EH7 ....18 B5
Spier's Pl LEITH EH6 ....18 B5
The Spinney GIL/MOR EH17 ..60 B3
Spittal St EDNT/CEDW EH3 ..2 B6
Spottiswoode Rd NWGTN EH9 ..43 G1
Spottiswoode St NWGTN EH9 ..43 G1
Springfield LEITH EH6 ......18 B4
Springfield Crs QFRY EH30 ..6 A4
Springfield La LEITH EH6 ..18 B4
Springfield Lea QFRY EH30 ..6 A4
Springfield Pl CORBR EH23 ..79 F5
QFRY EH30 ....6 A4
ROSLIN EH25 ....73 H2
Springfield Rd QFRY EH30 ..6 A4
Springfield St LEITH EH6 ..18 B4
Springfield Ter QFRY EH30 ..6 A4
Springfield Vw QFRY EH30 ..6 A4
Spring Gdns HLYRPK/NF EH8 ..28 C2
Springvalley Gdns
MCH/MOR/FMHD EH10 ....43 E3
Springvalley Ter
MCH/MOR/FMHD EH10 ....43 E3
Springwell Pl
DAL/STH/STNH EH11 ....26 D5
Springwood Pk LIB/NID EH16 ..59 H1
Spylaw Av COLIN EH13 ......56 C2
Spylaw Bank Rd COLIN EH13 ..56 C2
Spylaw Pk COLIN EH13 ......56 C3
Spylaw Rd
MCH/MOR/FMHD EH10 ....42 D2
Spylaw St COLIN EH13 ......56 C3
The Square DLKTH EH22 ......61 F1
Stable La
MCH/MOR/FMHD EH10 ....43 E3
Stair Pk MRYFD/COR EH12 ..26 A4
TRNT EH33 ....50 D1
Standingstane Rd KLSTN EH29 ..12 A3
Stanedykehead LIB/NID EH16 ..59 H3
Stanhope Pl MRYFD/COR EH12 ..26 C4
Stanhope St MRYFD/COR EH12 ..26 C4
Stanley Rd LEITH EH6 ......17 G2
Stanley St PBLO/DUD EH15 ..30 A4
Stanwell St LEITH EH6 ......18 B4
Stapeley Av RSTRC EH7 ....29 G1
Starbank Rd CNTN EH5 ......17 G2
Station Loan BAL/CUR EH14 ..53 E1
Station Rd CPS/PPNS EH32 ..34 B5
DLKTH EH22 ....68 A2
GORBR EH23 ....79 G3
KLSTN EH29 ....21 F1
LNHD EH20 ....66 A4
MRYFD/COR EH12 ....25 E5
MUS EH21 ....48 A1
QFRY EH30 ....6 D4
RATHO EH28 ....21 G5
ROSLIN EH25 ....73 H2
Station Ter KLSTN EH29 ....21 F2
Steads' Pl LEITH EH6 ....18 B4
Steele Av DLKTH EH22 ......77 H1
Steel's Pl
MCH/MOR/FMHD EH10 ....43 F3
Steil Gv TRNT EH33 ....51 F3
The Steils
MCH/MOR/FMHD EH10 ....42 D5
Stenhouse Av
DAL/STH/STNH EH11 ....41 G2
Stenhouse Av West
DAL/STH/STNH EH11 ....41 G2
Stenhouse Cottages
DAL/STH/STNH EH11 ....41 G2
Stenhouse Crs
DAL/STH/STNH EH11 ....41 G2
Stenhouse Dr
DAL/STH/STNH EH11 ....41 G2
Stenhouse Gdns
DAL/STH/STNH EH11 ....41 G2
Stenhouse Gdns North
DAL/STH/STNH EH11 ....41 G2
Stenhouse Gv
DAL/STH/STNH EH11 ....41 G2
Stenhouse Mill Crs
DAL/STH/STNH EH11 ....41 G3

Stenhouse Mill La
  DAL/STH/STNH EH11 ....41 H3
Stenhouse Mill Wynd
  DAL/STH/STNH EH11 ....41 H3
Stenhouse Pl East
  DAL/STH/STNH EH11 ....41 G2
Stenhouse Pl West
  DAL/STH/STNH EH11 ....41 G2
Stenhouse St East
  DAL/STH/STNH EH11 ....41 G2
Stenhouse St West
  DAL/STH/STNH EH11 ....41 F3
Stenhouse Ter
  DAL/STH/STNH EH11 ....41 H2
Stennis Gdns *LIB/NID* EH16 ....60 A2
Stevenlaw's Cl *EDOT* EH1 ....3 F4
Stevenson Av
  DAL/STH/STNH EH11 ....42 A1
Stevenson Dr
  DAL/STH/STNH EH11 ....41 G2
Stevenson Gv
  DAL/STH/STNH EH11 ....42 A1
Stevenson La *DLKTH* EH22 ....76 D3
Stevenson Pl *LSWD* EH18 ....74 B1
Stevenson Rd
  PNCK EH26 ....71 E1
Stevenson Ter
  DAL/STH/STNH EH11 ....42 A1
Stewart Av *BAL/CUR* EH14 ....53 C1
Stewart Clark Av *QFRY* EH30 ....6 D5
Stewart Crs *BAL/CUR* EH14 ....54 C5
Stewartfield *LEITH* EH6 ....17 H4
Stewart Gdns *BAL/CUR* EH14 ....54 C5
Stewart Gv *DLKTH* EH22 ....61 E1
Stewart Pl *BAL/CUR* EH14 ....53 C1
  KLSTN EH29 ....21 F1
Stewart Rd *BAL/CUR* EH14 ....53 C1
Stewart Ter
  DAL/STH/STNH EH11 ....42 B1
  QFRY EH30 ....6 C4
Stirling Rd *LEITH* EH5 ....17 F2
Stobhill Rd *DLKTH* EH22 ....76 D4
Stone Av *DLKTH* EH22 ....77 F1
Stone Crs *DLKTH* EH22 ....77 F1
Stone Pl *DLKTH* EH22 ....77 F2
Stoneybank Av *MUS* EH21 ....47 G2
Stoneybank Ct *MUS* EH21 ....47 G2
Stoneybank Crs *MUS* EH21 ....47 H2
Stoneybank Dr *MUS* EH21 ....47 G1
Stoneybank Gdns *MUS* EH21 ....47 G1
Stoneybank Gdns North
  MUS EH21 ....47 G1
Stoneybank Gdns South
  MUS EH21 ....47 H2
Stoneybank Gv *MUS* EH21 ....47 H2
Stoneybank Pl *MUS* EH21 ....47 H2
Stoneybank Rd *MUS* EH21 ....47 H2
Stoneybank Ter *MUS* EH21 ....47 H2
Stonycroft *QFRY* EH30 ....6 C4
Stoneyflatts *QFRY* EH30 ....6 B4
Stoneyflatts Pk *QFRY* EH30 ....6 B5
Stonyhill Av *MUS* EH21 ....47 G1
Stonyhill Ct *MUS* EH21 ....47 G1
Stonyhill Dr *MUS* EH21 ....47 G1
Stonyhill Farm Rd *MUS* EH21 ....47 H1
Stonyhill Gv *MUS* EH21 ....47 G1
Stonyhill Pl *MUS* EH21 ....47 G1
Stonyhill Ri *MUS* EH21 ....47 G1
Stonyhill Rd *MUS* EH21 ....47 G1
Stonyhill Ter *MUS* EH21 ....47 G1
Stonyhill Wynd *MUS* EH21 ....47 G1
Strachan Gdns *EDNW* EH4 ....25 G1
Strachan Rd *EDNW* EH4 ....25 G1
Straiton Jct *LNHD* EH20 ....65 G3
Straiton Mains *LNHD* EH20 ....65 G3
Straiton Pk *LNHD* EH20 ....65 G3
Straiton Pl *PBLO/DUD* EH15 ....30 B2
Straiton Rd *LNHD* EH20 ....65 G3
Strathalmond Ct *EDNW* EH4 ....13 H5
Strathalmond Gn *EDNW* EH4 ....13 H5
Strathalmond Pk *EDNW* EH4 ....23 H1
Strathalmond Rd *EDNW* EH4 ....13 H5
Strathearn Pl
  MCH/MOR/FMHD EH10 ....43 F2
Strathearn Rd *NWGTN* EH9 ....43 G2
Strathesk Gv *PNCK* EH26 ....71 E3
Strathesk Pl *PNCK* EH26 ....71 E3
Strathesk Rd *PNCK* EH26 ....71 E3
Strathfillan Rd *NWGTN* EH9 ....43 G2
Straton Park Wy *LNHD* EH20 ....65 G3
Strawberry Bank *DLKTH* EH22 ....68 A3
Stuart Crs *MRYFD/COR* EH12 ....24 B3
Stuart Gn *MRYFD/COR* EH12 ....24 B3
Stuart Pk *MRYFD/COR* EH12 ....24 B3
Stuart Sq *MRYFD/COR* EH12 ....24 B3
Stuart Wynd *MRYFD/COR* EH12 ....24 B3
Succoth Av *MRYFD/COR* EH12 ....26 B3
Succoth Gdns
  MRYFD/COR EH12 ....26 B3
Succoth Pk *MRYFD/COR* EH12 ....26 A3
Succoth Pl *MRYFD/COR* EH12 ....26 B3
Suffolk Rd *LIB/NID* EH16 ....44 B5
Suffolk Road La *LIB/NID* EH16 ....44 C3
Summer Bank
  EDNT/CEDW EH3 ....27 G1
Summerfield Gdns *LEITH* EH6 ....18 D4
Summerfield Pl *LEITH* EH6 ....18 D4
Summerhall Pl *NWGTN* EH9 ....44 A1
Summerhall Sq *NWGTN* EH9 ....44 A1
Summerlee *CPS/PPNS* EH32 ....34 A4
Summerside Pl *LEITH* EH6 ....17 H5
Summertrees Ct *LIB/NID* EH16 ....45 G3
Sunbury Pl *EDNW* EH4 ....26 D3
Sunbury St *EDNW* EH4 ....26 D3
Sunnyside *RSTRG* EH7 ....28 D2
Sunnyside *RSTRG* EH7 ....28 C1
Sutherland St
  MRYFD/COR EH12 ....26 D4
Suttieslea Crs *DLKTH* EH22 ....77 F1
Suttieslea Dr *DLKTH* EH22 ....77 F1
Suttieslea Pl *DLKTH* EH22 ....77 F1
Suttieslea Rd *DLKTH* EH22 ....77 F1
Swan Crs *GORBR* EH23 ....79 E1
Swanfield *LEITH* EH6 ....18 B3
Swan Rd *TRNT* EH33 ....51 E3
Swan Spring Av
  MCH/MOR/FMHD EH10 ....58 A2

Swanston Av
  MCH/MOR/FMHD EH10 ....58 A4
Swanston Crs
  MCH/MOR/FMHD EH10 ....58 A4
Swanston Dr
  MCH/MOR/FMHD EH10 ....58 B4
Swanston Gdns
  MCH/MOR/FMHD EH10 ....58 A4
Swanston Gn
  MCH/MOR/FMHD EH10 ....58 A4
Swanston Gv
  MCH/MOR/FMHD EH10 ....58 B4
Swanston Loan
  MCH/MOR/FMHD EH10 ....58 A4
Swanston Muir
  MCH/MOR/FMHD EH10 ....57 G4
Swanston Pk
  MCH/MOR/FMHD EH10 ....58 A4
Swanston Pl
  MCH/MOR/FMHD EH10 ....58 A4
Swanston Rd
  MCH/MOR/FMHD EH10 ....57 H5
Swanston Rw
  MCH/MOR/FMHD EH10 ....58 A4
Swanston Ter
  MCH/MOR/FMHD EH10 ....58 B4
Swanston Vw
  MCH/MOR/FMHD EH10 ....58 A4
Sycamore Av *CPS/PPNS* EH32 ....35 F2
Sycamore Gdns
  MRYFD/COR EH12 ....24 D5
Sycamore Rd *DLKTH* EH22 ....77 G1
Sydney Pk *RSTRG* EH7 ....29 G1
Sydney Pl *RSTRG* EH7 ....29 G1
Sydney Ter *RSTRG* EH7 ....29 G1
Sylvan Pl *NWGTN* EH9 ....43 H1
Syme Crs
  MCH/MOR/FMHD EH10 ....57 G1
Syme Rigg
  MCH/MOR/FMHD EH10 ....57 G1

T

Tait Dr *PNCK* EH26 ....70 D4
Tait St *DLKTH* EH22 ....68 C1
Talisman Pl *LIB/NID* EH16 ....44 D5
Tantallon Pl *NWGTN* EH9 ....43 H1
Tarvit St *EDNT/CEDW* EH3 ....2 C7
Taylor Gdns *LEITH* EH6 ....18 B3
Taylor Pl *DLKTH* EH22 ....69 E2
Tay St *DAL/STH/STNH* EH11 ....42 D1
Teiferton *RSTRG* EH7 ....29 F4
Telford Dr *EDNW* EH4 ....16 B5
Telford Gdns *EDNW* EH4 ....16 B5
Telford Pl *EDNW* EH4 ....16 B5
Telford Rd *EDNW* EH4 ....26 A1
Templar's Cramond *EDNW* EH4 ....14 A4
Templeland Gv
  MRYFD/COR EH12 ....24 D4
Templeland Rd
  MRYFD/COR EH12 ....24 C4
Temple Park Crs
  DAL/STH/STNH EH11 ....42 D1
Tennant St *LEITH* EH6 ....18 B4
Tenth St *DLKTH* EH22 ....76 D1
Terrars Cft *HLYRPK/NF* EH8 ....3 J7
Terregles *PNCK* EH26 ....70 B3
Teviotdale Pl *EDNT/CEDW* EH3 ....27 F1
Teviot Gv *PNCK* EH26 ....70 D2
Teviot Pl *EDOT* EH1 ....2 E6
Third Gait *BAL/CUR* EH14 ....54 C2
Third St *DLKTH* EH22 ....76 C3
Thirlestane La *NWGTN* EH9 ....43 G2
Thirlestane Rd *NWGTN* EH9 ....43 G1
Thistle Pl *DAL/STH/STNH* EH11 ....43 E1
Thistle St *CED/PRST* EH2 ....2 D2
Thistle Street North East La
  CED/PRST EH2 ....2 C2
Thistle Street North West La
  CED/PRST EH2 ....2 C2
Thistle Street South East La
  CED/PRST EH2 ....2 D2
Thistle Street South West La
  CED/PRST EH2 ....2 C2
Thomson Dr *BAL/CUR* EH14 ....55 F4
  CPS/PPNS EH32 ....35 F1
Thomson Pl *BAL/CUR* EH14 ....55 F4
Thomson Gv *BAL/CUR* EH14 ....55 F4
Thomson Rd *BAL/CUR* EH14 ....55 F4
Thorburn Gv *COLIN* EH13 ....57 E3
Thorburn Rd *COLIN* EH13 ....56 D2
Thornburn Ter *PNCK* EH26 ....70 D5
Thorntree Crs *CPS/PPNS* EH32 ....34 D4
Thorntree St *LEITH* EH6 ....18 C5
Thorntreeside *LEITH* EH6 ....18 C5
Thorntree St *LEITH* EH6 ....18 C4
Thornybauk *EDNT/CEDW* EH3 ....2 B7
Thornyhall *DLKTH* EH22 ....63 E5
Threipmuir Av *BAL/CUR* EH14 ....53 E4
Threipmuir Gdns
  BAL/CUR EH14 ....53 E4
Threipmuir Pl *BAL/CUR* EH14 ....53 E4
Timber Bush *LEITH* EH6 ....18 C2
Tintо Pl *LEITH* EH6 ....18 A4
Tipperlinn Rd
  MCH/MOR/FMHD EH10 ....43 E2
Toddshill Rd *KLSTN* EH29 ....21 F1
Toll House Gv *TRNT* EH33 ....51 F3
Torduff Rd *COLIN* EH13 ....56 C5
Torphichen St *EDNT/CEDW* EH3 ....27 E4
Torphin Bank *COLIN* EH13 ....56 B4
Torphin Rd *COLIN* EH13 ....56 A4
Torrance Pk *EDNW* EH4 ....24 C2
Torrance Medway *PNCK* EH26 ....72 B5
Torsonce Rd *DLKTH* EH22 ....68 B2
Tower Pl *LEITH* EH6 ....18 C2
Tower St *LEITH* EH6 ....18 C2
Tower Wynd *LEITH* EH6 ....18 C2
Trafalgar La *LEITH* EH6 ....17 H3
Traprain Ter *LNHD* EH20 ....66 A5
Traquair Pk East
  MRYFD/COR EH12 ....25 F5
Traquair Pk West
  MRYFD/COR EH12 ....25 E5
Trelawney Ter *PNCK* EH26 ....71 E1
Trench Knowe
  MCH/MOR/FMHD EH10 ....58 A4
Tressilian Gdns *LIB/NID* EH16 ....44 D5

Trinity Ct *GNTN* EH5 ....17 E3
Trinity Crs *GNTN* EH5 ....17 F2
Trinity Gv *GNTN* EH5 ....17 F2
Trinity Mains *GNTN* EH5 ....17 F3
Trinity Rd *GNTN* EH5 ....17 F2
Trinity Wy *GNTN* EH5 ....17 F3
Tryst Pk
  MCH/MOR/FMHD EH10 ....57 H4
Turner Av *BAL/CUR* EH14 ....52 D1
Turner Pk *BAL/CUR* EH14 ....52 D1
Turnhouse Farm Rd
  MRYFD/COR EH12 ....23 E2
Turnhouse Rd
  MRYFD/COR EH12 ....22 D2
Turret Gdns *CPS/PPNS* EH32 ....34 B5
Tyler's Acre Av
  MRYFD/COR EH12 ....41 E1
Tyler's Acre Gdns
  MRYFD/COR EH12 ....41 E1
Tyler's Acre Rd
  MRYFD/COR EH12 ....41 E1
Tynecastle La
  DAL/STH/STNH EH11 ....42 C1
Tynecastle Ter
  DAL/STH/STNH EH11 ....42 C1
Tytler Ct *HLYRPK/NF* EH8 ....28 C2
Tytler Gdns *HLYRPK/NF* EH8 ....28 C2

U

Ulster Crs *HLYRPK/NF* EH8 ....29 F3
Ulster Dr *HLYRPK/NF* EH8 ....29 F3
Ulster Gdns *HLYRPK/NF* EH8 ....29 F4
Ulster Gv *HLYRPK/NF* EH8 ....29 F4
Ulster Ter *HLYRPK/NF* EH8 ....29 F4
Union St *EDOT* EH1 ....27 H1
Upper Bow *EDOT* EH1 ....2 E4
Upper Broomieknowe
  BNYRG EH19 ....67 E5
Upper Coltbridge Ter
  ....26 B4
Upper Craigour *GIL/MOR* EH17 ....60 C1
Upper Craigour Wy
  GIL/MOR EH17 ....45 G5
Upper Dean Ter *EDNT/CEDW* EH4 ....27 E2
Upper Gilmore Pl
  MCH/MOR/FMHD EH10 ....27 F5
Upper Gilmore Ter
  EDNT/CEDW EH3 ....27 F5
Upper Gray St *NWGTN* EH9 ....44 A1
Upper Grove Pl
  EDNT/CEDW EH3 ....27 E5

V

Valleyfield Rd *PNCK* EH26 ....70 D5
Valleyfield St *EDNT/CEDW* EH3 ....27 F5
Valley Field Vw *PNCK* EH26 ....70 D5
Vanburgh Place La *LEITH* EH6 ....18 C4
Vandeleur Av *RSTRG* EH7 ....29 C2
Vandeleur Gv *RSTRG* EH7 ....29 C2
Vandeleur Pl *RSTRG* EH7 ....29 C1
Veitch's Sq *EDNW* EH4 ....27 F1
Ventnor Pl *NWGTN* EH9 ....44 C2
Ventnor Ter *NWGTN* EH9 ....44 B2
Vexhim Pk *PBLO/DUD* EH15 ....46 B1
Victoria Gdns *DLKTH* EH22 ....76 B1
Victoria Rd *DLKTH* EH22 ....76 B2
Victoria St *EDOT* EH1 ....2 E5
  GORBR EH23 ....78 D1
  RSWL EH24 ....74 B5
Victor Park Ter
  MRYFD/COR EH12 ....24 D4
Viewbank Dr *BNYRG* EH19 ....67 G4
Viewbank Rd *BNYRG* EH19 ....67 F4
Viewbank Vw *BNYRG* EH19 ....67 G4
Viewcraig Gdns
  HLYRPK/NF EH8 ....3 H5
Viewcraig St *HLYRPK/NF* EH8 ....3 H5
Viewfield *BNYRG* EH19 ....67 H4
Viewfield Av *BNYRG* EH19 ....67 H4
Viewfield Rd *BAL/CUR* EH14 ....56 A2
Viewforth *CPS/PPNS* EH32 ....35 F1
  DAL/STH/STNH EH11 ....27 E5
Viewforth Bank *QFRY* EH30 ....6 C4
Viewforth Gdns
  MCH/MOR/FMHD EH10 ....43 F1
  TRNT EH33 ....51 E2
Viewforth Pl *QFRY* EH30 ....6 C5
Viewforth Rd *QFRY* EH30 ....6 C5
Viewforth Sq
  MCH/MOR/FMHD EH10 ....43 E1
Viewforth Ter *EDNT/CEDW* EH3 ....43 E1
Viewpark Gdns *BNYRG* EH19 ....67 F4
Villa Rd *QFRY* EH30 ....6 C4
Vivian Ter *EDNW* EH4 ....15 F5
Vogrie Crs South *GORBR* EH23 ....79 F3
Vogrie Pl *GORBR* EH23 ....79 F3
Vogrie Rd *GORBR* EH23 ....79 F3

W

Wadingburn La *LSWD* EH18 ....66 C3
Wadingburn Rd *LNHD* EH20 ....66 C4
Wakefield Av *RSTRG* EH7 ....29 H1
Walker Crs *DLKTH* EH22 ....67 H5
Walker Rd *DLKTH* EH22 ....6 B4
Walker Pl *LSWD* EH18 ....74 C1
Walkers St *BAL/CUR* EH14 ....41 E5
Walkers Rig *BAL/CUR* EH14 ....41 E5
Walker St *EDNT/CEDW* EH3 ....27 E5
Wallace Av *MUS* EH21 ....49 E2
Wallace Crs *ROSLIN* EH25 ....73 H1
Wallace Pl *TRNT* EH33 ....51 E1
Walter Scott Av *LIB/NID* EH16 ....44 D5
Wanless Ct *MUS* EH21 ....32 B5
Warden's Cl *EDOT* EH1 ....2 E5
Wardie Av *GNTN* EH5 ....17 E3
Wardieburn Dr *GNTN* EH5 ....16 D2
Wardieburn Pl East *GNTN* EH5 ....16 D2

Wardieburn Pl North
  GNTN EH5 ....16 D2
Wardieburn Pl South
  GNTN EH5 ....16 D2
Wardieburn Pl West *GNTN* EH5 ....16 C2
Wardieburn Rd *GNTN* EH5 ....16 C2
Wardieburn St East *GNTN* EH5 ....16 C2
Wardieburn St West *GNTN* EH5 ....16 C2
Wardieburn Ter *GNTN* EH5 ....16 C2
Wardie Crs *GNTN* EH5 ....16 D2
Wardie Dell *GNTN* EH5 ....17 E2
Wardie Gv *GNTN* EH5 ....16 D2
Wardie Gv *GNTN* EH5 ....16 D2
Wardie House La *GNTN* EH5 ....17 E2
Wardie Pk *GNTN* EH5 ....17 E3
Wardie Rd *GNTN* EH5 ....17 E3
Wardie Sq *GNTN* EH5 ....17 E2
Wardlaw Pl
  DAL/STH/STNH EH11 ....42 C1
Wardlaw St
  DAL/STH/STNH EH11 ....42 C1
Wardlaw Ter
  DAL/STH/STNH EH11 ....42 C1
Warrender Park Crs
  NWGTN EH9 ....43 F1
Warrender Park Rd
  NWGTN EH9 ....43 F1
Warrender Park Ter
  NWGTN EH9 ....43 G1
Warriston Crs *EDNT/CEDW* EH3 ....17 G4
Warriston Crs *EDNT/CEDW* EH3 ....17 G5
Warriston Dr *EDNT/CEDW* EH3 ....17 G4
Warriston Farm Rd
  BAL/CUR EH14 ....54 A3
Warriston Gdns
  EDNT/CEDW EH3 ....17 F4
Warriston Gv *EDNT/CEDW* EH3 ....17 F4
Warriston Rd *EDNT/CEDW* EH3 ....17 G5
Warriston Ter *EDNT/CEDW* EH3 ....17 F4
Washington La
  DAL/STH/STNH EH11 ....26 D5
Waterfront Av *GNTN* EH5 ....16 B1
Waterfront Bank *PNCK* EH26 ....70 D5
Waterfront Broadway
  ....16 B2
Waterloo Pl *EDOT* EH1 ....3 F2
Water of Leith Walkway
  COLIN EH3 ....56 B3
Waters' Cl *LEITH* EH6 ....18 C3
Water St *LEITH* EH6 ....18 C3
Watertoun Rd *NWGTN* EH9 ....44 A3
Watson Crs
  DAL/STH/STNH EH11 ....42 D1
Watson St *PNCK* EH26 ....70 C4
Watt Dr *DLKTH* EH22 ....77 F2
Watt Pk *DLKTH* EH22 ....76 D3
Watt's Cl *MUS* EH21 ....31 H5
Wauchope Av *LIB/NID* EH16 ....45 H2
Wauchope Crs *LIB/NID* EH16 ....45 G2
Wauchope Pl *LIB/NID* EH16 ....45 H2
Wauchope Rd *LIB/NID* EH16 ....45 G2
Wauchope Sq *LIB/NID* EH16 ....45 H2
Wauchope Ter *LIB/NID* EH16 ....45 H2
Waulkmill Dr *PNCK* EH26 ....70 D5
Waulkmill Loan *BAL/CUR* EH14 ....53 G1
Waulkmill Rd *PNCK* EH26 ....70 D4
Waulkmill Vw *PNCK* EH26 ....70 D4
Waverley Br *EDOT* EH1 ....2 E3
Waverley Ct *BNYRG* EH19 ....75 G1
Waverley Crs *BNYRG* EH19 ....67 G5
Waverley Dr *BNYRG* EH19 ....67 G5
Waverley Pk *BNYRG* EH19 ....67 G5
  DLKTH EH22 ....77 F1
  HLYRPK/NF EH8 ....28 C2
Waverley Pl *RSTRG* EH7 ....28 C2
Waverley Rd *BNYRG* EH19 ....67 G5
  DLKTH EH22 ....68 F2
Waverley St *DLKTH* EH22 ....77 F2
Waverley Ter *BNYRG* EH19 ....67 F1
  DLKTH EH22 ....77 F1
Weavers' Knowe Crs
  BAL/CUR EH14 ....53 G4
Wedderburn Ct *MUS* EH21 ....48 B3
Wedderburn Ter *MUS* EH21 ....48 B3
Wee Brae *LSWD* EH18 ....66 E3
Weir Crs *DLKTH* EH22 ....68 A2
Wellflats Rd *KLSTN* EH29 ....21 F2
Wellhead Cl *QFRY* EH30 ....7 E5
Wellington Pl *LEITH* EH6 ....18 C4
Wellington St *RSTRG* EH7 ....28 B1
Well Wynd *TRNT* EH33 ....51 F2
Wemyss Gdns *MUS* EH21 ....49 G1
Wemyss Pl *CPS/PPNS* EH32 ....35 E1
  EDNT/CEDW EH3 ....2 B2
Wemyss Place Ms
  EDNT/CEDW EH3 ....2 B2
Wesley Crs *BNYRG* EH19 ....75 H1
West Adam St *HLYRPK/NF* EH8 ....3 G5
West Annandale St *RSTRG* EH7 ....17 H5
West Approach Rd
  DAL/STH/STNH EH11 ....26 B5
  EDNT/CEDW EH3 ....2 A5
Westbank Loan
  PBLO/DUD EH15 ....30 A2
Westbank Pl *PBLO/DUD* EH15 ....30 A2
Westbank St *PBLO/DUD* EH15 ....30 A2
West Bow *EDOT* EH1 ....2 D5
West Bowling Green St
  LEITH EH6 ....18 A3
West Brighton Crs
  PBLO/DUD EH15 ....30 A3
West Bryson Rd
  DAL/STH/STNH EH11 ....42 D1
Westburn Av *BAL/CUR* EH14 ....55 G1
Westburn Gv *BAL/CUR* EH14 ....55 G1
Westburn Middlefield
  BAL/CUR EH14 ....55 G1
Westburn Pk *BAL/CUR* EH14 ....55 H1
West Calder Crs *PNCK* EH26 ....70 C3
West Calystane Rd
  MCH/MOR/FMHD EH10 ....58 A3
West Camus Rd
  MCH/MOR/FMHD EH10 ....58 A3
West Carnethy Av *COLIN* EH13 ....56 C4
West Castle Rd
  MCH/MOR/FMHD EH10 ....43 E1
West Catherine Pl
  MRYFD/COR EH12 ....26 C4
West Cherrybank *LEITH* EH6 ....17 G2
West Coates *MRYFD/COR* EH12 ....26 C4

West College St *EDOT* EH1 ....3 F5
West Ct *EDNW* EH4 ....26 A2
West Craigs Av
  MRYFD/COR EH12 ....23 H5
West Craigs Crs
  MRYFD/COR EH12 ....23 H5
West Cft *RATHO* EH28 ....38 A4
West Crosscauseway
  HLYRPK/NF EH8 ....3 G7
West End Pl
  DAL/STH/STNH EH11 ....26 D5
Wester Broom Av
  MRYFD/COR EH12 ....40 C1
Wester Broom Dr
  MRYFD/COR EH12 ....40 C1
Wester Broom Gdns
  MRYFD/COR EH12 ....40 C1
Wester Broom Gv
  MRYFD/COR EH12 ....40 C1
Wester Broom Pl
  MRYFD/COR EH12 ....24 C5
Wester Broom Ter
  MRYFD/COR EH12 ....40 C1
Wester Coates Av
  MRYFD/COR EH12 ....26 C4
Wester Coates Gdns
  MRYFD/COR EH12 ....26 C4
Wester Coates Pl
  MRYFD/COR EH12 ....26 C3
Wester Drylaw Av *EDNW* EH4 ....15 H5
Wester Drylaw Dr *EDNW* EH4 ....15 H5
Wester Drylaw Pk *EDNW* EH4 ....16 A5
Wester Drylaw Pl *EDNW* EH4 ....15 H5
Wester Hailes Dr
  BAL/CUR EH14 ....55 H1
Wester Hailes Pk
  BAL/CUR EH14 ....56 A1
Wester Hailes Rd
  BAL/CUR EH14 ....55 H1
  DAL/STH/STNH EH11 ....40 C4
Wester Hl
  MCH/MOR/FMHD EH10 ....57 F1
Western Gdns
  MRYFD/COR EH12 ....26 A4
Western Harbour Dr *LEITH* EH6 ....17 H1
Western Pl *MRYFD/COR* EH12 ....26 A4
Wester Steil
  MCH/MOR/FMHD EH10 ....42 C5
Wester Fairbrae Crs
  DAL/STH/STNH EH11 ....41 E3
Wester Fairbrae Dr
  DAL/STH/STNH EH11 ....41 E3
West Ferryfield *GNTN* EH5 ....16 D4
Westfield Av
  DAL/STH/STNH EH11 ....42 B1
Westfield Bank *DLKTH* EH22 ....68 A3
Westfield Ct *DLKTH* EH22 ....68 A3
Westfield Gv *DLKTH* EH22 ....68 A3
Westfield Pk *DLKTH* EH22 ....68 A3
Westfield Rd
  DAL/STH/STNH EH11 ....42 B1
Westfield St
  DAL/STH/STNH EH11 ....42 B1
Westgarth Av *COLIN* EH13 ....56 D3
West Gorgie Pk *BAL/CUR* EH14 ....42 A3
West Gorgie Pl *BAL/CUR* EH14 ....42 A3
West Grange Gdns *NWGTN* EH9 ....43 H5
West Granton Access
  EDNW EH4 ....16 B3
West Granton Rd *GNTN* EH5 ....16 C2
Westhall Gdns
  MCH/MOR/FMHD EH10 ....43 F1
West Harbour Rd
  CPS/PPNS EH32 ....34 D1
  GNTN EH5 ....16 C1
West Holmes Gdns *MUS* EH21 ....31 H5
Westhouses Rd *DLKTH* EH22 ....77 C2
West Loan *CPS/PPNS* EH32 ....34 B4
West Lorimer Pl
  CPS/PPNS EH32 ....34 D1
West Mains Rd *NWGTN* EH9 ....44 A4
West Maitland St
  MRYFD/COR EH12 ....27 E4
West Mayfield *NWGTN* EH9 ....44 B2
West Mill La *EDNW* EH4 ....27 E3
West Mill Rd *COLIN* EH13 ....56 B3
West Montgomery Pl
  RSTRG EH7 ....28 B1
West Newington Pl
  NWGTN EH9 ....44 A1
West Nicolson St
  HLYRPK/NF EH8 ....3 G6
West Park Pl
  DAL/STH/STNH EH11 ....26 D4
West Pilton Av *EDNW* EH4 ....16 A4
West Pilton Bank *EDNW* EH4 ....15 H3
West Pilton Bray *EDNW* EH4 ....16 B3
West Pilton Crs *EDNW* EH4 ....15 H3
West Pilton Crossway
  EDNW EH4 ....16 A3
West Pilton Dr *EDNW* EH4 ....16 B3
West Pilton Gdns *EDNW* EH4 ....16 A3
West Pilton Gn *EDNW* EH4 ....16 A3
West Pilton Gv *EDNW* EH4 ....16 A3
West Pilton Lea *EDNW* EH4 ....16 A3
West Pilton Loan *EDNW* EH4 ....16 A3
West Pilton March *EDNW* EH4 ....16 B2
West Pilton Pk *EDNW* EH4 ....16 A3
West Pilton Pl *EDNW* EH4 ....16 B3
West Pilton Ri *EDNW* EH4 ....16 A3
West Pilton St *EDNW* EH4 ....16 A3
West Pilton Ter *EDNW* EH4 ....16 A3
West Port *EDNT/CEDW* EH3 ....2 C6
West Powburn *NWGTN* EH9 ....44 A3
West Preston St *NWGTN* EH9 ....44 A1
West Register St *CED/PRST* EH2 ....3 E2
West Relugas Rd *NWGTN* EH9 ....43 H3
West Richmond St
  HLYRPK/NF EH8 ....3 G6
West Savile Rd *NWGTN* EH9 ....44 B3
West Savile Ter *NWGTN* EH9 ....44 A3
West Scotland Street La
  EDNT/CEDW EH3 ....27 G1
West Seaside *CPS/PPNS* EH32 ....34 A4
West Shore Rd *GNTN* EH5 ....15 H2
West Silvermills La
  EDNT/CEDW EH3 ....27 F1
West St *PNCK* EH26 ....70 C5

West Telferton *RSTRG* EH7 ....29 H2
West Tollcross *EDNT/CEDW* EH5 ....2 D7
West Werberside *EDNW* EH4 ....16 C4
West Windygoul *TRNT* EH33.............50 D3
West Windygoul Gdns
  TRNT 50 D4
West Winnelstrae *EDNW* EH5..........16 D4
West Woods *EDNW* EH4.....................16 C5
Wheatfield Gv *LNHD* EH20...............65 G4
Wheatfield Loan *LNHD* EH20..........65 H3
Wheatfield Rd
  DAL/STH/STNH EH11.......................42 B1
Wheatfield St
  DAL/STH/STNH EH11.......................42 B1
Wheatfield Ter
  DAL/STH/STNH EH11.......................42 B1
Wheatfield Wk *LNHD* EH20.............65 G4
Wheatsheaf La *DLKTH* EH22..........62 C5
Whinneyknowe *DFLS* EH11.............4 C4
Whinny Hill Crs *DFLS* KY11 ....4 B1
Whin Pk *CPS/PPNS* EH32.................34 D2
Whins Pl *PBLO/DUD* EH15................30 A2
Whitecraig Av *MUS* EH21.................63 G1
Whitecraig Crs *MUS* EH21..............48 C5
Whitecraig Gdns *MUS* EH21...........48 C5
Whitecraig Gdns East
  MUS EH21..48 C5
Whitecraig Rd *MUS* EH21...............48 C5
Whitecraig Ter *MUS* EH21...............48 C5
Whitedales
  MCH/MOR/FMHD EH10..................58 C4
Whitehead Gv *QFRY* EH30................6 D5
Whitehill Av *MUS* EH21.....................47 G2
Whitehill Dr *DLKTH* EH22.................69 F2
Whitehill Farm Rd *MUS* EH21..........47 G2
Whitehill Gdns *MUS* EH21...............47 G2
Whitehill Gv *DLKTH* EH22.................69 F2
Whitehill Rd *DLKTH* EH22................46 C3
  MUS EH21..46 D1
Whitehouse Loan *NWGTN* EH9........43 F1
Whitehouse Rd *EDNW* EH4...............14 A5
Whitehouse Ter *NWGTN* EH9...........43 G2
Whitelea Crs *BAL/CUR* EH14............53 E4

Whitelea Rd *BAL/CUR* EH14.............52 D4
White Pk *DAL/STH/STNH* EH11.........42 C1
White's Cl *DLKTH* EH22....................68 C1
Whitson Crs
  DAL/STH/STNH EH11.......................41 H1
Whitson Gv
  DAL/STH/STNH EH11.......................41 H1
Whitson Pl East
  DAL/STH/STNH EH11.......................41 H1
Whitson Pl West
  DAL/STH/STNH EH11.......................41 H1
Whitson Rd
  DAL/STH/STNH EH11.......................41 G1
Whitson Ter
  DAL/STH/STNH EH11.......................41 H1
Whitson Wk
  DAL/STH/STNH EH11.......................41 G1
Whitson Wy
  DAL/STH/STNH EH11.......................41 H1
Wilkieston Rd *RATHO* EH28..............37 G4
William Black Pl *QFRY* EH30.............6 D5
William St *EDNT/CEDW* EH3............27 E3
William Street North East La
  EDNT/CEDW EH3.............................27 E3
William Street North West La
  EDNT/CEDW EH3.............................27 E3
William Street South East La
  EDNT/CEDW EH3.............................27 E3
William Street South West La
  EDNT/CEDW EH3.............................27 E4
Willow Av *BNYRG* EH19.....................75 F1
Willowbank Rw *LEITH* EH6...............17 H2
Willowbrae Av *HLYRPK/NF* EH8.......29 E3
Willowbrae Gdns
  HLYRPK/NF EH8...............................29 F3
Willowbrae Rd *HLYRPK/NF* EH8.......29 F3
Willow Rd *DLKTH* EH22......................77 G1
Willow Tree Pl *BAL/CUR* EH14..........53 F1
Wilson Av *CPS/PPNS* EH32..............34 B4
  DLKTH EH22......................................69 E1
Wilson Rd *GORBR* EH23.....................79 F1
Wilson's Pk *PBLO/DUD* EH15...........50 B2
Wilson St *PNCK* EH26.........................70 C4

Wilton Rd *LIB/NID* EH16...................44 C3
Windmill La *HLYRPK/NF* EH8............3 G7
Windsor Crs *PNCK* EH26...................71 E4
Windsor Dr *PNCK* EH26.....................71 E3
Windsor Gdns *MUS* EH21.................32 C5
Windsor Park Dr *MUS* EH21.............32 D5
Windsor Park Rd *MUS* EH21.............32 C5
Windsor Park Ter *MUS* EH21............32 C5
Windsor Pl *PBLO/DUD* EH15.............30 B3
Windsor Rd *PNCK* EH26....................71 E3
Windsor Sq *PNCK* EH26....................71 E3
Windsor Street La *RSTRG* EH7.........28 A1
Windsor Ter *PNCK* EH26...................71 E3
Windygoul Crs *TRNT* EH33...............51 G3
Winton Cl *TRNT* EH33.......................51 G4
Winton Ct *TRNT* EH33.......................51 G4
Winton Dr
  MCH/MOR/FMHD EH10..................58 C5
Winton Gdns
  MCH/MOR/FMHD EH10..................58 C5
Winton Gv
  MCH/MOR/FMHD EH10..................58 B4
  TRNT EH33...51 G4
Winton Loan
  MCH/MOR/FMHD EH10..................58 C5
Winton Pk *CPS/PPNS* EH32.............35 E2
Winton Pl *TRNT* EH33........................51 F2
Winton Ter
  MCH/MOR/FMHD EH10..................58 C5
Winton Wy *TRNT* EH33.....................51 F4
Wishart Av *BNYRG* EH19...................67 H4
Wishart Pl *DLKTH* EH22.....................68 A2
Wishaw Ter *RSTRG* EH7.....................28 D2
Wisp Gn *PBLO/DUD* EH15.................46 B2
The Wisp *PBLO/DUD* EH15................46 A2
Wolrige Rd *LIB/NID* EH16.................59 G1
Wolseley Crs *HLYRPK/NF* EH8.........29 E2
Wolsey Av *BNYRG* EH19....................75 G1
Woodburn Av *DLKTH* EH22...............69 E1
Woodburn Bank *DLKTH* EH22..........69 E1

Woodburn Dr *DLKTH* EH22...............68 D1
Woodburn Gdns *DLKTH* EH22.........69 E1
Woodburn Gv *DLKTH* EH22..............69 E1
Woodburn Loan *DLKTH* EH22..........69 E1
Woodburn Medway
  DLKTH EH22......................................69 E2
Woodburn Pk *DLKTH* EH22..............69 E1
Woodburn Pl *DLKTH* EH22...............69 E1
Woodburn Rd *DLKTH* EH22.............69 E2
Woodburn St *DLKTH* EH22...............69 E1
Woodburn Ter *DLKTH* EH22.............69 F2
  MCH/FMHD EH10.............................43 F5
Woodburn Vw *DLKTH* EH22............69 F2
Woodend Pk *ROSLN* EH25................73 G3
Woodfield Av *COLIN* EH13................56 B3
Woodfield Pk *COLIN* EH13................56 B3
Woodhall Av *BAL/CUR* EH14...........55 H3
Woodhall Bank *COLIN* EH13...........56 B3
Woodhall Dr *BAL/CUR* EH14............55 H3
Woodhall Gv *COLIN* EH13................56 B4
Woodhall Millbrae
  BAL/CUR EH14.................................56 A3
Woodhall Rd *COLIN* EH13................56 A4
Woodhall Ter *BAL/CUR* EH14...........55 H3
Woodlands Gv *PBLO/DUD* EH15......29 G4
Woodrow *GORBR* EH23......................79 E1
Woodside Dr *PNCK* EH26..................70 A1
Woodside Gdns *MUS* EH21..............32 C5
Woodside Ter *PBLO/DUD* EH15........30 C4
Woolmet Crs *DLKTH* EH22...............61 F1
Wyvern Pk *NWGTN* EH9...................43 H2

Yewlands Gdns *LIB/NID* EH16.........59 H2
York La *EDOT* EH1................................3 F1
York Pl *EDOT* EH1................................3 F1
York Rd *GNTN* EH5.............................17 F2
Young Av *TRNT* EH33.........................51 F5
Young St *CED/PRST* EH2.....................2 B3
Young Street La
  CED/PRST EH2.................................2 B3
Young Street South La
  CED/PRST EH2.................................2 B3

Z

Zetland Pl *GNTN* EH5.........................17 F2

Index - featured places

Abbeyhill Industrial Estate
  HLYRPK/NF EH8 ....28 C2
Abbeyhill Primary School
  RSTRG EH7 ....3 K1
Abercorn Sports Club
  HLYRPK/NF EH8 ....29 F3
Academy Sports Centre
  EDNT/CEDW EH3 ....17 E4
Ainslie Park Leisure Centre
  GNTN EH5 ....16 C3
Albion Business Centre
  RSTRG EH7 ....28 C1
Alva Business Centre
  EDNT/CEDW EH3 ....2 C1
Apex European Hotel
  MRYFD/COR EH12 ....26 D4
Apex International Hotel
  EDOT EH1 ....2 D5
Arniston Rangers Junior FC
  GORBR EH23 ....78 D2
Astley Ainsley Hospital
  MCH/MOR/FMHD EH10 ....43 G3
Baberton Golf Club
  BAL/CUR EH14 ....55 H3
Baird Road Health Centre
  RATHO EH28 ....37 H4
Balerno High School
  BAL/CUR EH14 ....53 E2
Balerno Primary School
  BAL/CUR EH14 ....53 E2
Balgreen Primary School
  MRYFD/COR EH12 ....42 A1
The Balmoral Hotel
  CED/PRST EH2 ....2 E2
Bangholm Loan Medical Centre
  GNTN EH5 ....17 G3
The Basil Paterson
  Tutorial College
  EDNT/CEDW EH3 ....2 C1
BBC Scotland
  LIB/NID EH16 ....44 B1
Beaverbank Business Park
  RSTRG EH7 ....17 G5
Bedlam Theatre
  EDOT EH1 ....2 E6
Beeslack Community
  High School
  PNCK EH26 ....71 E2
Belgrave Business Centre
  CED/PRST EH2 ....2 C2
Bellevue Medical Centre
  EDOT EH1 ....28 A1
Best Western Bruntsfield Hotel
  MCH/MOR/FMHD EH10 ....43 F1
Blackford Hill
  MCH/MOR/FMHD EH10 ....43 G4
Blackhall Medical Centre
  EDNW EH4 ....25 H1
Blackhall Primary School
  EDNW EH4 ....25 G2
Bonaly Primary School
  COLIN EH13 ....56 C4
The Bonham Hotel
  EDNT/CEDW EH3 ....27 E3
Bonnington Business Centre
  LEITH EH6 ....18 B4
Bonnington Industrial Estate
  LEITH EH6 ....18 A4
Bonnington Mills
  Business Centre
  LEITH EH6 ....18 A3
Bonnington Primary School
  LEITH EH6 ....18 A4
Bonnyrigg Health Centre
  BNYRG EH19 ....67 F5
Bonnyrigg Primary School
  BNYRG EH19 ....75 G1

Borders College
  EDNT/CEDW EH3 ....2 D1
Boroughmuir High School
  MCH/MOR/FMHD EH10 ....43 F1
Boroughmuir RFC
  (Colinton Road)
  BAL/CUR EH14 ....42 B3
Braidburn Special School
  RSTRG EH7 ....57 F1
Braid Hills Golf Course
  MCH/MOR/FMHD EH10 ....58 B1
Braid Hills Hotel
  MCH/MOR/FMHD EH10 ....58 A1
Broomhouse Health Centre
  DAL/STH/STNH EH11 ....41 E3
Broomhouse Primary School
  DAL/STH/STNH EH11 ....41 E3
Broomieknowe Golf Club
  LSWD EH18 ....67 G2
Broughton Health Clinic
  EDOT EH1 ....3 F1
Broughton High School
  EDNW EH4 ....26 D1
Broughton Primary School
  RSTRG EH7 ....17 H5
Brunstane Primary School
  PBLO/DUD EH15 ....30 C5
Brunswick Business Centre
  RSTRG EH7 ....28 B1
Bruntsfield Health Centre
  MCH/MOR/FMHD EH10 ....43 F1
Bruntsfield Links
  Golfing Society
  EDNW EH4 ....14 D4
Bruntsfield Primary School
  MCH/MOR/FMHD EH10 ....43 E1
Bryans Primary School
  DLKTH EH22 ....69 G5
Buckstone Primary School
  MCH/MOR/FMHD EH10 ....58 C3
Burdiehouse Primary School
  GIL/MOR EH17 ....59 H5
Burgh Primary School
  MUS EH21 ....32 A5
Butlerfield Industrial Estate
  BNYRG EH19 ....76 C4
Cairnpark Special School
  BAL/CUR EH14 ....41 H5
Cameo Cinema
  EDNT/CEDW EH3 ....2 B7
Camera Obscura
  & World of Illusions
  EDOT EH1 ....2 D4
Cameron Toll Shopping Centre
  LIB/NID EH16 ....44 C3
Campie Primary School
  MUS EH21 ....31 H5
Canal View Primary School
  BAL/CUR EH14 ....41 E5
Canongate Kirk
  HLYRPK/NF EH8 ....3 H3
Canonmills Special School
  EDNT/CEDW EH3 ....27 G1
Capital Hotel
  MRYFD/COR EH12 ....25 E2
Cargilfield School
  EDNW EH4 ....14 C4
Carlton CC
  NWGTN EH9 ....43 H2
Carrick Knowe Golf Course
  MRYFD/COR EH12 ....41 G1
Carrick Knowe Primary School
  MRYFD/COR EH12 ....41 F1
Castlebrae Business Centre
  LIB/NID EH16 ....45 F2
Castlebrae Business Park
  LIB/NID EH16 ....45 G1

Castlebrae Community
  High School
  LIB/NID EH16 ....45 G3
Castleview Primary School
  LIB/NID EH16 ....45 G3
Cavalry Park RFC
  PBLO/DUD EH15 ....45 F1
Chalmers Hospital
  EDNT/CEDW EH3 ....2 D6
Channings Hotel
  EDNW EH4 ....27 E2
Child & Family Mental
  Health Service
  NWGTN EH9 ....43 G2
Cineworld & Megabowl
  DAL/STH/STNH EH11 ....27 E5
City Art Centre
  EDOT EH1 ....3 F4
City Hospital
  MCH/MOR/FMHD EH10 ....57 G1
City Hotel
  EDNT/CEDW EH3 ....2 C6
Clermiston Primary School
  EDNW EH4 ....24 C1
Clifton Hall School
  RATHO EH28 ....36 B4
Clifton Trading Estate
  RATHO EH28 ....36 D3
Clinic Health Centre
  MRYFD/COR EH12 ....24 B3
Clovenstone Primary School
  BAL/CUR EH14 ....56 A1
Cockenzie Business Centre
  CPS/PPNS EH32 ....35 E1
Cockenzie & Port Seton
  Health Centre
  CPS/PPNS EH32 ....35 E1
Cockenzie Primary School
  CPS/PPNS EH32 ....35 E2
Cockpen School
  BNYRG EH19 ....75 G1
Colinton Primary School
  COLIN EH13 ....57 F2
Collegiate Church
  CPS/PPNS EH32 ....35 H2
Cornbank St James
  Primary School
  PNCK EH26 ....70 A3
Corstorphine Hill Cemetery
  MRYFD/COR EH12 ....24 C3
Corstorphine Hospital
  MRYFD/COR EH12 ....25 F4
Corstorphine Primary School
  MRYFD/COR EH12 ....24 D5
Corstorphine Rugby FC
  MRYFD/COR EH12 ....41 F1
Cowgate Medical Centre
  EDOT EH1 ....2 E5
Craigentinny Golf Course
  RSTRG EH7 ....19 F5
Craigentinny Primary School
  RSTRG EH7 ....29 F1
Craigleith Retail Park
  EDNW EH4 ....26 A1
Craiglockhart
  Primary School
  DAL/STH/STNH EH11 ....42 C2
Craigmillar Castle
  LIB/NID EH16 ....45 F4
Craigmillar Park Golf Club
  NWGTN EH9 ....44 A4
Craigmount High School
  MRYFD/COR EH12 ....24 A4
Craigour Park Primary School
  GIL/MOR EH17 ....60 C2
Craigroyston Health Clinic
  EDNW EH4 ....16 A4

Craigroyston High School
  EDNW EH4 ....15 H4
Craigroyston Primary School
  EDNW EH4 ....15 H4
Cramond Primary School
  EDNW EH4 ....14 B3
Crewe Medical Centre
  EDNW EH4 ....16 B2
Cuiken House
  PNCK EH26 ....70 B3
Currie Cemetery
  BAL/CUR EH14 ....55 F5
Curriehill Health Centre
  BAL/CUR EH14 ....54 D5
Curriehill Primary School
  BAL/CUR EH14 ....54 D5
Dalhousie Castle Hotel
  BNYRG EH19 ....76 A3
Dalhousie Country Park
  DLKTH EH22 ....62 D4
Dalkeith High School
  DLKTH EH22 ....63 F4
Dalkeith Leisure Centre
  DLKTH EH22 ....68 D2
Dalkeith Medical Centre
  DLKTH EH22 ....68 C1
Dalkeith RFC
  DLKTH EH22 ....68 B1
Dalkeith Schools Community
  Campus
  DLKTH EH22 ....63 F4
Dalmeny House
  QFRY EH30 ....8 C4
Dalmeny Primary School
  QFRY EH30 ....12 A1
Dairy Cemetery
  DAL/STH/STNH EH11 ....26 D5
Dalry Primary School
  DAL/STH/STNH EH11 ....26 D5
Dalry Swimming Pool
  DAL/STH/STNH EH11 ....26 D5
Danderhall Leisure Centre
  DLKTH EH22 ....61 G2
Danderhall Primary School
  DLKTH EH22 ....61 F1
Davidsons Mains
  Primary School
  EDNW EH4 ....15 F5
Deaconess Hospital
  HLYRPK/NF EH8 ....3 H6
Dean Park Primary School
  BAL/CUR EH14 ....52 D4
Deep Sea World
  DFLS KY11 ....4 D5
D Napier & Son Health Clinic
  EDOT EH1 ....3 F6
Dominion Cinema
  MCH/MOR/FMHD EH10 ....43 F3
Donaldsons College
  MRYFD/COR EH12 ....26 C4
Dovecot
  MRYFD/COR EH12 ....24 D5
Dr Bells Primary School
  LEITH EH6 ....18 B3
Drum Brae Leisure Centre
  EDNW EH4 ....24 C2
Drumbrae Primary School
  MRYFD/COR EH12 ....24 C2
Drum Mohr Caravan Park
  MUS EH21 ....33 H4
Drummond Community
  High School
  RSTRG EH7 ....27 H1
Duddingston Golf Club
  PBLO/DUD EH15 ....45 G1
Duddingston Primary School
  HLYRPK/NF EH8 ....29 G4

Dumbryden Industrial Estate
  BAL/CUR EH14 ....41 F5
Dundas Castle
  QFRY EH30 ....10 D2
Dundas Parks Golf Club
  QFRY EH30 ....11 E2
Dunedin School
  LIB/NID EH16 ....44 C4
Dynamic Earth
  HLYRPK/NF EH8 ....3 J4
Eagle Rock
  QFRY EH30 ....14 A1
East Craigs Primary School
  MRYFD/COR EH12 ....24 B3
Eastern Cemetery
  LEITH EH6 ....18 C5
Eastern General Hospital
  LEITH EH6 ....19 F5
Eastfield Clinic
  PNCK EH26 ....70 D3
Eastfield Industrial Estate
  PNCK EH26 ....70 D3
Eastfield Medical Centre
  PNCK EH26 ....70 D3
Eastfield Primary School
  PNCK EH26 ....70 D3
Easthouses Industrial Estate
  DLKTH EH22 ....69 F4
Echline Primary School
  QFRY EH30 ....6 A4
Edenhall Hospital
  MUS EH21 ....48 C2
Edgefield Road
  Industrial Estate
  LNHD EH20 ....66 A3
Edinburgh Academical
  Sports Centre
  EDNW EH4 ....27 E1
The Edinburgh Academy
  EDNT/CEDW EH3 ....3 H4
Edinburgh Airport
  MRYFD/COR EH12 ....22 B3
Edinburgh Airport
  Terminal Building
  MRYFD/COR EH12 ....22 B3
Edinburgh Business Centre
  LEITH EH6 ....18 C3
Edinburgh Butterfly
  & Insect World
  LSWD EH18 ....67 G1
Edinburgh Castle
  EDOT EH1 ....2 C4
Edinburgh College of Art
  EDNT/CEDW EH3 ....17 F4
Edinburgh Crystal
  Visitor Centre
  PNCK EH26 ....70 D3
The Edinburgh Dungeon
  EDOT EH1 ....2 E4
Edinburgh Festival Centre
  (The Hub)
  EDOT EH1 ....2 C5
Edinburgh Festival Theatre
  HLYRPK/NF EH8 ....3 F6
The Edinburgh Holistic
  Health Centre
  EDNT/CEDW EH3 ....17 F4
Edinburgh International
  Conference Centre
  EDNT/CEDW EH3 ....2 A5
Edinburgh Natural
  Health Centre
  EDNT/CEDW EH3 ....27 E3
Edinburgh Park Business Park
  MRYFD/COR EH12 ....39 H2
Edinburgh Peoples Theatre
  NWGTN EH9 ....44 B2

Edinburgh Playhouse Theatre
EDT EH1 .... 3 G1
Edinburgh Reivers RFC
MRYFD/COR EH12 .... 26 D3
The Edinburgh Rudolf
Steiner School
DAL/STH/STNH EH11 .... 42 D2
Edinburgh Telford College
EDNW EH4 .... 16 C4
Edinburgh Zoo
MRYFD/COR EH12 .... 25 F4
Eldin Industrial Estate
MUS EH20 .... 66 A2
Eskbridge Medical Centre
MUS EH21 .... 32 A5
Esk Medical Centre
MUS EH21 .... 32 A5
Exhibition Hall
RATHO EH28 .... 22 A4
The Eye Clinic
CED/PRST EH2 .... 2 B3
Ferryhill Primary School
EDNW EH4 .... 15 H5
Ferrymuir Retail Park
QFRY EH30 .... 11 F1
Festival Square
EDNT/CEDW EH3 .... 2 C5
Fettes College
EDNW EH4 .... 16 C5
Fettes College
Preparatory School
EDNW EH4 .... 16 C5
Filmhouse Cinema
EDNT/CEDW EH3 .... 2 A5
Firrhill High School
BAL/CUR EH14 .... 57 F1
Firrhill Medical Centre
COLIN EH13 .... 57 F2
Fisherrow Industrial Estate
MUS EH21 .... 31 G5
Fleets Industrial Estate
TRNT EH33 .... 51 E5
Flora Stevenson
Primary School
EDNW EH4 .... 26 D1
Foot Health Centre
MUS EH21 .... 31 H5
Forecourt Leisure Centre
LEITH EH6 .... 18 A4
Forrester High School
MRYFD/COR EH12 .... 40 D2
Forth Industrial Estate
GNTN EH5 .... 16 C1
Forthview Primary School
EDNW EH4 .... 16 B4
Fort Kinnaird Retail
& Leisure Park
PBLO/DUD EH15 .... 46 B2
Fort Primary School
LEITH EH6 .... 18 A2
Fox Covert Primary School
EDNW EH4 .... 25 C2
Freemasons Hall
CED/PRST EH2 .... 2 C3
The Fruitmarket Gallery
EDOT EH1 .... 2 E3
Gateway Theatre
RSTRG EH7 .... 28 A1
George Heriots RFC
EDNT/CEDW EH3 .... 17 F4
George Heriots School
EDNT/CEDW EH3 .... 2 D6
George Inter-Continental Hotel
CED/PRST EH2 .... 2 D2
George Watson's College
MCH/MOR/FMHD EH10 ..... 43 E3
George Watson's School
MCH/MOR/FMHD EH10 ..... 42 D3
Georgian House
CED/PRST EH2 .... 2 A3
Gilmerton Primary School
GIL/MOR EH17 .... 60 B3
Gladstone's Land
EDOT EH1 .... 2 E4
Glencorse Golf Club
PNCK EH26 .... 72 C5
Glencorse Industrial Estate
PNCK EH26 .... 72 C5
Gorebridge Health Centre
GORBR EH23 .... 79 E2
Gorebridge Primary School
GORBR EH23 .... 79 E1
Gracemount High School
LIB/NID EH16 .... 59 H3
Gracemount Leisure Centre
LIB/NID EH16 .... 59 H4
Gracemount Primary School
LIB/NID EH16 .... 59 H3
Grange Cemetery
NWCTN EH9 .... 43 H2
Grannies Park Industrial Estate
DLKTH EH22 .... 68 B1
Granton Primary School
GNTN EH5 .... 16 D2
Greendykes Clinic
LIB/NID EH16 .... 45 G2
Greendykes Primary School
LIB/NID EH16 .... 45 H3
Gylemuir Primary School
MRYFD/COR EH12 .... 40 C1
Hardengreen Business Park
DLKTH EH22 .... 68 A3
Hardengreen Industrial Estate
DLKTH EH22 .... 68 A3
Harewood School
LIB/NID EH16 .... 45 G2
Harmeny School
BAL/CUR EH14 .... 53 F4
Hawthornden Primary School
BNYRG EH19 .... 74 D1
Heart of Midlothian FC
DAL/STH/STNH EH11 .... 42 B1
Heriot Watt University
BAL/CUR EH14 .... 54 C2
EDOT EH1 .... 2 C6
Hermitage Park
Primary School
LEITH EH6 .... 18 C5
Hibernian FC (Easter Road)
RSTRG EH7 .... 28 C1

Hillwood Primary School
RATHO EH28 .... 37 G1
HM General Register House
CED/PRST EH2 .... 3 F2
HM Prison
BAL/CUR EH14 .... 41 G3
Holy Cross & Cricket Clubs
EDNT/CEDW EH5 .... 17 E4
Holy Cross RC Primary School
GNTN EH5 .... 17 E4
Holyrood Business Park
LIB/NID EH16 .... 45 E2
Holyrood Park
HLYRPK/NF EH8 .... 3 J4
Holy Rood RC High School
PBLO/DUD EH15 .... 29 F5
Hopefield Primary School
BNYRG EH19 .... 75 E1
Hotel Ibis
EDOT EH1 .... 3 G4
The Howard Hotel
EDNT/CEDW EH3 .... 27 G1
Huntly House Museum
HLYRPK/NF EH8 .... 3 H4
IKEA Store Edinburgh
LNHD EH20 .... 65 G3
Innkeeper's Lodge
MRYFD/COR EH12 .... 24 D5
QFRY EH30 .... 6 C4
QFRY EH30 .... 7 E4
Inveresk Industrial Estate
MUS EH21 .... 48 A1
Inveresk Lodge Garden (NTS)
MUS EH21 .... 48 B2
Inveresk Mills Industrial Park
MUS EH21 .... 47 H1
Jack Kane Sports Centre
LIB/NID EH16 .... 46 A2
Jackson Street School
PNCK EH26 .... 70 C4
James Gillespies High School
NWCTN EH9 .... 43 G1
James Gillespies
Primary School
MCH/MOR/FMHD EH10 ..... 43 F1
Jewel & Esk Valley College
DLKTH EH22 .... 68 B3
PBLO/DUD EH15 .... 30 D5
PNCK EH26 .... 70 C4
John Cotton Business Centre
RSTRG EH7 .... 28 C1
John Knox House
EDOT EH1 .... 3 G4
Juniper Green Primary School
BAL/CUR EH14 .... 55 H3
Jurys Inn
EDOT EH1 .... 3 G3
Kaimes Special School
LIB/NID EH16 .... 60 A3
Kings Acre Golf Course
& Academy
LSWD EH18 .... 67 E1
Kings Hall
HLYRPK/NF EH8 .... 28 A5
King's Haugh
LIB/NID EH16 .... 45 E2
Kingsinch School
LIB/NID EH16 .... 44 C4
Kingsknowe Golf Club
BAL/CUR EH14 .... 56 C1
Kings Manor Hotel
PBLO/DUD EH15 .... 30 D5
Kings Park Primary School
DLKTH EH22 .... 68 C2
Kings Theatre
EDNT/CEDW EH3 .... 27 G5
Kirkliston Health Centre
KLSTN EH29 .... 21 E1
Kirkliston Primary School
KLSTN EH29 .... 20 D2
Kirkliston Sports Centre
KLSTN EH29 .... 20 D1
Lady Victoria Business Centre
NBNG EH23 .... 76 C3
Ladywell Medical Centre
MRYFD/COR EH12 .... 24 C5
Ladywood Leisure Centre
PNCK EH26 .... 71 E2
Ladywood Primary School
PNCK EH26 .... 71 E3
Langlaw Primary School
DLKTH EH22 .... 69 F4
Lasswade High School
BNYRG EH19 .... 75 E1
Lasswade Primary School
BNYRG EH19 .... 67 G4
Lasswade RFC
BNYRG EH19 .... 75 E1
Lauder College
DLKTH EH22 .... 69 E1
Lauriston Castle
EDNW EH4 .... 15 E3
Leith Academy
LEITH EH6 .... 18 C5
Leith Primary School
LEITH EH6 .... 18 C4
The Leith School of Art
LEITH EH6 .... 18 A2
Leith Walk Business Centre
LEITH EH6 .... 18 B4
Leith Walk Primary School
RSTRG EH7 .... 28 A1
Liberton Golf Club
LIB/NID EH16 .... 45 E5
Liberton High School
LIB/NID EH16 .... 60 A1
Liberton Hospital
LIB/NID EH16 .... 59 H2
Liberton Primary School
LIB/NID EH16 .... 44 D4
Liberton RFC
LIB/NID EH16 .... 44 C5
Lismore Primary School
MUS EH21 .... 32 A1
Lismore Primary School
PBLO/DUD EH15 .... 29 H5
Loanhead Clinic
LNHD EH20 .... 65 H4
Loanhead Hospital
LNHD EH20 .... 66 B4

Loanhead Leisure Centre
LNHD EH20 .... 65 H4
Loanhead Primary School
LNHD EH20 .... 66 A4
Loanhead Town Hall
LNHD EH20 .... 66 A4
Lochend Industrial Estate
RATHO EH28 .... 37 F1
Longstone Primary School
BAL/CUR EH14 .... 41 G5
Loretto Gallery
MUS EH21 .... 32 B5
Loretto Junior School
MUS EH21 .... 32 A5
Loretto RC Primary School
MUS EH21 .... 32 B5
Loretto School
MUS EH21 .... 32 B5
Lorne Primary School
LEITH EH6 .... 18 B5
Lothianburn Golf Club
MCH/MOR/FMHD EH10 ..... 64 B1
Mackenzie Medical Centre
HLYRPK/NF EH8 .... 3 G6
Malleny Garden (NTS)
BAL/CUR EH14 .... 53 F2
Malmaison Hotel
LEITH EH6 .... 18 C2
Mannafields Christian School
RSTRG EH7 .... 28 B1
Marco Leisure Centre
EDNT/CEDW EH5 .... 27 E4
Marco's Leisure Centre
BAL/CUR EH14 .... 42 A3
Marriott Hotel
MRYFD/COR EH12 .... 24 A5
The Mary Erskine School
EDNW EH4 .... 25 H2
The Mary Erskine & Stewarts
Melville Junior School
EDNW EH4 .... 25 H3
Mauricewood Primary School
PNCK EH26 .... 70 D2
Mayfield Industrial Estate
DLKTH EH22 .... 76 D2
Mayfield Leisure Centre
DLKTH EH22 .... 77 F1
Mayfield Primary School
DLKTH EH22 .... 77 F2
McEwan Hall
HLYRPK/NF EH8 .... 3 F6
McLeod Street Sports Centre
DAL/STH/STNH EH11 .... 26 C5
Meadowbank Stadium
& Sports Centre
RSTRG EH7 .... 28 D2
Meadowmill Sports Centre
TRNT EH33 .... 35 E4
Medical School
LIB/NID EH16 .... 45 F4
Megabowl
PBLO/DUD EH15 .... 46 B2
Melville Castle Hotel
LSWD EH18 .... 67 G1
Menzies Belford Hotel
EDNW EH4 .... 26 D3
Merchants of Edinburgh
Golf Club
MCH/MOR/FMHD EH10 ..... 42 C5
Merchiston Castle School
COLIN EH13 .... 56 D2
Midlothian Ski Centre
MCH/MOR/FMHD EH10 ..... 64 A2
Mid Road Industrial Estate
CPS/PPNS EH32 .... 34 B5
Moray House
College of Education
HLYRPK/NF EH8 .... 3 H4
LIB/NID EH16 .... 44 C3
Moredun Primary School
GIL/MOR EH17 .... 60 B1
Morningside Cemetery
MCH/MOR/FMHD EH10 ..... 43 E4
Morningside Health Centre
MCH/MOR/FMHD EH10 ..... 43 E2
Mortonhall Cemetery
LIB/NID EH16 .... 59 F4
Mortonhall Crematorium
LIB/NID EH16 .... 59 F4
Mortonhall Golf Club
LIB/NID EH16 .... 58 B2
Mount Vernon Cemetery
LIB/NID EH16 .... 59 H1
Murrayburn Primary School
DAL/STH/STNH EH11 .... 40 D4
Murrayfield Golf Club
EDNW EH4 .... 25 H3
Murrayfield Hospital
MRYFD/COR EH12 .... 25 G4
Murrayfield Ice Rink
MRYFD/COR EH12 .... 26 A5
Murrayfield Indoor
Sports Club
MRYFD/COR EH12 .... 26 B5
Murrayfield Medical Centre
MRYFD/COR EH12 .... 25 H5
Murrayfield Stadium
MRYFD/COR EH12 .... 26 A5
Museum of Childhood
EDOT EH1 .... 3 G4
Museum of Edinburgh
HLYRPK/NF EH8 .... 3 H4
Museum of Lighting
EDNT/CEDW EH3 .... 27 F1
Musselburgh Golf Club
MUS EH21 .... 47 H3
Musselburgh Grammar School
MUS EH21 .... 48 A1
Musselburgh Links,
The Old Golf Course
MUS EH21 .... 32 C4
Musselburgh Racecourse
MUS EH21 .... 32 C4
Musselburgh RFC
MUS EH21 .... 31 G5
Musselburgh Sports Centre
MUS EH21 .... 48 A1
Napier University
BAL/CUR EH14 .... 42 B5
DAL/STH/STNH EH11 .... 40 C4

MCH EH4 .... 26 C1
MCH/MOR/FMHD EH10 ..... 42 C4
MCH/MOR/FMHD EH10 ..... 43 E2
NWGTN EH9 .... 43 G1
National Galleries of Scotland
RSTRG EH7 .... 17 H5
National Gallery of Scotland
CED/PRST EH2 .... 2 D4
National Monument
EDOT EH1 .... 3 H2
National War
Museum of Scotland
EDOT EH1 .... 2 C4
The Natural Health Centre
EDNT/CEDW EH5 .... 27 F5
Nelson Monument
RSTRG EH7 .... 3 H2
Netherbow Arts Centre
& Theatre
EDOT EH1 .... 3 G4
Nether Currie Primary School
BAL/CUR EH14 .... 55 F4
Newbattle Community
High School
DLKTH EH22 .... 69 E5
Newbattle Golf Club
DLKTH EH22 .... 68 C2
Newbridge Industrial Estate
RATHO EH28 .... 36 C2
New Cemetery
EDNT/CEDW EH5 .... 27 F2
Newcraighall Primary School
MUS EH21 .... 47 E2
Newhailes Industrial Estate
MUS EH21 .... 47 F1
Newhailes (NTS)
MUS EH21 .... 47 F1
Newhaven Heritage Museum
LEITH EH6 .... 17 G1
Newtongrange Leisure Centre
DLKTH EH22 .... 76 C2
Newtongrange
Primary School
DLKTH EH22 .... 76 C2
Niddrie Mill Primary School
LIB/NID EH16 .... 46 A2
North Merchiston Cemetery
DAL/STH/STNH EH11 .... 42 C1
North Queensferry
Primary School
DFLS KY11 .... 4 C4
Norton House Hotel
RATHO EH28 .... 37 H2
Novotel
EDNT/CEDW EH3 .... 2 C6
Oaklands School
DAL/STH/STNH EH11 .... 41 E3
Observatory
RSTRG EH7 .... 3 G2
Ocean Terminal
LEITH EH6 .... 18 A1
Odeon Cinema
BAL/CUR EH14 .... 55 H1
CED/PRST EH2 .... 2 B6
Old Waverley Hotel
CED/PRST EH2 .... 2 E3
Olivebank Retail Park
MUS EH21 .... 31 G5
Omni Leisure Cinema
& Entertainment Complex
EDOT EH1 .... 3 G3
Open University
EDNT/CEDW EH3 .... 27 E3
Oxgangs Primary School
COLIN EH13 .... 57 F1
Palace of Holyrood House
HLYRPK/NF EH8 .... 3 K3
Paradykes Primary School
LNHD EH20 .... 65 H4
Paramount Carlton Hotel
EDOT EH1 .... 3 F4
Park Leisure Centre
MRYFD/COR EH12 .... 39 H2
Parkside Bowling Club
LIB/NID EH16 .... 28 B5
Parliament House
EDOT EH1 .... 2 E5
Parliament Visitor's Centre
HLYRPK/NF EH8 .... 3 K4
Parsons Green
Primary School
HLYRPK/NF EH8 .... 29 F4
Peffermill Primary School
LIB/NID EH16 .... 45 F3
Penicuik Health Centre
PNCK EH26 .... 70 D4
Penicuik High School
PNCK EH26 .... 70 C4
Pennypit Sports Centre
CPS/PPNS EH32 .... 34 A4
Pennywell Clinic
EDNW EH4 .... 16 A4
Pentlandfield Business Park
ROSLIN EH25 .... 72 D1
Pentland Industrial Estate
PNCK EH26 .... 65 F5
Pentland Primary School
COLIN EH13 .... 57 H1
The People's Story
HLYRPK/NF EH8 .... 3 H3
Pilrig Park School
LEITH EH6 .... 18 A4
Pinkie St Peters
Primary School
MUS EH21 .... 32 C5
Pirniehall Primary School
EDNW EH4 .... 16 A3
Pleasance Festival Theatre
HLYRPK/NF EH8 .... 3 G5
Plus Health Clinic
NWGTN EH9 .... 44 A1
Pollock Halls of Residence
LIB/NID EH16 .... 44 C1
Portobello Cemetery
PBLO/DUD EH15 .... 31 E5
The Portobello Gallery
PBLO/DUD EH15 .... 30 B3
Portobello Golf Course
PBLO/DUD EH15 .... 30 A4

Portobello High School
PBLO/DUD EH15 .... 29 H4
Portobello Swimming Pool
PBLO/DUD EH15 .... 30 C3
Portobello Town Hall
PBLO/DUD EH15 .... 30 A3
Premier Lodge
EDNT/CEDW EH3 .... 2 C6
Premier Travel Inn
EDNT/CEDW EH3 .... 27 E4
HLYRPK/NF EH8 .... 29 C4
LEITH EH6 .... 17 C1
MUS EH21 .... 48 C4
QFRY EH30 .... 6 B5
Prestonfield Golf Club
LIB/NID EH16 .... 44 C1
Prestonfield Hotel
LIB/NID EH16 .... 44 D1
Prestonfield Primary School
LIB/NID EH16 .... 44 D3
Prestongrange Industrial
Heritage Museum
CPS/PPNS EH32 .... 33 G3
Preston Lodge High School
CPS/PPNS EH32 .... 34 C4
Preston Market Cross
CPS/PPNS EH32 .... 34 B4
Prestonpans Industrial Estate
CPS/PPNS EH32 .... 34 B5
Prestonpans Infant School
CPS/PPNS EH32 .... 34 B4
Prestonpans Primary School
CPS/PPNS EH32 .... 34 C5
Prestonpans Town Hall
CPS/PPNS EH32 .... 34 C4
Preston Street Primary School
LIB/NID EH16 .... 44 B1
Preston Tower (NTS)
CPS/PPNS EH32 .... 34 A4
Princes Mall
EDOT EH1 .... 2 E3
Prospect Bank School
LEITH EH6 .... 18 D4
Quality Hotel
RATHO EH28 .... 22 A4
Quartermile
EDNT/CEDW EH3 .... 2 E7
Queen Margaret
University College
LEITH EH6 .... 18 C4
MRYFD/COR EH12 .... 24 D3
Queensferry High School
DFLS KY11 .... 7 E5
The Queensferry Hotel
DFLS KY11 .... 4 C4
Queensferry Museum
QFRY EH30 .... 6 D4
Queensferry Primary School
QFRY EH30 .... 6 D4
Queensferry Recreation Centre
QFRY EH30 .... 7 E5
Queens Hall
HLYRPK/NF EH8 .... 28 A5
Queensway Leisure Centre
PNCK EH26 .... 70 C2
Ramada Hotel
CED/PRST EH2 .... 2 D3
Ratho Park Golf Club
RATHO EH28 .... 38 B4
Ratho Primary School
RATHO EH28 .... 37 H4
Ratho Viaduct
RATHO EH28 .... 36 C1
Ravelston Golf Club
EDNW EH4 .... 25 G2
The Real Mary King's Close
EDOT EH1 .... 2 E4
Reception Business Centre
MRYFD/COR EH12 .... 26 D4
Restairig Park Medical Centre
LEITH EH6 .... 18 D5
Riccarton Primary School
BAL/CUR EH14 .... 54 D4
The Rolling Stone Gallery
EDOT EH1 .... 2 D5
Rosebank Cemetery
RSTRG EH7 .... 18 A4
Roseburn Primary School
MRYFD/COR EH12 .... 26 B5
Rosewell Primary School
RSWL EH24 .... 74 C5
Roslin Glen Country Park
ROSLIN EH25 .... 73 G4
Roslin Primary School
ROSLIN EH25 .... 73 G3
Ross High RFC
TRNT EH33 .... 51 E3
Ross High School
TRNT EH33 .... 51 E2
Rowanfield School
EDNW EH4 .... 16 A5
The Roxburghe Hotel
CED/PRST EH2 .... 2 B3
Royal Alexandra Eye Pavilion
EDNT/CEDW EH3 .... 2 C6
Royal Blind School
MCH/MOR/FMHD EH10 ..... 43 F3
The Royal Blind School
NWGTN EH9 .... 44 B3
Royal Botanic Garden
EDNT/CEDW EH3 .... 17 F5
Royal Burgess Golfing Society
of Edinburgh
EDNW EH4 .... 14 B5
Royal College of Nursing
EDNT/CEDW EH3 .... 43 G3
Royal College of Surgeons
of Edinburgh
HLYRPK/NF EH8 .... 3 G5
Royal Commonwealth Pool
LIB/NID EH16 .... 44 B1
Royal Edinburgh Hospital
MCH/MOR/FMHD EH10 ..... 42 D4
Royal Highland Showground
RATHO EH28 .... 22 A4
The Royal High
Primary School
HLYRPK/NF EH8 .... 29 F2
The Royal High School
EDNW EH4 .... 14 D5

Royal Hospital
for Sick Children
NWGTN EH9 ....43 H1
The Royal Infirmary
of Edinburgh
LIB/NID EH16 ....45 G4
Royal Lyceum
Theatre Company
EDOT EH1 ....2 B5
Royal Mile Primary School
HLYRPK/NF EH8 ....3 J3
Royal Museum Cinema
EDOT EH1 ....2 E5
Royal Museum of Scotland
EDOT EH1 ....2 E5
Royal Musselburgh Golf Club
CPS/PPNS EH52 ....33 H3
Royal Observatory
Visitor Centre
NWGTN EH9 ....43 H4
Royal School
of Veterinary Studies
NWGTN EH9 ....28 A5
Royal Scottish Academy
CED/PRST EH2 ....2 D3
Royal Terrace Hotel
RSTRG EH7 ....3 J1
Royal Victoria Hospital
EDNW EH4 ....26 C1
The Royal Yacht Britannia
LEITH EH6 ....18 B1
Royal Zoological Society
of Scotland
MRYFD/COR EH12 ....25 F5
Royston Primary School
GNTN EH5 ....16 B2
Rural Centre
RATHO EH28 ....22 A5
SAC Centre for Study
NWGTN EH9 ....44 B5
Sacred Heart RC
Primary School
PNCK EH26 ....70 B4
St Andrews College
NWGTN EH9 ....43 G2
St Andrew's House
EDOT EH1 ....3 G2
St Andrews RC Primary School
GORBR EH23 ....76 D4
St Augustines RC High School
MRYFD/COR EH12 ....40 C2
St Bernard's Well
EDNT/CEDW EH3 ....27 E2
St Brides Cinema
DAL/STH/STNH EH11 ....26 D5
St Catherines RC
Primary School
LIB/NID EH16 ....59 H4
St Crispins Special School
NWGTN EH9 ....44 A3
St Cuthbert's RC
Primary School
BAL/CUR EH14 ....42 B2
St Davids RC High School
DLKTH EH22 ....63 F4
St Davids RC Primary School
DLKTH EH22 ....69 E2
EDNW EH4 ....16 A3
St Denis & Cranley School
MCH/MOR/FMHD EH10 ....42 D2
St Francis RC Primary School
LIB/NID EH16 ....45 G2

St Gabriels RC Primary School
CPS/PPNS EH32 ....34 B5
St Georges School for Girls
MRYFD/COR EH12 ....26 B4
St Giles Cathedral
EDOT EH1 ....2 E4
St James Shopping Centre
EDOT EH1 ....3 F2
St Johns RC Primary School
PBLO/DUD EH15 ....29 H4
St John Vianney RC
Primary School
LIB/NID EH16 ....44 D5
St Katharines School
LIB/NID EH16 ....59 G4
St Leonards Medical Centre
HLYRPK/NF EH8 ....3 H6
St Lukes RC Primary School
DLKTH EH22 ....77 F1
St Margarets RC
Primary School
LNHD EH20 ....65 H3
OFRY EH30 ....6 D4
St Margarets School
LIB/NID EH16 ....44 C3
St Marks RC Primary School
COLIN EH13 ....57 G2
St Martins RC Primary School
TRNT EH33 ....51 G2
St Marys Episcopal Cathedral
MRYFD/COR EH12 ....27 E4
St Marys (Leith) RC
Primary School
LEITH EH6 ....18 D3
St Marys Music School
MRYFD/COR EH12 ....26 D4
St Marys RC Cathedral
EDOT EH1 ....3 F1
St Marys RC Primary School
BNYRG EH19 ....75 F1
RSTRG EH7 ....27 H1
St Matthews RC
Primary School
RSWL EH24 ....74 C5
St Nicholas Special School
DAL/STH/STNH EH11 ....42 A1
St Ninians RC
Primary School
RSTRG EH7 ....29 E1
St Peters RC Primary School
MCH/MOR/FMHD EH10 ....43 F3
St Serfs School
MRYFD/COR EH12 ....26 C4
St Thomas of Aquins
High School
DAL/STH/STNH EH11 ....42 D1
St Thomas of Aquins RC
High School
EDNT/CEDW EH3 ....2 C7
St Triduana's Chapel
RSTRG EH7 ....29 E2
Saltersgate School
DLKTH EH22 ....62 B5
Saughton Athletic Track
DAL/STH/STNH EH11 ....41 H2
Saughton Cemetery
BAL/CUR EH14 ....41 H3
Saughton Mains
Industrial Estate
DAL/STH/STNH EH11 ....41 F2
Sciennes Primary School
NWGTN EH9 ....43 H1

Scotch Whisky
Heritage Centre
EDOT EH1 ....2 D5
The Scotsman
EDOT EH1 ....3 F4
Scottish Agricultural College
PNCK EH26 ....72 B2
Scottish Executive
LEITH EH6 ....18 B2
Scottish Mining Museum
BNYRG EH19 ....76 C3
Scottish National Gallery
of Modern Art
MRYFD/COR EH12 ....26 C3
Scottish National
Portrait Gallery
CED/PRST EH2 ....2 D1
Scottish Parliament Building
HLYRPK/NF EH8 ....3 J3
Scott Monument
CED/PRST EH2 ....2 E3
Seafield Cemetery
LEITH EH6 ....19 E4
Seafield Crematorium
LEITH EH6 ....19 E4
Seafield Industrial Estate
PBLO/DUD EH15 ....29 H1
Seton Sands Holiday Village
CPS/PPNS EH52 ....35 H1
The Sheraton Grand Hotel
EDNT/CEDW EH3 ....2 A5
Sherwood Industrial Estate
BNYRG EH19 ....67 G5
Sighthill Health Centre
DAL/STH/STNH EH11 ....40 D4
Sighthill Primary School
DAL/STH/STNH EH11 ....40 C5
Sighthill Shopping Centre
DAL/STH/STNH EH11 ....40 D4
Silverknowes Golf Course
EDNW EH4 ....15 F3
Smith & Saunders
Business Centre
DAL/STH/STNH EH11 ....53 E3
Southfield Hospital
GIL/MOR EH17 ....60 A2
The South Gyle
Shopping Centre
MRYFD/COR EH12 ....40 A1
South Morningside
Primary School
MCH/MOR/FMHD EH10 ....43 E4
Springwell Medical Centre
DAL/STH/STNH EH11 ....42 C1
Stenhouse Primary School
DAL/STH/STNH EH11 ....41 G2
Stepping Stones Theatre
EDOT EH1 ....2 E5
Stevenson College
BAL/CUR EH14 ....54 C5
DAL/STH/STNH EH11 ....26 C5
DAL/STH/STNH EH11 ....40 D5
DAL/STH/STNH EH11 ....41 G2
LEITH EH6 ....18 C4
Stewart Melville RFC
EDNW EH4 ....16 D4
Stewarts Melville College
EDNW EH4 ....26 D2
Stills Gallery
EDOT EH1 ....3 F4
Stobhill Primary School
GORBR EH23 ....79 F2

Stockbridge
Primary School
EDNT/CEDW EH3 ....27 F1
Stoneyhill Primary School
MUS EH21 ....47 G1
Summerside Medical Centre
LEITH EH6 ....18 A3
Suntrap Garden
MRYFD/COR EH12 ....39 G4
Theatre Du Pif
GNTN EH5 ....16 B4
Thistle Hotel
EDOT EH1 ....3 F2
Thornybank
Industrial Estate
DLKTH EH22 ....63 F5
Tollcross Primary School
EDNT/CEDW EH3 ....2 A7
Torphin Hill Golf Club
COLIN EH13 ....56 B4
Towerbank Primary School
PBLO/DUD EH15 ....30 B2
Tranent FC
TRNT EH33 ....51 F2
Tranent Primary School
TRNT EH33 ....51 F1
Travelodge
COLIN EH13 ....57 F4
EDOT EH1 ....3 G4
MUS EH21 ....47 H4
Traverse Theatre
EDOT EH1 ....2 B5
Trinity Acadamicals RFC
GNTN EH5 ....17 G3
Trinity Academy
LEITH EH6 ....17 H2
Trinity Primary School
LEITH EH6 ....17 H2
Turnhouse Business Park
MRYFD/COR EH12 ....23 E3
Turnhouse Golf Club
MRYFD/COR EH12 ....23 F3
UCI Cinema
PBLO/DUD EH15 ....46 C2
University of Edinburgh
EDNT/CEDW EH3 ....2 E6
EDOT EH1 ....2 D4
EDOT EH1 ....3 G5
LIB/NID EH16 ....44 C5
University of Edinburgh
(Kings Building)
NWGTN EH9 ....44 B4
University of Edinburgh
Sports Centre
HLYRPK/NF EH8 ....3 H5
Usher Hall
EDOT EH1 ....2 B5
Victoria Primary School
LEITH EH6 ....17 H1
Vue Cinema
LEITH EH6 ....18 A1
Wallace Tutorial College
EDOT EH1 ....2 E5
Wallyford Industrial Estate
MUS EH21 ....49 F1
Wallyford Primary School
MUS EH21 ....49 F1
Wardie Primary School
GNTN EH5 ....17 E2
Warrender Baths
Swimming Pool
NWGTN EH9 ....43 G1

Warriston Cemetery
EDNT/CEDW EH3 ....17 G4
Warriston Crematorium
RSTRG EH7 ....17 G4
Waterfront Edinburgh
GNTN EH5 ....16 B1
Water of Leith Visitor Centre
BAL/CUR EH14 ....42 A3
Watsonians RFC
BAL/CUR EH14 ....42 C3
Waverley Lawn Tennis Squash
& Sports Club
NWGTN EH9 ....44 B3
Westburn Primary School
DAL/STH/STNH EH11 ....40 D5
West Craigs Industrial Estate
MRYFD/COR EH12 ....23 H5
Wester Hailes
Education Centre
BAL/CUR EH14 ....40 C5
Wester Hailes Health Centre
BAL/CUR EH14 ....55 H1
Westerlea Special
Education Unit
MRYFD/COR EH12 ....26 A4
Western General Hospital
EDNW EH4 ....16 B5
West One Business Park
DAL/STH/STNH EH11 ....40 B4
West Register House
CED/PRST EH2 ....2 A3
West Shore Road
Trading Estate
GNTN EH5 ....16 A1
Wetherby Business College
EDOT EH1 ....3 G4
Whin Park Industrial Estate
CPS/PPNS EH32 ....34 D2
Whin Park Medical Centre
DAL/STH/STNH EH11 ....41 F3
Whitecraig Primary School
MUS EH21 ....63 G1
Whitehill Industrial Estate
DLKTH EH22 ....69 G2
Wilkie House Theatre
EDOT EH1 ....3 F5
Willowbrae School
HLYRPK/NF EH8 ....29 E2
Willowpark School
DAL/STH/STNH EH11 ....42 B1
The Witchery
by the Castle Hotel
EDOT EH1 ....2 C4
Woodburn Primary School
DLKTH EH22 ....69 E1
The Writer's Museum
EDOT EH1 ....2 E4

Acknowledgements

Schools address data provided by Education Direct

Petrol station information supplied by Johnsons

Garden centre information provided by:

Garden Centre Association Britains best garden centres

Wyevale Garden Centres

The statement on the front cover of this atlas is sourced, selected and quoted
from a reader comment and feedback form received in 2004

Notes

Street by Street QUESTIONNAIRE

Dear Atlas User
Your comments, opinions and recommendations are very important to us.
So please help us to improve our street atlases by taking a few minutes
to complete this simple questionnaire.

You do not need a stamp (unless posted outside the UK). If you do not want to remove this page from your street atlas, then photocopy it or write your answers on a plain sheet of paper.

Send to: Marketing Assistant, AA Publishing, 14th Floor Fanum House,
Freepost SCE 4598, Basingstoke RG21 4GY

ABOUT THE ATLAS...

Please state which city / town / county you bought:

_____

Where did you buy the atlas? (City, Town, County)

_____

For what purpose? (please tick all applicable)

To use in your local area ☐   **To use on business or at work** ☐

Visiting a strange place ☐   **In the car** ☐   **On foot** ☐

Other (please state)

_____

Have you ever used any street atlases other than AA Street by Street?

Yes ☐   **No** ☐

If so, which ones?

_____

Is there any aspect of our street atlases that could be improved?
(Please continue on a separate sheet if necessary)

_____
_____
_____

ML67y

continued overleaf

Please list the features you found most useful:

_____

_____

Please list the features you found least useful:

_____

_____

_____

LOCAL KNOWLEDGE...

Local knowledge is invaluable. Whilst every attempt has been made to make the information contained in this atlas as accurate as possible, should you notice any inaccuracies, please detail them below (If necessary, use a blank piece of paper) or e-mail us at _streetbystreet@theAA.com_

_____

_____

_____

ABOUT YOU...

Name (Mr/Mrs/Ms) _____

Address _____

          Postcode _____

Daytime tel no _____

E-mail address _____

Which age group are you in?

Under 25 ☐   **25-34** ☐   **35-44** ☐   **45-54** ☐   **55-64** ☐   **65+** ☐

Are you an AA member? **YES** ☐   **NO** ☐

Do you have Internet access? **YES** ☐   **NO** ☐

_____

Thank you for taking the time to complete this questionnaire. Please send it to us as soon as possible, and remember, you do not need a stamp (unless posted outside the UK).

We may use information we hold about you to, telephone or email you about other products and services offered by the AA, we do NOT disclose this information to third parties.

Please tick here if you do not wish to hear about products and services from the AA. ☐